Library of Shakespearean Biography and Criticism

I. PRIMARY REFERENCE WORKS ON SHAKESPEARE

II. CRITICISM AND INTERPRETATION

    A. Textual Treatises, Commentaries
    B. Treatment of Special Subjects
    C. Dramatic and Literary Art in Shakespeare

III. SHAKESPEARE AND HIS TIME

    A. General Treatises. Biography
    B. The Age of Shakespeare
    C. Authorship

Series II, Part B

SHAKESPEAREAN TRAGEDY
AND THE
ELIZABETHAN COMPROMISE

Library of Shakespearean Biography and Criticism

SHAKESPEAREAN TRAGEDY
AND THE
ELIZABETHAN COMPROMISE

PAUL N. SIEGEL

 BOOKS FOR LIBRARIES PRESS
FREEPORT, NEW YORK

Copyright © 1957 by
New York University Press, Inc.

Reprinted 1972 by arrangement.

To my daughter Rosalind,
but for whom this book would have been completed sooner

INTERNATIONAL STANDARD BOOK NUMBER:
0-8369-6810-7

LIBRARY OF CONGRESS CATALOG CARD NUMBER:
78-39208

PRINTED IN THE UNITED STATES OF AMERICA
BY
NEW WORLD BOOK MANUFACTURING CO., INC.
HALLANDALE, FLORIDA 33009

PREFACE

This book is concerned with the relation between Shakespearean tragedy and the society of which it was a product. Its purpose is not to examine the tragedies as social documents but to analyze them as works of art forming a magnificent edifice which, no matter how loftily it towers or how richly enchanting a pleasure dome it has proved to be through the ages, rests on the foundation provided by the social structure. It seeks, to vary the figure, to display their subtle inner workings, observing how these are governed in a general way by the tastes, attitudes, ideas, and expectations of the audience for which they were written, and how these, in turn, were formed by the intellectual and emotional environment created for this audience by the social system.

Its thesis, briefly and all too schematically stated, is that the Elizabethan social order was based on a social, political, and religious compromise dependent on the fact that the old pre-Tudor aristocracy, the new Tudor aristocracy, and the bourgeoisie balanced one another in strength and that the continuation of this compromise was rendered impossible when the bourgeoisie grew in power after the defeat of the Spanish Armada. The destruction of the Elizabethan compromise brought with it questionings of the Christian humanist world view, a rationalization of the social position of the new aristocracy that dominated the thought of the time. Shakespearean tragedy expresses this world view and the philosophical and emotional reverberations caused by the breaking up of its material basis.

In making this study of Shakespearean tragedy I am undertaking to enlarge a great creative synthesis of Shakespearean scholarship, Theodore Spencer's *Shakespeare and the Nature of Man,* and to supplement a great work of Shakespearean criticism, A. C. Bradley's *Shakespearean Tragedy.* Profiting from the scholarship on Elizabethan psychology, social theory, and cosmology of Ruth Anderson, Lily B. Campbell, and James Emerson Phillips, Jr., among others, and from his own research, Spencer re-created a setting against which Shakespearean drama casts off new lights. Today, thanks to him and to E. M. W. Tillyard, whose *Elizabethan World Picture* appeared shortly after Spencer's book, we are so cognizant of the importance of the Elizabethan concept of hierarchy in human nature, society, and the universe that we can scarcely comprehend how it was almost entirely passed by before. But Spencer only partly fulfilled his purpose of presenting "the historical—the intellectual, social, and emotional—background" which Shakespeare "was able to use, and out of which he grew," [1] for, interested primarily in intellectual history and literary criticism, he confined his comments on Shakespeare's social background to a few perfunctory sentences. I have sought not only to fill in further details in the Elizabethan pattern of belief which he displayed but to show the social causes for the development of this pattern and for the age's intense awareness of the possibilities and consequences of its violation.

Bradley's *Shakespearean Tragedy* came after nearly a century of analysis of Shakespeare's characters and of attempts to extract aesthetic and ethical systems from his plays. Al-

[1] Theodore Spencer, *Shakespeare and the Nature of Man* (New York, 1943), p. vii.

PREFACE

though much of this is worthless romantic impressionism, German pedantry, and Victorian moralizing, the work of such men as Coleridge, Hazlitt, Schlegel, and Dowden furnished valuable critical insights that Bradley used in his book, which culminates the tradition. *Shakespearean Tragedy,* despite the scorn cast on it some years ago by those who would read the tragedies solely as poems and not as dramas, retains today its vitality as a classic. Its opening lecture on the nature of Shakespearean tragedy, which reveals a remarkable power for critical analysis and generalization, is one on which all subsequent writers must in some measure base themselves. However, the work of recent critics and scholars, notably G. Wilson Knight and S. L. Bethell, has shown Christian overtones in the tragedies of which Bradley was unaware or only dimly aware. By examining the Christian humanist basis of the tragedies I have sought to rectify the inadequacies of Bradley's description of Shakespeare's tragic vision and to re-interpret the four great plays he discussed.

In working out my thesis and my interpretations of the tragedies I have drawn heavily upon the publications of scholars in the fields of economic, social, intellectual, literary, and theatrical history as well as upon those of Shakespearean critics. Although I believe I have mentioned here or in my footnotes the works to which I am most indebted, it is impossible to acknowledge in detail the extent to which I have profited from the enormous labors of the many others who have worked in these fields. Suffice it to say that the fact that I have not referred to a book or an article does not mean that I did not consult it or that I did not learn from it.

I wish also to express my gratitude here to Douglas Bush, Wallace K. Ferguson, J. H. Hexter, Roy W. Battenhouse, and Basil Busacca, who were kind enough to read sections of my manuscript and give me the benefit of their opinions about them. I am indebted to them for both kind encouragement and trenchant criticism—criticism which was as valuable to me when it caused me to seek to reinforce my position to meet objections as it was when it caused me to modify it. Thanks are also due to the Fund for the Advancement of Education, which granted me a fellowship for 1952–1953 for the study of the history of the Renaissance. Although the fellowship was not for the purpose of writing this book, the study which I conducted as a result of the generosity of the Fund helped me in the formulation of some of the ideas contained in it. Finally, the editors of *Journal of the History of Ideas, PMLA, Shakespeare Quarterly,* and *Notes and Queries* kindly granted me permission to use as portions of this book articles published in their periodicals.

ANALYTICAL TABLE OF CONTENTS

CONTENTS

xiii

CONTENTS

Part I

THE ELIZABETHAN COMPROMISE AND ITS DISSOLUTION

Chapter I

THE ELIZABETHAN
COMPROMISE

1

Elizabeth's absolutism was of a limited kind. Unlike the modern dictators, she ruled without a local bureaucracy, all-pervading police agents, and a standing army. The secret of her power lay in the fact that the bourgeoisie was not yet strong enough to rule directly but required a strong centralizing force to maintain the "king's peace" and protect trade; that the old aristocracy, which had been weakened by its own internal struggles of the previous century, was too weak to challenge Elizabeth successfully; that the new aristocracy gained too much from the Tudor monarchy to do so; and that all of the upper classes needed the monarchy to enforce the vagabond laws against the dispossessed peasants.[1] Elizabeth took advantage of this temporary balance of classes to mediate between them, endeavoring to raise herself above them, but serving, in the long run, the interests of the dominant class—that of the enterprising gentry, the class engaged in "a more businesslike agriculture,"[2] particularly its most powerful and privileged section, the new aristocracy. Her reign was one of social, political, and religious compromise, based on this balance of classes.

Notes to this chapter begin on page 189.

2

The center of Elizabethan political life was the court. The importance of the court derived from the continued predominance of agriculture and the landowning classes in the national life. One of its most outstanding characteristics was that it was divided into factions, each of which exerted pressure on the queen in favor of its policies. Indeed, it is one of the features of the Elizabethan compromise that she controlled these factions, yielding to one or the other as she saw fit. "The principal note of her reign," writes a contemporary observer of the court, "will be that she ruled much by faction and parties, which herself both made, upheld, and weakened, as her own great judgment advised." [3] A contemporary letter filled with court gossip pictures the shifting strength and the intrigues of the various factions:

> My Lord of Sussex goeth with the tide, and helpeth to back others; but his own credit is sober, considering his estate. . . . My lord of Oxford is lately grown into great credit; for the Queen's Majesty delighteth more in his personage and his dancing and valiantness than any other. I think Sussex doth back him all he can; if it were not for his fickle head, he would surely pass any of them shortly. . . . Now is there devices, chiefly by Leicester (as I suppose), and not without Burghley's knowledge, how to make Mr. Edward Dyer as great as ever was Hatton; for now, in this time of Hatton's sickness, the time is convenient. [4]

Thomas Howard, Duke of Norfolk, and his cousin, Thomas Radcliffe, Earl of Sussex, were leaders of the faction which desired to retain the privileges of the old aristocracy against monarch, parliament, and "saucy upstart courtiers." The Duke of Norfolk was able to boast of revenues almost as large as those of the kingdom of Scotland.

4

Elizabeth at first acted very cautiously in regard to this powerful faction. In 1572, however, after the failure of the revolt of the Catholic grandees of northern England whom Elizabeth had employed as her officials, allowing them to exert their old feudal influence, Norfolk was sent to the Tower on charges of being involved in the conspiracy. "The North Parts" received other officials, loyal to Elizabeth, but it remained half feudal up to the time of the Civil War, when the Earl of Newcastle, the Earl of Worcester, and the Earl of Derby were able to bring to Charles's army large numbers of tenants and dependents. At Elizabeth's court Sussex, seconded now by the Earl of Oxford, the Duke of Norfolk's cousin, continued to head the faction representing the old aristocracy.

Elizabeth's policy toward this faction was to tame it, making it forget its dreams of bygone glories by offering it a prominent place in her brilliant court. "It was part of her natural propension," says Naunton, "to grace and support ancient nobility, where it did not intrench, neither invade her interest. . . ." [5] While making it dependent on her good will, she used it as a counterweight to the bourgeoisie. She sought to stem the pressure from below by using the old nobility as a bulwark. The old nobility, shorn of its previous overweening greatness, was to be a citadel of conservatism and a symbol of order in a changing society. "She did not suffer the nobility to be servant one to another," writes one of her principal courtiers, "neither did her gentry wear their liveries as in the ages before; their number and wealth was moderate, and their spirits and powers counterpoised with her majesty, from being authors of any new barons' wars, and yet reserved as brave half paces between a throne and a people." [6]

The arch-rival of Sussex was Robert Dudley, created by Elizabeth the Earl of Leicester, whose family owed its power and prestige to the Tudors. Leicester was the leader of the second principal court faction. Amid all the personal rivalries and feuds these two factions maintained an enduring enmity. Leicester championed the cause of the new aristocracy, which had attained its position under Elizabeth's father, and upheld advanced reform in religion. His faction grew in power after the first years of Elizabeth's rule until his death, although its influence was threatened during the negotiations for the French marriage.

It would be wrong to draw an absolutely hard-and-fast line between the new and the old aristocracy. They were both landowners of consequence; they were members of the same court; many of the new aristocracy had been ennobled by Henry VIII and a few by Elizabeth; some had married into noble families. In short, there was a partial amalgamation between them, as there often is between the members of two upper classes, wealth and power attracting to each other. Nevertheless, each tended to have a social, religious, and political outlook different from the other, and this difference had an economic basis.

The old aristocracy had long since accommodated itself to a money economy, accepting the fixed payments of its tenants in cash instead of in kind, but its conservative mode of managing its estates was reflected in its declining economic position, which forced many to turn to the ascending capitalists for money to meet their current expenses. Land being the safest long-term investment and important for social prestige, although the least fluid form of capital, landowners generally borrowed freely to meet higher prices. But, although borrowing on land was general, it was "the wealth of some of the nobility, and especially of the older families," that was most "locked up in frozen assets—immobilized in sumptuous appurtenances, at once splendid and unrealizable. More important, the whole structure and

6

organization of their estates was often of a kind which, once a pillar of the social system, was now obsolescent. Side by side with more lucrative possessions, their properties included majestic but unremunerative franchises—hundreds, boroughs, fairs, and markets; a multitude of knights' fees, all honour and no profit. . . ." [7] These "frozen assets" militated against the old aristocracy's reorganizing its estates and investing in industry.

Such difficulties confronted all conservative landowners, both peers and commoners, in proportion to the magnitude of their commitments and the rigidity of their incomes. . . . The former usually carried more sail than the latter, and found it, when the wind changed, more difficult to tack. . . . It would be easy to find noble landowners who move with the times, and make the most of their properties. . . . The smaller the part, nevertheless, played by passive property, as compared with active enterprise, the larger the opportunities of rising; and the increased rewards to be reaped by the improving landlord favored classes still ascending the ladder compared with those already at the summit. [8]

The very size of their estates, the fact that they were scattered over a dozen different counties, the cumbersomeness of their administrative machines, the opportunities afforded to their stewards to fleece their absentee lords made drastic reorganization exceedingly difficult. And the old aristocracy, a rentier class with feudalistic traditions, did not readily turn to business methods. [9]

When Lord Cobham appointed an expert to reorganize his finances, he was told that his employees were cheating him right and left. . . . When the Earl of Derby carried out a similar survey, the results were even more startling. One tenant . . . paid the Earl a rent of £2 and sublet it for £70. If some were thus incompetent, others were merely old-fashioned. Prices trebled in half a century, but Lord Darcy could still boast complacently "I have lived as my father did before me, of the old rents of my land." [10]

On the other hand, the rise in farm prices favored those who were able to commercialize their holdings. The dissolution of the monasteries had given a great impetus to a process that had been going on for more than two centuries. From 1536 to 1556 one fifth of the available land of England changed hands. The largest individual grants went to noblemen, but the largest total amount went to members of the gentry (the lesser landowners with the title of "gentleman" but without patents of nobility), with merchants and wealthy yeomen (prosperous free landowners not of gentle birth, who, possessing the middle-class virtues, "got down to making profits, not just subsistence out of the land" [11]) also getting a share [12] ; however, by the beginning of the seventeenth century most of the monastic land that had gone to the nobility and city speculators had been acquired by members of the gentry. Although the lay agents of the monks had enclosed land and converted arable to pasture,[13] this movement was greatly accelerated by the rapid turnover of the monastic property, as land prices rose and each buyer sought to profit from his purchase. The men who acquired the monastic lands confiscated by Henry VIII were the most aggressive in applying capitalist methods of estate management. "Consider you," exclaimed a writer of the time, "what a wickedness is commonly used through the realm unpunished, in the inordinate enhancing of rents and taking of unreasonable fines, and every day worse than other; and even of them especially to whom the king hath given and sold the lands of those imps of anti-Christ, abbeys and nunneries." [14] Thus, too, his contemporary, the preacher Thomas Becon, contrasting "our newcome gentleman" with the "true gentlemen," who study how "to profit many, to do good to the country, to maintain the poor, to relieve the succourless, to nourish the weak, to cherish their needy tenants," indignantly describes the business zeal of the enterprising gentry:

They are such as this common proverb noteth:

As riseth my good,
So riseth my blood.

They think all nobility to consist in the abundance of worldly goods. . . . Yea, they move every stone, as they say, to maintain and set forth their unnoble nobility, not caring how they come by it, so they have it. . . . If they buy any tenement and let it out again to the poor man, O how they do rack and stretch out the rents thereof, almost from a penny to a pound! Yea, and some of them, buying house and land in a town, suffer the houses to fall down and turn the ground into pasture, the poor not having where to hide his head.[15]

The commercialization of agriculture advanced most rapidly in areas close to London and the ports, which furnished a market for food and wool that encouraged an entrepreneurial rather than a dominantly subsistence system.[16] Most of all this was true of the counties around London. Where capital from capitalist farming or other sources was available, estates could more readily be modernized. Long leases could be waited out, and rents could then be raised or the tenants evicted. Where little capital was available, however, the temptation was to accept large fines in return for long leases. And in northern England, where the border fighting made a numerous tenantry necessary for military reasons, customary tenures, and with them feudal obligations, remained relatively unchanged, although even there heavy fines provoked peasant discontent.[17]

Thus, what with the smallness of the available local market and lack of capital, many of the gentry, like the old aristocracy, had difficulty in reorganizing their mode of production, with commercialization being effected most widely in the south and in the east. In these economically changing areas the gentry, constantly recruiting from the wealthy yeomen, from lawyers and to some extent from the merchants, especially the London merchants, who more than took the place of those of the gentry who foundered, grew in numbers and in wealth. Many of them engaged in trade and carried on mining; many obtained lucrative local offices. For offices, as well as for trade and industry, it was necessary to have capital, since they were sold at stiff, competitive prices by the crown, courtiers, or the previous holder. Moreover, education was a necessary qualification, and "education was expensive: the mere gentry of the north and west could not always afford to send their sons to Oxford and Cambridge. . . ." [18]

In sum, it may be said that very many of "the older gentry, on their smaller scale, were in the same predicament as the older aristocracy" and that "both classes were being transformed at an unequal rate." [19] So, too, Tawney asserts: "There was a struggle for survival, not only between large landowners and small, but between different categories among the former. It was primarily a struggle between economies of different types, which corresponded more closely with regional peculiarities than with social divisions. There are plenty of gentry who stagnate or go downhill." [20] The difference between the economies of two large landowners of north and south is illustrated by Rowse:

> The striking contrast between the value of North Country lands and those in the South may be seen by comparing the Survey of Northumberland's estates, or Westmoreland's, with those of the Earl of Bedford. Though Northumberland lived like a prince in his castle at Alnwick, with his feudal retinue

. . . when the Rising caught him he could raise hardly any ready money and was forced to pawn his George and let off his Yorkshire demesnes on lease. . . . For all the princely position of the Percys in Northumberland and Cumberland, the new southern Earl could have bought them up several times over.[21]

The new aristocracy represented the topmost reaches of the enterprising gentry. The territorial foundation which it had gained as a result of the great land expropriations had enabled it to forget its obscure gentry, lawyer, merchant, and yeomen forebears.

Those who have watched the uncouth, rough-handed master of a backward industry, who has wrought among his workmen as a friend or a tyrant, blossom, under the fertilizing influence of expanding markets, into the sedate suburban capitalist who sets up a country house in the second generation and sends his sons to Oxford in the third, and who scientifically speeds up his distant operatives through the mediation of an army of managers and assistant-managers and foremen, will not need to be reminded that economic changes which bring civilization to one class may often be fraught with ruin to another. . . . An Earl of Pembroke has been given immortality by Shakespeare. But the first of his name had founded the family on estates which had belonged to the Abbey of Wilton, and by his exactions had provoked the Wiltshire peasants into rebellion. The Raleigh family—it was a Raleigh's chance gibe at the old religion which set the West in a blaze in 1549—had endowed itself with a manor torn from the see of Wells, as the Grenvilles had done with the lands of Buckland Abbey. The gentle Sidney's *Arcadia* is one of the glories of the age, and it was composed, if we may trust tradition, in the park at the Herberts' country-seat at Washerne, which they had made by enclosing a whole village and evicting the tenants.[22]

Sussex might sneer at Leicester as a man with only two noble ancestors, but the new aristocracy could always find one strain or another in its ancestry to justify its claim to noble or at least ancient gentry lineage. The wife of Lord Berkeley, sister of the Duke of Norfolk, might refuse Leicester's suggestion of marriages between her daughters and his nephews and heirs, the Sidneys, but this snobbishness meant only that Berkeley, in losing a lawsuit to Leicester, did not retain the property in the family. Indeed, the day when the old nobility could wave aside the new aristocracy, ennobled or gentle, was gone. When Elizabeth chided Sir Philip Sidney for his quarrel with the Earl of Oxford, reminding him of "the difference in degree between earls and gentlemen," Sidney "did instance the government of K. Henry the Eighth, who gave the gentry free and safe appeal to his feet against the oppression of the grandees and found it wisdom by the stronger corporation in number to keep down the greater in power, inferring else that, if they should unite, the overgrown might be tempted, by still coveting more, to fall as the angels did by affecting equality with their Maker." [23]

The ranks of the new aristocracy were frequently replenished from the enterprising gentry. Sir Walter Ralegh, for instance, came to court the youngest son of an obscure country gentleman and by sheer dint of his extraordinary personality became for a time the reigning favorite. By and large, however, the new aristocracy was a small, specially privileged, self-perpetuating conservatized group within the enterprising gentry. It assimilated many of the feudal traditions while modifying the spirit of feudal militarism by the humanism of the universities, reviving chivalric usages such as the tourney in an effort to connect itself with the past. And, in accordance with the idea that one must live up to his position accepted by gentlemen as well as by nobles, the members of the new aristocracy, as the bright stars of a brilliant court, spent money lavishly and practiced old-time hospitality. The second Earl of Bedford dispensed largess so widely that he was charged by Elizabeth with encouraging beggary.

The new aristocracy was the great balance wheel of the Elizabethan compromise. Henry VIII had sought to stabilize the changing social structure by building up a new aristocracy from among the men he had raised to eminence by enforcing primogeniture in the transmission of their estates. It was this aristocracy which produced the great courtiers and administrators of Elizabeth's reign. It was able to maintain itself as a privileged section of the enterprising gentry by reason of the exclusiveness of the court.

One entered the court through patronage and attached oneself to the faction of the patron. Leicester introduced Dyer, Sidney, Essex, and probably Ralegh to court. Most of the higher members of the fifteen hundred or so persons who comprised the court were related to one another, either through blood or through marriage. The new aristocracy, like the old aristocracy, intermarried within itself. Sidney was Leicester's nephew. He married Sir Francis Walsingham's daughter, who, after Sidney's death, married Essex. Essex was Leicester's stepson and a kinsman of Sir Fulke Greville. Essex's sister, the Stella of the sonnets, was at one time spoken of as a prospective match for Sir Philip Sidney.

Similarly, a large part of the professional administrator section of the new aristocracy under Elizabeth was composed of men whose older relations had been in Henry VIII's service and whose sons and nephews came into office in her later years. The Cecils and the Bacons are the most well-known of these. The temporary stabilization of the social structure after the expropriation of the church estates had closed the floodgates. Although position at court under Elizabeth was insecure, abrupt rises and falls such as those of

13

Wolsey and Cromwell were characteristic of her father's reign rather than hers.

The new aristocracy was intimately involved with the development of commerce and industry.

> The great industrial and commercial expansion of the time was financed and directed behind artificial barriers which confined investment and control to some two or three score of great London merchants, a few enterprising courtiers like Burghley and Leicester, and a handful of progressive-minded industrialists and land-owners. Extensive economic control and a measure of social conservatism were achieved at the price of a free hand for big business.[24]

It was the members of the Leicestrian faction who furnished a large part of the subscription to the Frobisher and Drake expeditions (the Drake voyage returned dividends of some 4,700 per cent to the shareholders), the London merchants making up most of the balance. Sidney, especially, gave encouragement to the "merchant adventurers" and at one time tried to command a colonizing expedition as Ralegh did, but was prevented from doing so by the queen. His purpose was the seizure of one of the Spanish Indies, Nombre de Dios, which he argued would give England a strategic base and "an emporium for the confluence of all nations that love or profess any kind of virtue or commerce." Such a project would offer to the military adventurer glory and riches, to the religious divines conversion of the heathen from paganism and the "idolatry of Rome," to "the ingeniously industrious, variety of natural richesses for new mysteries and manufactures to work upon," and to "the merchant, with a simple people a fertile and unexhausted earth." [25]

By virtue of its dominant political position the new aristocracy acted as the senior partner in its alliance with the bourgeoisie.[26] Its special privileges were justified by its greater weight in the political scale. Especially did it speak not only for itself but for the bourgeoisie in the matter of foreign policy.

Elizabeth's foreign policy mirrored her domestic policy. She did not take an open anti-Spanish position at the outset of her reign, holding out promise of a marriage to Philip, just as she acted cautiously toward the great Catholic lords at home. Gradually she came to give aid to the Netherlands, with whom England had, as Fulke Greville said, a "league of religion and traffic," in their struggle against Spain, but not to the extent that the Leicestrian faction desired and not as part of a great Protestant League together with the French Huguenots and the free German princes. Her basic strategy was to maneuver between France and Spain, encouraging the suit of each in accordance with the needs of the moment. The high-school pupil who wrote "Elizabeth was called the Virgin Queen. As a queen she was a great success" did not do her full justice. In one respect, at least, she was also a conspicuous success as a virgin: as a marriageable spinster she dazzled the eyes of the rulers of France and Spain and held them back from war. Each hoped to gain England by marriage rather than by ravage. At one point she almost fell into the arms of the Duke D'Alençon, provoking a domestic crisis, as the Leicester faction thought that such a marriage, backed by the Sussex faction, was as bad as an alliance with Spain.

"A meeting was held . . . at the Earl of Pembroke's house," reported the Spanish ambassador, "there being present Lord Sidney [sic] and other friends and relatives. They no doubt discussed the matter, and some of them afterwards remarked that Parliament would have something to say whether the Queen married or not. The people in general seem to threaten revolution about it." [27] Leicester's young political lieutenant, however, was not content with talk. He wrote a letter to the queen unexampled in its frankness.

In his letter Sidney warned Elizabeth that the Protestants had so grown in importance and numbers as a result of Elizabeth's policy that she was "entrapped": she could not afford to alienate those who constituted her chief, if not her sole, strength. He warned also that the Catholics would rally to D'Alençon as their head and hinted that Elizabeth might be deposed by him, citing the example of "Lewis the French King's son, in Henry the Third's time, who, having no show of title, yet he did cause the nobility and more to swear direct fealty and vassalage. . . ."[28]

Fulke Greville adds what Sidney could not very well have written to the queen, that he feared that as a consequence of a French marriage England would follow the example of France. Common law would be disregarded, parliament and pulpit suppressed, England's "moderate form of monarchy" transformed into "a precipitate absoluteness," and the people taxed till they were reduced to the level of the French peasantry for the benefit of a few favorites, "only to fill up a Danaus' sieve of prodigality, and thereby to secure the old age of tyranny from that which is never old: I mean danger of popular inundations." [29] Sidney's understanding of the direction of France's development and of the dangers of England's proceeding along the same line is remarkable and justifies the Prince of Orange's, Leicester's, and Walsingham's encomia of him as a political analyst.[30] The Stuarts, however, unlike the Bourbons, were unable to shore up the bourgeois revolution, for commerce and industry had grown to a greater extent under the Tudors than they had under the Valois. But if France's "popular inundation" came almost a century and a half later than it did in England, the deluge which Louis XV foresaw was all the more far-sweeping.

3

The strength of the Elizabethan bourgeoisie was concentrated in London, which, with its corporate authority and its citizen militia bands, was highly independent. "London is most opulent," wrote the Italian ambassador,

> not only from her trade and great commerce with other countries, but by the many privileges enjoyed by all the inhabitants themselves without exception, that is to say, by the commonalty, merchants and artificers, from among whom some twenty-five persons, called "Aldermen," elected from among the wealthiest and most moneyed among them, rule the city with supreme power, almost like a Republic, neither the King nor his ministers interfering in any way.[31]

The importance of London is illustrated by the fact that it was Essex's failure to receive its support, on which he had relied, which made his rebellion a fizzle. When Elizabeth stood in immediate and drastic need of money, her financial counselor, Sir Thomas Gresham, the great merchant and founder of the Royal Exchange, would obtain a state loan from the Merchant Adventurers and other wealthy companies and from individual merchants. Gresham worked through the city authorities, whose practice seems to have been to assess shares to the various companies. These good relations with the mercantile community were cemented by Elizabeth's fostering of international trade through the improvement of harbors, the imposition of custom rates against foreign competitors, and the granting of bounties on new ships. "The merchant part of her kingdom was oppressed with few impositions," writes Greville, "the companies free to choose their own officers, to fashion their trade, assisted with the name and countenance of her ambassadors, the custom and return of their industry and adventures, contenting them in a free market without any nearer cutting of peoples' industry to the quick." [32] Elizabeth herself was one of those who invested in the joint-stock companies which financed Drake's and Frobisher's voyages.

If Elizabeth encouraged mercantile capital, however, she did not apply the same liberal principles of the free market to usurers' capital and the transformation of both of these forms of capital into industrial capital.

The great increase of capital caused by the expansion of commerce, the profits of the African slave trade, and the influx of gold and silver from the New World had brought into being new forms of credit. "The transactions ranged from those of the most disreputable class of money-lenders, who specialized in ruining young spendthrifts, to the mortgaging by nobles of thousands of acres to capitalists with an international reputation." [33]

An even more important consequence of the tremendous growth of capital was "a great industrial expansion which began . . . in the forties of the sixteenth century and was most rapid between about 1575 and 1620." [34] Important sections of commercial capital assumed increasing control over industrial production by providing the master craftsman with the raw material, the markets, and the credit which were necessary now that he was no longer producing for local consumption. In the great textile and the new extractive industries, the craftsmen and "free miners" were reduced from independent producers financed by the merchant to outright wage earners. "The transference of the control of industry from the individual producer to the commercial capitalist," writes Tawney, "was the most conspicuous result of the industrial revolution of the sixteenth century." This movement "rendered more acute the problem of maintaining the independence of the craftsman against the financier which had given its edge to the suspicion of the usurer, and created in the higher ranges of economic organization conditions in which that traditional sentiment lost much of its point." [35]

By 1575 foreign trade had also reached such proportions that brokers did a profitable business financing it. These were drawn from the ranks of the successful merchants who knew the market and found it more worth their while to finance new business than to engage directly in trade.

Because of this economic revolution the government had to make new regulations about the taking of interest. Much as Elizabeth and her Privy Council might fear these transactions, which were dislocating previous economic relations and provoking the resentment of the nobility, part of the gentry, master craftsmen, and many small traders, there seemed to be no way of preventing a "black market" in money. It was argued that circumvention of the statutes by concealed loans actually made the rates of interest higher than they were in countries where a maximum limit for interest had been fixed and that this gave foreign merchants an advantage over the English in the competition for international markets. Moreover, the government itself had to come to the great capitalists for public loans which the prohibition of interest would make difficult to float. "If we were not, the state as I take it, could hardly stand. . . . Where is money to be had in time of need if the city should fail?" [36] Calvin was also cited as allowing interest within limits.[37] The upshot of the debate was what Tawney calls "the compromise of 1571," which did not go so far as the commercial magnates wished, but legalized interest up to 10 per cent and permitted debtors to recover the interest under certain circumstances. In practice, as well as theory, however, the Act of 1571 was a turning point, for the debtor usually stood too much in need of his creditor for further advances to take legal proceedings to regain his interest. Moreover, in the interpretations of the common-law courts, the maximum interest came to be regarded as the normal.[38]

The other great problem which Elizabeth was confronted with as a result of the growth of capital was the regulation of the new industries. These industries—coal, saltpeter, glass, alum, soap, steel, sugar refining, saltmaking, and others— were established in the country districts or in seaports to avoid the guild restrictions of the craftsmen of the old corporate towns. Elizabeth attempted to control industry for her own purposes by assuming the powers formerly held by the medieval feudal, ecclesiastical, and municipal authorities. She adopted the policy of granting patents selling exclusive privileges to individuals or groups in one industry or another. By this means she was able to gain revenue and at the same time to reward her courtiers for their public services. The courtier who received the monopoly generally entered into a partnership with a "projector" or businessman to whom he offered his influence in return for capital. Such monopolies served to foster industry by attracting to it capital assured of freedom from competition. With the increase of capital, however, this system came to hamper industry rather than to foster it, as the fields for investment were closed by the monopolists.

Elizabeth also attempted to control industry through a comprehensive system of regulations, the Statute of Artificers, which "aimed at stabilizing the existing class structure, the location of industry, and the flow of labour supply by granting privileges and by putting hindrances in the way of mobility and freedom of contract." [39] The regulations had the support of master craftsmen and particular strata of the established industrial entrepreneurs, whom it protected against new competitors. But as in the case of the Usury Act of 1571, the regulations in practice did not prove so effective a brake on capital investments as they did on paper.

For the officials on whom Elizabeth was dependent for their enforcement, the justices of the peace, the city aldermen, and the common-law judges, were members of the gentry and of the wealthy merchant class whose interests were often opposed to applying strictly the regulations to the mining and new manufacturing industries.[40]

Politically, the power of the enterprising gentry and of the bourgeoisie was expressed in the House of Commons. In the first year of her reign Elizabeth re-established with its help the supremacy of the national state and of its servant, the national church. The House of Lords, with difficulty, was brought to accept these changes. At the same time, Elizabeth exerted a restraining force upon the House of Commons. The English Prayer Book was restored and its use enforced in accordance with the wishes of the Protestants, but the alterations of its language were designed to conciliate the Catholics as much as possible.[41] The rest of Elizabeth's long life was spent in maintaining this political and religious compromise.

Her methods, as well as her realization of the dangers to her throne from the religious extremists of both sides, can be seen in her handling of the petitions of the House of Commons of 1584 against various practices of the episcopacy. The House of Lords and the Archbishop of York rejected the petitions, but Elizabeth acknowledged that they might be justified and threatened the episcopacy with deposition if it did not grant the demands "without heedless or open exclamation." She warned, however, that, though she did not mean to encourage "Romanism," she would not tolerate "newfangleness." "I mean to guide them both," she declared, "by God's holy true rule. In both parts be perils, and of the latter I must pronounce them dangerous to a kingly rule, to have every man according to his own censure to make a doom of the validity and privity of his Prince's government with a common veil and cover of God's word. . . ." [42]

In her relations with Parliament Elizabeth combined tact, professions of love for her subjects, and bluster. Since the time of Henry VIII the spirit of independence in the House of Commons had grown so that the Elizabethan Arthur Hall caustically remarked that Commons was a new member in the Trinity.[43] It extended the conception of "matters of commonwealth" which had been regarded as coming within the province of its petitions to include "matters of state" which the crown had maintained as its own prerogative. Its petitions, moreover, were now drawn as bills ready to be enforced as law once Elizabeth had given her assent rather than as requests for legislation. The actual legislative body of the land was the queen's Privy Council, chosen by herself, mainly from members of the new aristocracy with administrative training and skill, but Elizabeth could not disregard the Commons' "petitions." Often she would accede to their wishes, but when, stirred by Puritan agitation, they passed bills encroaching upon her ecclesiastical supremacy, she warned them "as a mother over her children" not to proceed in this direction. [44] "By a certain amount of coercion, by practical concessions, and by astonishing tact, Elizabeth generally got her way," but her tactics "hurried on the growth of the house of commons, as a hot-house hastens the growth of a plant." [45] "By these degrees," wrote James Harrington two generations later, referring to Elizabeth's concessions and the "perpetual love tricks that passed between her and her people," "came the House of Commons to raise that head, which since has been so formidable to their princes that they have looked pale upon those assemblies." [46]

4

The Protestant bourgeoisie of Elizabethan England did not suffer the severe setback that the French Huguenots did on St. Bartholomew's Eve, for England's strategic geographical position and her well-indented coast line—as compared with the great unbroken rural expanse of France—made her seaport population a much stronger factor in national life than Admiral Coligny's followers were. England was spared the bloody carnage of the religious wars of Renaissance France. To the Elizabethans this seemed little less than a miracle. In spite of all the weaknesses and uncertainties of England's position at the beginning of Elizabeth's reign, in spite of the predictions that her rule would not last more than thirteen years, in spite of conspiracies, plots, attempted assassinations, and abortive rebellions, she had survived, and after 1575 England entered upon the "eleven wonderful years," a period of prosperity such as it had never seen before. It is no wonder that Elizabeth was an object of adulation.

But the Elizabethan compromise, always precarious, was undermined by this very prosperity. The new industries absorbed a large part of the floating labor class which had been brought into being by the great enclosures, the dissolution of feudal retainer bands, and the expropriation of the monasteries earlier in the century. The growth of London and other cities created an added demand for foodstuffs which turned the pasture lands back to arable, this time on a large-scale capitalist basis,[47] absorbing the remainder of the unemployed. Thus that mass of social discontent which had threatened all of the upper classes with revolution and had strengthened Tudor absolutism by creating a desire for strong government was eliminated. At the same time the rise in prices, which enriched those engaged in commerce, industry, and capitalist farming, weakened the economic position, by reducing the value of feudal dues and long-term rents, not only of the feudalistic gentry and the old aristocracy, as Sir Thomas Wilson noted in 1600,[48] but of the monarchy, dependent on its revenue from the crown lands and judicial fines. It was to this process of enrichment of the middle class and impoverishment of the crown that James Harrington was to trace the final decline of the monarchy in his day.

Chapter II

THE DISSOLUTION OF THE ELIZABETHAN COMPROMISE

1

Three years before the sailing of the Spanish Armada the English Jesuit leader, Father Parsons, urging the Pope and Philip of Spain to attack England immediately, wrote for their benefit a résumé of the balance of forces in England. He maintained that at least two thirds of England was Catholic at heart and would support a Spanish invasion if it were sanctioned by the Pope.

The counties specially Catholic are the most warlike. . . . The north towards the Scotch border has been trained in constant fighting. The Scotch nobles on the other side are Catholic and will lend their help. So will all Wales. The inhabitants of the midland and southern provinces, where the taint is deepest, are indolent and cowardly, and do not know what war means. But the strength of England does not lie, as on the Continent, in towns and cities. The town population are merchants and craftsmen, rarely or never nobles or magnates. The nobility, who have the real power, reside with their retinues in castles scattered over the land. The wealthy yeomen are strong and honest, all attached to the ancient faith, and may be counted on when an attempt is made for the restoration of it. The knights and gentry are generally well affected

Notes to this chapter begin on page 196.

also, and will be well to the front. . . . Of the great peers, marquises, earls, viscounts, and barons, part are with us, part against us. But the latter sort are new creations, whom the Queen has promoted either for heresy or as her personal lovers, and therefore universally abhorred. . . . Besides those who will be our friends for religion's sake we shall have others with us—neutrals or heretics of milder sort, or atheists, with whom England now abounds, who will join us in the interest of the Queen of Scots. Among them are the Marquis of Winchester, the Earls of Shrewsbury, Derby, Oxford, Rutland, and several other peers. . . . The enemies that we shall have to deal with are the more determined heretics whom we call Puritans, and certain creatures of the Queen, the Earls of Leicester and Huntingdon, and a few others.[1]

When Philip attacked three years later, the civil war which Parsons had envisaged failed to materialize. The execution of Mary of Scotland, which Elizabeth, guided by her fear of foreign intervention and of setting an example of regicide, had steadfastly opposed and to which she had sullenly assented only under the united pressure of her Council, Commons, and the people of London, had deprived the moderate Catholics of a claimant to the throne round whom they could rally. Moreover, it is clear that Parsons in his zeal had exaggerated the Catholic strength. Protestant-ism must have been far more widespread among the gentry than he indicated. Above all, Parsons had underestimated the Puritan "seadogs." The war was fought at sea. No army invaded England to test its unity.

However, if Parsons proved to be wrong in his anticipa-tion of a civil war, his analysis shows which classes were the most determined antagonists of Spain. Elizabeth, under pressure from Walsingham and Leicester's faction, had given grudging support to the revolt of the Netherlands, as "a bridle of Spain, which kept war out of our own gate," but sought a peace which would leave them a continued weapon against Spain. The control of events, however, passed out of her hands. The bourgeoisie refused to accede to the monopoly of the New-World trade granted to Spain by the Pope and was engaged in its own private war with Philip. Elizabeth, like an inwardly timid schoolboy egged into a fight by his zealous supporters, was finally pushed into a war which she did not want.

While Elizabeth dribbled out her secret aid to the Prince of Orange, the London traders sent him half-a-million from their own purses, a sum equal to a year's revenue of the Crown. . . . Privateers brought back tales of English seamen who had been seized in Spain and the New World, to linger amidst the tortures of the Inquisition, or to die in its fires. In the presence of this steady drift of popular passion the diplomacy of Elizabeth became of little moment. . . . The Papal decree which gave the New World to Spain, and the threats of Philip against any Protestant who should visit its seas, fell idly on the ears of English seamen. . . . The profits of the trade were large enough to counteract its perils; and the bigotry of Philip was met by a bigotry as merciless as his own. The Puritanism of the seadogs went hand in hand with their love of adventure. To break through the Catholic monopoly of the New World, to kill Spaniards, to sell negroes, to sack gold-ships, were in these men's minds a seemly work for the "elect of God." [2]

Elizabeth was forced to heed the clamor of the "seadogs," the more enterprising members of the gentry of the coastal regions who commanded the merchant marine. She permitted Drake to gather a fleet financed by the merchants of London and Plymouth to raid the West Indies as revenge for the seizure of English vessels in a Spanish port, although she warned him she would disown him if necessary. When Philip massed his Armada, she sent Drake to reconnoiter.

Characteristically, she appointed one of her regular officers vice-admiral as a check on him. It was her settled policy not to allow the "seadogs" too much power. "When the course of times," writes Greville, "made them [her 'gallantest sea commanders'] in power and gain, seem or grow too exorbitant . . . she striving . . . to allay that vast power of place with some insensible counterpoise, many times joined an active Favourite with that sea Neptune of hers, making credit, place, and merit, finely competitors in her service." [3] In spite of his vice-admiral's advice, Drake exceeded his commission by his raid on Philip's shipping at Cádiz, which materially delayed the sailing of the Armada. Elizabeth, however, continued to negotiate for peace up till the last moment. Only five months before the Armada sailed, she ordered her fleet to be dismantled as a friendly gesture and told the Prince of Parma, commanding Philip's forces in the Netherlands, that Drake had made his raid on Cádiz against her orders. She listened to the counsel of her negotiator, Sir James Crofts, that Drake and Hawkins wanted war because it was their business. When she did refit her fleet, she allowed it food and powder for only a limited time so that when the Armada arrived the crew of the English Navy was on half rations and lacked sufficient shot.

The vast majority of the fleet which faced and defeated the Spanish Armada, however, was composed of armed merchant ships, which came from every port in England. "The English fleet consisted of 195 ships (all told) and 15,334 men, of which only 61 ships and 7,901 men were in the direct pay of the Government. . . . The majority were vessels supplied by various ports and places in England, to contribute which was in many instances a great hardship." [4] London played a prominent part in the organization of defensive measures. It supplied ground forces of 19,000 men from its trained bands, many of the officers of which were sent to command the national levies in other parts of the country. "The Lord Mayor, further, called upon the City Companies, and the members put down their names for £54,000. The 'Twelve' great Livery Guilds (among 219 members) alone subscribed £43,700. . . . On the 3rd of April, the Corporation of London had resolved to fit out 16 of the largest ships and 4 pinnaces, and in July, it was reported that these 20 vessels (with 2,140 men) were costing the citizens £2,291 per month. . . ." [5]

The defeat of the Spanish Armada was a victory primarily for those classes which were later to conduct the war against Charles I. For Parsons did not prove so far wrong, after all. Catholicism suffered a decisive blow with the defeat of Spain, but the struggle between the old aristocracy and the bourgeoisie and its allies assumed new forms. The war with Spain was in reality the first phase of the English Civil War. Some fifty years after Parsons wrote his résumé the division of forces in the Civil War he had predicted proved to be substantially that which he expected—the parliamentary forces were strongest in the commercially developed Midlands and the south, especially among the merchants and craftsmen of the towns, and had with them a few peers of Tudor creation such as the Earl of Essex and his cousin, the sailor Earl of Warwick; [6] the royalist forces were strongest in the poor but warlike west and north and were led by the nobility, among them the heirs of the Marquis of Winchester and the Earl of Derby whom Parsons had mentioned as favorable to the Catholic cause. And it is significant that the outbreak of the Civil War found the entire royal navy, as well as every large seaport, on Parliament's side.

2

Pollard writes:

The year 1588 is perhaps more important as a landmark in England's domestic annals than in the history of its war with Spain. . . . So far as any one year can be said to have done so, it opened a new chapter in the political and constitutional development of England. During these last fifteen years of her reign Elizabeth seems like an actor lingering on the stage after his part has been played. She loses touch with her people; crown and parliament come into sharper conflict; the breach with puritanism widens; there is even a rebellion in London, and protestants look forward to a change of sovereign. The house of commons is girding itself for its hundred years' war with the crown, and only refrains from pushing its attack, as it told James I, out of respect for the age and sex of the queen. The Tudor period is dissolving into the Stuart.[7]

In chemistry, the solution of certain crystals may be made more and more supersaturated, but at a given point the addition of a single crystal will cause a precipitation. The defeat of the Spanish Armada was the event in the historical process which crystallized the opposition of the bourgeoisie to the crown. The bourgeoisie's self-confidence had been increased by the elimination of Mary of Scotland as a center of Catholic and feudal intrigue. The war with Spain mobilized it and gave it a spirit of independence. The result was a new militancy that expressed itself inside and outside of Parliament. The issues on which the enterprising gentry in the House of Commons, backed by the bourgeoisie, clashed with Elizabeth—control of the church, monopolies, taxes, foreign policy, parliamentary rights, the royal succession—had previously been raised, but the bourgeoisie was in no mood now to be chided into submission. These were also the issues on which it clashed with the Stuarts, for they involved the whole question of state power, toward which the bourgeoisie was tentatively groping.

In the very year of the defeat of the Spanish Armada, the surreptitious publication of the Martin Marprelate tracts ushered in a new period in Elizabethan politics. Their virulent attack on the bishops, the ministers of the queen, was a challenge not only to the ecclesiastical but to the social order. Hooker, the great defender of the Anglican Church, showed in his prefatory address to the Puritans that he understood clearly that their attacks on the church hierarchy were a challenge to the queen and the nobility as well as to the bishops:

> The changes likely to ensue throughout all states and vocations within this land, in case your desire should take place, must be thought upon. First, concerning the supreme power of the Highest, they are no small prerogatives, which now thereunto belonging the form of your discipline will constrain to resign. . . . Again, it may be justly feared whether our English nobility, when the matter came in trial, would contentedly suffer themselves to be always at the call and to stand to the sentence of a number of mean persons assisted with the presence of their poor teacher. . . .[8]

Although the tracts were suppressed, they found a wide popular sympathy in London. In 1593 Elizabeth imprisoned a member of Parliament for introducing a bill designed to check Archbishop Whitgift's commissioners and instructed the speaker of the House not to accept any more bills "touching matters of state or reformation in causes ecclesiastical." [9]

It was against the monopolies, however, that Parliament waged its greatest fight. As the Commons voted for increased subsidies for campaigns against Ireland and Spain, Elizabeth found herself compelled to sell more and more monopolies for either exclusive privileges or licensing and regulatory rights in industry and commerce. These monopolies and the industrial regulations were often criticized in the House of Commons and in the common-law courts. In the Parliament of 1601 the fight against monopolies was fiercest. In spite of the arguments of Francis Bacon and others that the matter affected the queen's prerogative, members insisted on bringing it up. One of them exclaimed: "Mr. Speaker, I know the queen's prerogative is a thing curious to be dealt withal; yet all grievances are not comparcable [sic]." [10] Some wished to write a bill and see if the queen would veto it; others wanted the House itself to undertake to cancel the monopoly patents; others thought it best to petition the queen. The excitement was such that Cecil remonstrated:

> Never did I see the House in so great confusion. I believe, there was never, in any Parliament, a more tender point handled, than the liberty of the subject, and the prerogative royal of the prince: what an indignity then is it to the prince, and injury to the subject, that when any is discussing this point, he should be cried and coughed down? This is more fit for a grammar-school than a Parliament.[11]

The turbulent House was being in part pushed forward by the London masses. Cecil gravely warned the members against discussing state affairs outside of Parliament and expressed his fears of the masses invading the sacred precincts of politics.

> I fear, we are not secret among ourselves. . . . Why, Parliament matters are ordinarily talked of in the streets. I have heard myself, being in my coach, these words spoken aloud: "God prosper those that further the overthrow of these monopolies! God send the prerogative touch not our liberty." I will not wrong any so much, as to imagine he was of this House; yet let me give you this note, that the time was never

more apt to disorder, or make ill interpretations of good meanings. I think those persons would be glad that all sovereignty were converted into popularity. . . .[12]

The members of Commons put themselves at the head of the masses who felt that monopolies in such everyday articles of consumption as starch, fish, oil, vinegar, and salt were raising the cost of living to an unbearable degree. Fundamentally, however, their quarrel with the system of monopolies was that it was constricting trade and industry. As one speaker said, "The traffic is taken away by wars; the inward and private commodities dare not be used, without the licence of those monopolitans." [13] Bacon, as usual, hit the pith of the matter when he ironically remarked, "If her majesty makes a patent, or a monopoly, to any of her servants; that we must go and cry out against: but if she grants it to a number of burgesses, or corporation, that must stand; and that, forsooth, is no monopoly." [14] The bourgeoisie did not really object to monopoly on principle, for many of its members had shares in joint-stock companies which were given monopolistic rights. However, it was no longer disposed to regard itself as a junior partner in the affairs of the nation and could not see why it should pay an exorbitant toll to a courtier or crown servant for the privilege of engaging in its own business or why it should be excluded from certain industries.

For members of the new aristocracy sitting in the House the denunciations of the "bloodsuckers of the commonwealth" must have been highly embarrassing. The reporter states that when the monopoly of playing cards was mentioned, Sir Walter Ralegh turned red, and when the monopoly of tin was excoriated, he got up to say that it had been an ancient privilege of the Dukes of Cornwall, that since he had received it the wages of the workers had been raised, and that he would gladly give it up if all other possessors of monopolies gave up theirs. It is recorded that he spoke so sharply that a great silence followed his speech.

Elizabeth succumbed to the pressure of Parliament. She continued to assert her prerogative, but discovered that she had been ill-advised in the grants of many monopolies, graciously thanked her subjects for having brought the matter to her attention, and revoked the most obnoxious of the monopolies. She was storing up troubles for her successor by giving Parliament a taste of blood without satisfying it completely.

The uncertainty as to who would succeed the aged queen, which hung heavily over men's minds, added to the nervous tension of the political atmosphere of the nineties. The parliamentary champion and anti-Episcopalian, Peter Wentworth, was imprisoned for introducing a bill to entail the succession to the crown. Elizabeth was too wary to allow any successor to be named during her lifetime, as she was well aware that such a move would cause all parties to court her successor and weaken her own power. The bourgeoisie, although too powerful to have its wishes overlooked in the final choice of the Council, was left on the outside looking in on this vital question. Nashe, in 1592, charged the advanced bourgeoisie with secretly wishing to do away with nobility and monarchy: "They [the 'collian,' the 'club-fisted usurer' and those 'sprung up from base brokery'] care not if all the ancient houses were rooted out, so that, like the burgomasters of the Low Countries, they might share the government amongst them as states and be quartermasters of our monarchy." [15] However, if any of the bourgeoisie really dreamed of a plutocratic republic on the model of the Netherlands, these were merely dreams, and the bourgeoisie was overjoyed to get James, who had condoned his mother's execution, had maintained a benevolent neutrality

during the war with Spain, and was known to be a good
Calvinist, rather than the Infanta of Spain or the Earl of
Derby.

3

As her relations with Parliament became more difficult,
Elizabeth leaned more heavily on the church. She thus
constructed the beginnings of a new alliance of the crown
and the church against Parliament which superseded the
alliance of crown and Parliament against the church established by Henry VIII. The first sign of the new alliance was
the appointment of Archbishop Whitgift and his two
adherents, Lords Cobham and Buckhurst, to the Privy
Council in 1586, a new departure in Elizabeth's choice of
councilors. None of Elizabeth's previous archbishops had
been regular members of the Council. Whitgift's function
was to oppose the democratic tendencies of Puritanism.

> He was divided from his victims only by the question of
> church-government; he believed in monarchy, they had been
> driven into democratic principles. He was a pluralist, and he
> held medieval views of prelatical dignity. "He maintained an
> army of retainers. He travelled on the occasion of his triennial
> visitations with a princely retinue. His hospitality was pro-
> fuse. His stables and armoury were better furnished than those
> of the richest nobleman." To Elizabeth he commended him-
> self by his high opinion of royal prerogative and his abstinence
> from matrimony.[16]

Whitgift helped Sir Christopher Hatton, known to the
Puritans as "an enemy of the gospel," to secure the lord
chancellorship. Backed by Hatton, Whitgift turned his guns
on the Puritans in spite of the petitions of the House of
Commons and the opposition of the majority of the Privy
Council. The Court of High Commission, a weapon which

had been forged for use against the Catholics, was employed against the Puritans, as it was to be employed by Laud.

By 1591 Elizabeth's council and court were undergoing an ever-increasing change.[17] Leicester, Sidney, and Walsingham were dead. Their successors, Essex and Ralegh, sensing an alteration of the balance of forces, oscillated politically. They intrigued against each other and against Sir Robert Cecil, Burghley's son, the politic successor of a politic father.

Essex gained tremendous popularity in London by carrying on the war policy of Leicester and by his raid on Cádiz. When the queen, disturbed by Essex's strength, cut off most of his income by refusing to renew his wine monopoly, saying, "an unruly horse must be abated of his provender that he may be the easier managed," he attempted to rally all discontented elements around him—Puritan ministers, Catholic noblemen, courtiers out of favor, unemployed soldiers of fortune. But his adventuristic tactics failed to pay dividends when the London city authorities refused to support him and the populace did not rise in response to his wild charges of a plot to kill him and to sell England to the Infanta of Spain. London was ready to applaud him for his victories against Spain, but it was not ready to do battle to restore his wine monopoly or to further his personal ambition.[18]

Ralegh, too, sought to steer his political ship to a haven of security and power, but found it difficult to keep his rudder steady in riding the troubled waters. As a popular ballad of the time says, "Ralegh doth time bestride: / He sits 'twixt wind and tide: / Yet uphill he cannot ride." He supported Cecil against Essex and was said to have held that "after the queen's death the English people should keep the staff in their own hand and establish a commonwealth." [19] He commanded no popular support, however, because of his share in Essex's downfall and because of his tin monopoly.[20] He was unable, therefore, to offer any resistance to Cecil's negotiations with James. With the coming of James, Cecil freed himself of Ralegh by a trumped-up trial in which Ralegh was accused of being in the pay of Spain and plotting with Catholics.

The fact was that the new aristocracy was no longer a vital cog between the bourgeoisie and the monarchy, and it was ground to pieces between them when they came into conflict with each other. The question of the day now was whether the monarchy would become a tool in the hands of the bourgeoisie or maintain and reinforce its absolutism by upholding monopolistic privileges and restricting industry. The new aristocracy had fostered commerce and industry and supported the monarchy. But it was now impossible to do both at the same time. The bourgeoisie required its own parliamentary spokesmen, free of any ties to the monarchy; the monarchy required corrupt favorites, ready to accept its uncontested supremacy in return for the spoils of privilege. Having outlived its function as a mediator between the bourgeoisie and the monarchy, the new aristocracy was crushed as an independent force.

4

James completed the break between the monarchy and the bourgeoisie. His previous experience made him adopt the more eagerly the policies dictated by changed class relations. His struggle with the democratic kirk of Scotland, which reflected the sentiments of the impoverished peasants and burghers, had taught him to hate Presbyterianism. "No bishops, no king," was his watchword.

In carrying out his policies, James, with the aid of Cecil, changed the character of the court. He had secretly corresponded prior to the accession with Cecil, the Earl of Northumberland, and Lord Henry Howard, and Northumberland had written to him: "Of the nobility some are not satisfied. . . . The nobility are unsatisfied that . . . offices of trust are not laid in their hands to manage as they are wont, that her majesty is parsimonious and slow to relieve their wants, which from their own prodigalities they have burdened themselves withal." [21] Under James the dissatisfied members of the nobility had no reason to complain. "When, in 1604, Lord Sheffield told the King that 'he reckoned I had repaired the ruins of every nobleman's house in England except his,' James could think of no better retort than that he knew of one Lord at least, Lord Cromwell, who was still hard up." [22] Through a rain of patents and monopolies and of lavish gifts financed by the sale of crown lands the nobility was rehabilitated.

James brought to favor the great Howard family, members and kinsmen of which had long been the enemies of the new aristocracy. Lord Henry Howard—a younger son of the poet Earl of Surrey executed by Henry VIII, a brother of the Duke of Norfolk executed by Elizabeth, a cousin of the Earl of Oxford who was Sidney's foe, an uncle of the Catholic Earl of Arundel who had died in prison—was created the Earl of Northampton. Under Elizabeth he had supported the match with D'Alençon, had corresponded with Mary Stuart, had been three times arrested on charges of treason, and kept in custody in the country after 1583 until his readmission to the court in 1600. Now he intrigued to deprive Ralegh of his offices and thus reduce him to desperation. His nephew, Thomas Howard, a son of the executed Duke of Norfolk, was created Earl of Suffolk, lord chamberlain and later lord treasurer.

The new aristocracy was also weakened by the influx of James's Scottish courtiers. "And now the principal managers of the English affairs," writes a contemporary court chronicler,

> were Salisbury [Cecil], Suffolk, Northampton, Buckhurst, Eger-
> ton (Lord Keeper), Worcester and the old admiral [Howard,
> Earl of Effingham]; for the Scots, Sir George Hewme, now
> Earl of Dunbar, Secretary Elfeston, after Earl of Balmerino,
> . . . the Lord of Kinlosse. . . . You are now to observe that
> Salisbury had shaken off all that were great with him, and of
> his faction, in Queen Elizabeth's days, as Sir Walter Ralegh,
> Sir George Carew, the Lord Grey, the Lord Cobham.[23]

By enlarging the peerage [24] and choosing favorites from the new peers and the compliant ancient peers, James was able to build up gradually an entourage which was entirely subservient to him.

A section of the new aristocracy, primarily its professional administrators, such as Cecil and Bacon, and the younger and less prominent courtiers, accommodated itself to the new regime. Another section, made up of men such as Sir Edward Dyer, who was deprived of his post as steward of Woodstock one year after the king had assumed the throne, retired from court.

> It was no longer possible for him [James] to gratify the desires
> of his new courtiers without neglecting the claims of the old
> household of his predecessor; nor could he bestow lavish gifts
> of crown land on his favorites of today, without attempting
> cruel and arbitrary resumptions of the long established grants
> of former princes. A court letter of the period treats feelingly
> on these matters: "The old servants are in a manner rather
> neglected than in the least measure countenanced. . . . The
> oldest officers in court retire themselves, and those more young,
> with their money are suffered to purchase preferment. . . ." [25]

Thus the new aristocracy was broken up as an independent force. For a century it had been at the head of the enterprising gentry and the bourgeoisie, whom it had served while maintaining its own special privileges. As the representative at court of a gentry reinvigorated by yeoman and bourgeois infusions, it had built a brilliant culture and its theoreticians had shaped the world outlook which dominated the thought of the time. With the growth in power of the bourgeoisie and the dissolution of the Elizabethan compromise, it lost its dominant social and intellectual position. But the greatest literary expressions of its world outlook, which had been formulated in the treatises of the Christian humanists of the early sixteenth century and had made its way through sermons, histories, and serious literature, were produced only when the material base for it was disintegrating.

Chapter III

THE HUMANIST WORLD VIEW OF THE NEW TUDOR ARISTOCRACY

1

The theoreticians of the new aristocracy were the humanists. The humanists were not merely scholars. Sprung from the commercial classes, without feudal connections, learned in the literature of the ancient world to which the monarchs of the new centralized state looked for a model, they were the natural administrators of the first Tudors. Colet, the son of a knighted merchant who was several times lord mayor of London, and More and Elyot, the sons of leading lawyers, held prominent positions under Henry VIII. The "new men" had a monopoly of the "new learning." This was the justification for their elevation. Dudley, the hated tax collector of Henry VII and grandfather of Elizabeth's Earl of Leicester, had stated that as a result of the ignorance of the nobility "the children of poor men and mean folks are promoted to the promotion and authority that the children of noble blood should have if they were meet therefor."[1] Henry VIII made the same complaint[2] and Cecil, Elizabeth's minister, repeated it.[3]

The traditions of the old aristocracy were indeed opposed to their accepting the new learning. During the Middle Ages

Notes to this chapter begin on page 198.

the education of the knight had been quite distinct from that of the scholar. There is no hint of book learning in the accomplishments of Chaucer's knight or of worldly knowledge in the accomplishments of Chaucer's clerk. The merits of the two types of education were frequently debated in medieval literature, and the knight was represented as regarding the learning of the scholar as a useless acquirement, quite unbecoming a man of action, which could only make him effeminate and impractical. The attitude persisted throughout the sixteenth century. Richard Pace, More's friend and "other self," in a letter to Colet about 1500, described how a peer of the realm exclaimed to him that he would rather have his son hanged than become a scholar or know aught than to wind a horn or train a hawk. To which Pace retorted that it was just such ideas which caused men of humble origin to be administrators of the affairs of state.[4] Elyot deplored the pride of the nobility which caused them to affirm that "to a great gentleman it is a notable reproach to be well learned and to be called a great clerk." [5] And James Cleland wrote in the same vein in 1607: "False and fantastical opinion prevaileth so against reason nowadays that ignorance is thought an essential mark of a nobleman by many. If a young child loveth not a hawk and a dog while he sitteth upon his nurse's lap, it is a token, say they, he degenerates." [6]

It was to the "new monarch" and to the new men of power, the new landed aristocracy and the great merchant princes, that the bearers of the new learning looked.[7] The new aristocracy and the merchant princes allied with it enabled the humanism of the universities to spread by founding free grammar schools. A broadly humanistic program governed these schools, where sons of the gentry mingled with sons of merchants. Sir Philip Sidney attended Shrewsbury and Edmund Spenser went to the newly founded Merchant Taylors School, where he was one of Mulcaster's leading scholars.

The spread of education and the increased interest in literature meant the growth of professional writers who looked to the court for patronage, especially since the temporary stabilization of the social structure had closed many of the avenues for advancement in government. The chief dispensers of patronage were members of the new aristocracy. Sir Philip Sidney was the center of this circle of literary patrons. The other outstanding patrons were Sir Philip Sidney's sister, Mary, the wife of William Herbert, the Earl of Pembroke; Mary Sidney's son, William Herbert, the third Earl of Pembroke; the Earl of Leicester; the Earl of Essex; his intimate friend, the Earl of Southampton; the Countess of Bedford; the Countess of Cumberland.[8]

In *Colin Clouts Come Home Again* Spenser contrasted the followers of Lobbin (Leicester), who promote the causes of poor suitors and encourage learning in every way, with the "gracelesse men" who abuse the gifts God bestows on Cynthia's realm. Deception is the only art the latter study; the learned arts they hold in contempt and poets they shoulder out-of-doors. In *The Tears of the Muses* he described how the old nobility, "whom thou great *Ioue* by doome vniust / Didst to the tip of honour earst aduaunce," despise "the brood of blessed Sapience" and repress the "learned Impes that wont to shoote vp still / And grow to hight of kingdomes gouerment." [9] It behooves "mightie Peeres" to encourage learning and to be themselves learned, for "that is the girlond of Nobilitie." But they "to be learned it a base thing deme" and "onely boast of Armes and Auncestrie." However, he said at the conclusion of the poem, Elizabeth and "some few beside," "lightned with her beawties beme," support the cause of literature and learning.[10]

If humanism was not favored by the old aristocracy, how-

43

ever,[11] neither was it favored by the growing Puritan section of the bourgeoisie which was coming to a revolutionary position independent of the new aristocracy. Nashe writes:

> All arts to them [the "collian," the "clubfisted usurer" and those "sprung up from base brokery"] [12] are vanity; and if you tell them what a glorious thing it is to have Henry the Fifth represented on the stage, leading the French king prisoner and forcing both him and the Dauphin to swear fealty, "Aye, but," will they say, "what do we get by it," respecting neither the right of fame that is due to true nobility deceased nor what hope of eternity are to be proposed to adventurous minds to encourage them forward, but only their execrable lucre and filthy unquenchable avarice.[13]

Glory, honor, immortal fame? The clink of cold cash sounded louder than the music of these Renaissance ideals in the ears of the bourgeoisie. A class "on the make" cannot afford to be diverted by the graces of life or by promises of being immortalized in literature.

Christian humanism was the world view of the new aristocracy. "The humanistic synthesis [of 'Christian faith and classical reason'] was an aristocratic orthodoxy like early scholasticism, but a synthesis less subtly metaphysical and theological and more humane, literary, and utilitarian." [14] This synthesis was a modification of the basic substratum of medieval teaching by the newly discovered classical literature to suit the needs of the new aristocracy. It was a cosmology, social theory, and psychology which rationalized the new aristocracy's social position.

2

Christian humanist literature saw society as an integrated hierarchy which reflected the cosmological order and the psychological nature of man. This view was essentially the same as the medieval view. In medieval theory society was a hierarchy of social classes and of groups and orders within them, each of which had its own God-given function and peculiar privileges and which was bound to the other orders and classes by mutual obligations. Each class had its own place in the Christian Commonwealth, which united them all and directed them toward one single common end. The world had been made to serve man, and the whole course of nature moved toward this end, drawn by God's love of perfection. Everything in the universe, created as it was by the will of God, had a meaning in the drama of man's redemption and salvation; everything was tied up with everything else into a scheme which was absolute for the entire universe. The aim of learning, therefore, was not the observation of how things happen in order to control them but the discovery of the purposes things served in the divine scheme. From this frame of mind arose the reading of allegory into nature and books. Allegory assumed that the universe was a divine, elaborate pattern with meaning and beauty—a pattern whose many figures, large and small, of different orders of dignity, artfully repeated the details of each other. The social hierarchy reflected the celestial hierarchy, the cosmological hierarchy, the psychological hierarchy.

The Christian humanists, too, assumed that the universe was a divine pattern, but, rejecting the scholastic searchings for first causes as vain prying into the ways of God, did not try to trace out the minutiae within the large outlines. They were opposed to overelaborate allegorical readings of the Bible and nature, trying to find the plain word of God in each as it is given to the intelligence of man to understand it.[15] They accepted, however, the general outlines of the medieval picture of the universe, although they modified and simplified its details, and continued to use the analogy between the social hierarchy and the other hierarchies of nature to defend it. To this defense they added the citation of classical and biblical example. The conception of social order they derived from these sources they counterposed to the feudal anarchic strife of the War of Roses and the communistic uprisings of the German Anabaptists and of the peasant insurrectionists of 1549.[16]

Thus Sir Thomas Elyot argues that human society must be based on "discrepance of degrees," for from the social hierarchy proceeds order,

> which in things as well natural as supernatural hath ever had such a preëminence that thereby the incomprehensible majesty of God, as it were by a bright gleam of a torch or candle is declared to the blind inhabitants of this world. Moreover, take away order from all things, what should then remain? Certes, nothing finally, except some man would imagine eftsoons chaos. . . . Also where there is any lack of order needs must be perpetual conflict. And in things subject to nature nothing of himself only may be nourished; but, when he hath destroyed that wherewith he doth participate by the order of his creation, he himself of necessity must then perish; whereof ensueth universal dissolution.[17]

The last sentence is pregnant with implications. Since everything is dependent for its existence upon everything else in the great chain of being which is the universe, a deviation by any of the links of the chain from the natural law which governs all of creation would result in the destruction not only of that link but of the entire chain. Man's fall had corrupted man and nature so that now ruin perpetually threatens the universe. After the fall, men, their reason overthrown, became bestial and warred against each other. Society was born as a result of the desire of men to suppress this asocial condition in which men robbed their neighbors

and to live in a manner worthy of human beings.[18] The
state, with its social hierarchy, springs, therefore, from a
human instinct and is necessary in order that men might
fulfill the laws of their being; its abolition would call back
the social chaos of the period immediately following the fall
and would finally bring about the destruction of the universe
and the perpetual conflict of the warring elements. It is no
wonder, then, that Elyot concludes that those who believe
in communism are "moved more by sensuality than by any
good reason or inclination to humanity." [19] Communism
appeals not to the reason of men, which is the distinctive
attribute of humanity, but to their baser instincts by promising them what is not rightfully theirs; it would turn the
natural order based on reason topsy-turvy and allow the evil
passions to have free sway.

The same concept of social order is presented in the 1547
homily "Of Obedience," which was published on the accession of the nine-year-old Edward when the Pilgrimage of
Grace was very fresh in men's minds and which, together
with the 1571 "Homily Against Disobedience and Willful
Rebellion," was required to be read in all churches nine
times a year during Elizabeth's reign. "Take away kings,
princes, rulers, magistrates, judges, and such states of God's
order," the 1547 homilist exclaims, arguing that the disregard of the central authority must bring communism and
chaos, "no man shall ride or go by the highway unrobbed,
no man shall sleep in his own bed unkilled, no man shall
keep his wife, children and possessions in quietness, all
things shall be common, and there must needs follow all
mischief and utter destruction, both of the souls, bodies,
goods and commonwealths." [20] Thus, too, did Sir John
Cheke adjure the rebels of 1549 not to seek an unnatural
equality:

And think besides that riches and inheritance be God's providence and given to whom of his wisdom he thinketh good.
. . . Why do not we then, being poor, bear it wisely, rather than by lust seek riches unjustly, and show ourselves contented with God's ordinance, which we must either willingly obey, and we be wise, or else we must unprofitably strive withall, and then we be mad? [21]

3

Society, in the Christian humanist world view, is, then, an integrated hierarchy which is constantly threatened by chaotic disintegration, as indeed is the entire universal order. The apex of the pyramidal social hierarchy is the single person of the prince. Through him human society achieves unity, the same unity as have all things in heaven and earth, which are "governed by one God, by one perpetual order, by one providence." [22]

This argument is an adaptation of Dante's argument in *De Monarchia*, where he states that humanity can attain the supreme virtue of unity only through a universal monarch, the Holy Roman Emperor, whom Dante conceives of as a sort of super overlord crowning the feudal hierarchy. In the "new monarch" of the national state, however, was concentrated a power such as the medieval theoreticians never dreamed of. It was to the "new monarch," who seemed to control the destiny of the nation, that the humanists looked for the advancement of the cause of the "new learning." The ideal of the Christian prince who would rule the commonwealth as the head of the body politic in accordance with the laws of reason was as important a part of the Christian humanist world outlook as the ideal of the emperor who would bring all of mankind into a united Christendom over which he would rule in accordance with the teachings of the philosophers was of the medieval world outlook.

The humanists cast about the king a halo of divinity. He was no longer a mere overlord who could be deposed for violating the feudal contract. He was God's vicegerent on earth, and rebellion against him was a sin against God. At the same time the humanists did not permit the king the unlimited absolutism which was given him by the theory of the divine right of kings propounded during the Stuart period. The adherents of the theory of the divine right of kings emphasized that the king had absolute power as a hereditary right derived from the first monarch of remote antiquity, on whom it had been conferred by God. The theorists of the newly founded Tudor dynasty, however, did not speak of the origins of kingship and of hereditary rights.[23] They exalted the king, but they emphasized the medieval doctrine of the king's duty to make operative the law of nature [24] and of his responsibility to God. By exalting the king as God's vicegerent the humanists reinforced his authority against the old aristocracy and the Catholic Church; [25] by emphasizing his moral obligations they taught him that, under the penalty of incurring the wrath of God and the disaffection of his subjects, he was not to use this authority in an arbitrary manner but in accordance with the advice of those who were his eyes and ears, his ministers whom he was to choose for their learning and virtue—that is to say, in accordance with the advice of the "new men" who had assimilated the "new learning."

The concept of the Christian prince was fitted into the medieval universal pattern. The rule of a good prince, it was held, resembles the rule of reason over the passions in a man of well-balanced personality, and human society and man's inner nature are only parts of the harmonious order of the universe.[26] The prince, who by birth and breed-

49

ing excels the rest of mankind, has it as his duty to fashion a virtuous and harmonious society after his own image.[27] Setting the example, he should seek to display the three prime qualities of God: the highest power, the greatest wisdom, the greatest goodness.[28] Then will he fulfill his function as God's vicegerent and, as the sun is a likeness of God in the heavens, will he be an image of God among mortal men.[29] His laws will be based upon God's law of nature, and he himself will obey them.[30] Among God's natural laws is that of degree.[31] Each man in his kingdom, himself included, will perform the function pertaining to his station and will be honored in accordance with his degree.[32] The prince should see to it that no one is idle, including the members of the nobility, too many of whom do not have the virtues which gave their ancestors their honors and indulge in wanton nonsense instead of learning the principles of government.[33]

The antithesis of the Christian prince is the tyrant. The tyrant is unable to rule others, for he is unable to rule himself.[34] Swayed by his emotions rather than governed by his reason, he rules not in accordance with the natural law which is revealed by man's reason but in accordance with his arbitrary will. In doing so, he revolts against God, whose deputy he is, and disrupts the moral order of the universe. In this he resembles Lucifer.[35] Thinking only of satisfying his own evil passions, he destroys the harmony of the social order, for "when they which have rule, corrupt with ambition, envy or malice or any other like affect, look only to their own singular weal, pleasure, and profit, then this good order is turned into high tyranny; then is broken the rule of all good civility." [36] Unable to sleep for fear of his people, the tyrant persecutes the good and promotes the wicked, severing all ties which might unite men against him and sowing contention and strife to keep them divided

and weak.[37] Thus, like the good prince, he fashions his
kingdom in his own image.[38] Lacking emotional balance, he
promotes social disorder; violating the natural laws prescribed by the human conscience, he destroys the social
relations prescribed by man's nature.

4

Although monarchy is the ideal form of government,
therefore, its corruption leads to the worst possible form
of government—tyranny. In actuality, moreover, princes,
even when they are not tyrants, are not complete in all good
qualities. This being the case, "it will be better to have a
limited monarchy checked and lessened by aristocracy and
democracy. Then there is no chance for tyranny to creep
in, but just as the elements balance each other, so will the
state hold together under similar control." [39]
Most important of all, however, are the education of the
prince and of the men about him. To keep himself from
going astray from the paths of virtue and to maintain social
order the prince needs wise counselors and a ruling class
of "governors." These governors, Elyot recommends, should
be chosen from among those of gentle birth, although men
of base estate who possess exceptional virtue and learning
may be advanced to positions of responsibility in the government.[40]
The basis of all the conduct books which described how a
gentleman should behave was that, as a person of superior
reason and virtue, with rare opportunities furnished for the
development of his personality by his cultural milieu and
by the exemption from degrading manual labor which his
wealth made possible, he bore a responsibility to society.
The very titles of respect, "gentle" and "noble," had moral

connotations. The gentleman was to excel in virtue and to exercise a moral leadership over society, which he was to serve primarily through his participation in the state. There were, to be sure,

> certain occupations, such as agriculture, trade, and even medicine, which, calling forth no enthusiasm on the part of idealists, but rather apology and restriction, were accepted as honorable for the gentleman to pursue. . . . But after all was said that could be said for such occupations, the fact remains that for the sixteenth century the ideal service for the gentleman was public office, through which without wages he might directly work for the preservation of the state, and the welfare of the people.[41]

This emphasis on participation in state affairs of course reflected the new strength of the national state. Military service was superseded by civil service, the knight by the gentleman. The gentleman united the virtues of the knight with those of the humanistic scholar, just as the knight had united the virtues of the barbarian warrior with those of the Christian saint.

As the court became the center of political life from which the monarch drew his statesmen, the social graces, the polished urbanity, the easy nonchalance of the courtier were added to the virtues of the gentleman. In his famous description of the true courtier, which is undoubtedly an idealized portrait of Sidney, Spenser contrasts him with the Italianate courtier Ape,[42] as the humanists contrasted a harmonious society with mob rule and with a corrupt and factious oligarchy and as they contrasted the Christian prince with the tyrant.

The Italianate courtier Ape is a light-minded reveler who mocks God and religion and displays the old feudal contempt for the scholar. His "thriftles games" and "costly riotize" lure the "noble wits he led" from "desire of honor" and "loue of letters" and feed their "vaine humours" with "fruitles follies and vnsound delights." He often, to be sure, plays the poet, framing "fine louing verses," with the "'sugrie sweete" of which he allures "Chast Ladies eares to fantasies impure," but such verses are not genuine poetry and are an insult to the sacred muses.[43]

The ideal courtier, however, seeks to gain honor and high position in the service of his prince, not because he is materially ambitious or vain, but because he desires the esteem of his peers and regards honor as a sign of the grace of God.[44] An athlete and a warrior, a student of science, geography, history, government, and literature, he regards all of these accomplishments primarily as training for his function to act as the counselor of his prince in peace or war.

Castiglione's *Courtier,* in Hoby's translation of 1561, was the most influential source of this ideal of the courtier. Sidney, whom most of his contemporaries regarded as the embodiment of the ideal, was said to carry the book about with him constantly in his pocket. In the pages of the *Courtier,* the new aristocracy saw, as in a magic mirror, an image of itself and the world which conformed to all its dreams. The image it saw was that of a man who, partaking in martial exercises and in the games and conversation of polite society with equal facility, imparts to each action, slight as it may be, the same easy grace which is the result of serious, almost religious, study; a man who moves, as it were, in time to the music of existence and who teaches his prince to fashion his princedom into a harmoniously ordered society, a society whose harmony blends with the harmony of the universe.

5

The humanists, then, accepted the divinely ordered universe of the scholastic philosophers, simplifying its internal details, making the new national monarch, instead of Dante's world emperor, part of the universal pattern, and altering the nature of the aristocratic ideal while defending the social hierarchy as part of the natural scheme of things. The Christian humanist world view was largely medieval in spite of the important modifying elements it contained, just as Tudor England was largely medieval in its economic organization in spite of the growth of capitalism. The expropriation of the monastic estates by Henry VIII had been the first stage of the bourgeois revolution, as Harrington, looking back at the time of the Civil War, well realized. Following this first stage of the revolution, the social structure was temporarily stabilized, as the bourgeoisie first consolidated its position and then gradually extended it within the limits of the feudal framework. During this period the new aristocracy, the chief beneficiary of the first stage of the revolution, acting as the great balancing weight between the old aristocracy and the bourgeoisie, was the dominant social and intellectual force. Its world view, like itself, was the product of the transition between feudalism and capitalism.

Chapter IV

THE DISILLUSIONMENT OF THE INTELLECTUALS WITH HUMANIST IDEALS

1

With the growing dissolution of the Elizabethan compromise there came a growing disillusionment with humanist ideals among the young intellectuals arriving at maturity during this time of unrest. In the late 1590's there arose a group of writers, many of them, such as Marston, Hall, Guilpin, and Bastard, young men starting their literary careers fresh from the universities, who were highly conscious of themselves as the members of a new generation that differed in its outlook from the older generation of writers. The slogan of this new generation of professional writers was: the time for sonneteering has gone; now is the time for stripping bare the evils of the age.[1] In advancing this slogan, these writers took the significant step of turning away from aristocratic patronage to concentrate on writing for the general reading public.

Before this the professional writer had already been well under way to becoming a seller of commodities on the market. In a money economy the tradition of the bardic entertainer of the feudal household was breaking down. Patronage continued, but it was mostly in the form of grants

Notes to this chapter begin on page 207.

of money or other favors to whatever writer pleased the patron's fancy, flattered him in a dedication, or rendered him a service rather than in the form of a fixed subsistence for individual writers. As the number of writers increased, the competition for patrons by the writers, insufficiently paid by their publishers in a time of rising prices, became ever fiercer. In the 1590's complaints were voiced by Daniel, Churchyard, Lyly, Ocland, Peele, Arthur Hall, Henry Lok, Richard Robinson, and others about the increasing dearth of patronage.[2]

From the Parnassus trilogy, a group of university plays staged at Cambridge during the years 1598–1602 dealing with the life of the scholar at the university and after graduation, we get a picture of how social conditions made the "university wits" turn toward satire. In one scene Sir Raderick, a knight who has refused a poor scholar a benefice because he cannot pay a bribe for it, expresses his enmity toward university men. These ragged clerks, the sons of weavers and butchers, he says, are never contented. Before long each scholar will demand a triple benefice, "else with his tongue he'll thunderbolt the world." [3] Sir Raderick, an old lecher, complains of the epigrams that university men make at his expense. His recorder agrees that "this scorn of knights is too egregious," but, in an allusion to the governmental prohibition of satire in 1599, hints that action will shortly be taken against it: "Scholars are pried into of late and are found to be busy fellows, disturbers of the peace." Sir Raderick replies fervently: "I hope at length England will be wise enough. I hope so, i' faith. Then an old knight may have his wench in a corner without any satires or epigrams." [4]

Academico, the rejected applicant for the benefice, does not turn satirist. The typical scholar, he returns to the university to complete his studies, although it is a melancholy life with slim prospects. Not so his classmate Ingenioso, the typical "university wit." He is attracted to London, the magnet for men who wish to make a living by the products of their brains. There he leads an uncertain sort of existence as a pamphleteer, "bound to the right honorable printing house for his poor shifts of apparel" [5] and trying desperately to find a generous patron. Finally he manages to attach himself to Gullio, an upstart pretender to gentility, who maintains him in a very niggardly fashion. In return, Ingenioso must write sonnets for Gullio to present to his mistress, listen to his inane chatter, suffer his supercilious manner, and flatter him lavishly. At length, Gullio, in a fit of anger because his mistress has rejected some verses which Ingenioso delivered on his behalf, cashiers him. Ingenioso forgets to soothe him with flattery and instead tells Gullio what he really thinks of him. This is the turning point in Ingenioso's career. For, with the termination of his relationship with Gullio—and Gullio, as he makes clear, is not a single individual, but represents a class—he becomes a satirist:

> My freer spirit did lie in tedious woe
> Whiles it applauded bragging Gullio,
> Applied my vein to sottish Gullio,[6]
> Made wanton lines to please lewd Gullio.
> Attend henceforth on gulls for me who list,
> For Gullio's sake I'll prove a satirist.[7]

He writes verse satire, libelous pamphlets, and satiric plays. Writs are sent out for him, and he is forced to flee to the Isle of Dogs, where he is able to attack freely "our feared lordings' crying villainy." [8]

And so the Ingeniosos wrote their satirical pieces, castigating contemporary society and its lords. Satire became a sort of literary craze. The professional writers all lived in London, banded together in a confraternity of the pen.

Under these conditions one writer influenced the other, and literary fashions spread rapidly. The writers of satire had abandoned the quest for patronage and now wrote exclusively for the reading audience.[9] Satire sold well, especially the scurrilous kind.[10] Satirists, in attacking amorists and other types of gulls and gallants, were able to give vent to their often very genuine discontent with the existing social scheme and to fulfill a demand of their audience.

The general reading public was composed predominantly of the middle class, which in the nineties had begun to lose its taste for euphuistic romances written in accordance with the literary fashion of the court. Robert Greene, the Elizabethan writer most sensitive to the demands of the reading public, began his career in the 1580's with moralizing romances which, although purportedly addressed to "gentlemen readers," undoubtedly also enjoyed wide favor with the middle class; [11] he ended it in the 1590's writing pamphlets describing city life dedicated to "the young gentlemen, merchants, apprentices, farmers and plain countrymen." The turn from romance to realism marked the coming of age of the bourgeoisie. In the works of prose writers such as Greene, Deloney, and Dekker, with their realistic narrative, their sympathetic depiction of the bourgeois milieu, their exposés of London low life, their sensationalism and death-bed repentances, and their religiously couched diatribes against big-city corruption, the sixteenth-century citizen found matter which had for him a journalistic appeal.

The formal satirists, however, addressed themselves not so much to members of the broad middle class as to the students at the inns of courts and the universities. It was to them that Jonson dedicated his *Every Man Out of His Humor* and *Volpone*. The classical form of the verse satire, its deliberate obscurity and veiled allusions, its criticism of society at large, the clique quarrels of the satirists, all made it an *avant-garde* literature of the intellectuals, whose disillusionment with the prevailing ideology it marks.

2

"The central figure of Elizabethan satire," writes Alden, "is the gorgeous young gallant. . . . Closely akin to the gorgeous young gallant is the professedly traveled gentleman." [12] The "gorgeous young gallant" and the "professedly traveled gentleman" were descendants of the "Italianate Englishman" of Ascham's generation. To the characteristics of Ascham's Italianate Englishman—flaunting of foreign habits and railing at his native country; esoteric vices; epicureanism; atheism; pretended Catholicism; political discontent; assumed wisdom about politics and life generally; libelous and seditious speech; flattery; specious courtesy; Machiavellianism—the malcontent traveler, as the Italianate Englishman came to be called in the nineties,[13] added that of melancholy, which had been implicit from the first. He assumed the Byronic pose of standing aloof from society, gloomily contemplating it while wrapped in meditations unintelligible to the ordinary man.[14]

Italianism was, as we have seen, an aristocratic fashion which was set by the faction at court led by Oxford, who, although secretly a Catholic for political reasons, was said to be an atheist and was certainly a skeptical freethinker. Although Catholicism and free thought seem to be strange bedfellows, their conjunction was not at all unusual during the Renaissance. The religious disbelief of the period was primarily the product of the old aristocracy with Catholic sympathies or traditions, as the material conditions from which it derived its power disintegrated and with them the ideas which sprang from these conditions. Young aristocrats of Oxford's type, lacking the profound religious faith that

59

animated each of Sir Philip Sidney's actions, practiced the vices they had learned in decadent Italy as a mark of their emancipation and as a relief from the tedium of their idle lives.

Italianism, however, was not confined to the court. The gallants of the court had their imitators among the young men of London,[15] which had sucked into itself from all parts of the country a motley crew of fortune seekers—younger sons of noble families, soldiers returned from foreign wars, and graduates of the universities and the Inns of Court whose fathers, rich yeomen and well-to-do merchants, had labored to give them the advantages of education and travel. Most of them were unable to find their place in court or city. Without recognized status in society, discontented with their lot, they formed one of the most serious problems of Elizabethan England. They crowded the playhouses, roistered in the taverns, and haunted the ordinaries of London, asserting their personalities by making themselves conspicuous and copying the Italianate manners of the court. Although many of these sword-wearing braggarts made pretensions to gentility, the most desperate and impoverished of them were the very dregs of society. Members of a declassed group, dissatisfied, cynical, without moral scruples or political principles, they were always ready to sell themselves to the highest bidder. Many of them joined the militant Catholics; [16] others became *agents provocateurs* for the government.[17]

The different kinds of "gulls," as the would-be city gallants were called,[18] were the satirists' main objects of scorn, for they were easier and less dangerous targets than the courtiers. However, the satirists not only derided the shams and impostors; they attacked as false and vicious the standards to which the gulls were endeavoring to conform. These standards, in fact, were regarded as corrupting and undermining society.

The point of view which Ascham had designated as Italianate, however, was regarded as only one of the two principal threats to the social order. The other threat was that of Puritanism. Like the Italianate, the Puritan was a nonconformist who dressed and acted differently from everyone else, although he had a trick of speaking through his nose rather than lisping affectedly. Like the Italianate, he was a carping critic of those in authority who regarded himself as possessing an esoteric wisdom and would introduce into England all sorts of newfangled innovations, although his came from Geneva rather than from Rome. And, like the Italianate, he was a scheming hypocrite, for his sober demeanor was a mask for his covetousness and his religious zeal a mask for his seditious purposes.[19] Gorinius the usurer, the father of Roberto in Greene's *Groat's Worth of Wit*, who dies advising his sons to think only of acquiring wealth and getting ahead in this world by trickery and dissimulation and to learn wisdom by reading Machiavelli, is a good example of the satirically drawn Puritanical hypocrite: "Wise he was, for he bore office in his fox-furred gown, as if he had been a very upright-dealing burgess. He was religious, too, never without a book at his belt and a bolt in his mouth, ready to shoot through his sinful neighbor." [20]

Both the Italianates and the Puritans were attacked as "Machiavellians" and "malcontents." Both of these words were highly charged with meaning. Machiavelli had studied statecraft as a pure science, entirely apart from considerations of morality. Such a point of view could not but have been shocking to the Elizabethans, who had been trained to think that the existence of human society, which was the natural corollary of man's God-given rational faculty and power of speech, could be maintained only if society as a whole followed the path of virtue indicated by reason. To discuss the exercise of state power as if it were unconcerned with moral laws was, for the Elizabethans, to deny God's order of nature. For them the Machiavellian was an atheist ready to commit any crime to advance his purposes or any enormity to gratify his desires.

The word "malcontent," although it was used to refer to anyone who was melancholy or in any way dissatisfied, had from the beginning the specialized meaning of political discontent. Apparently, the Elizabethans felt the same way as the police agent who arrested Mazzini because he kept to himself, read a lot, and took long, solitary walks in the evening—suspicious conduct, unnatural for a young man. The malcontent was a dangerous person, a troublemaker, one who was dissatisfied with his place in society, who wished to pull down those above him and crush those below —in short, one who refused to accept the social hierarchy which constituted part of the divine order of the universe.

Both Italianism and Puritanism were inimical to humanism. Each in its own way was an unbridled individualism which was destructive to the ideal of an integrated hierarchical society. Each was gaining strength in the nineties; with Elizabeth growing old and demanding more flattery and the great courtiers and statesmen of her reign dying off, the court degenerated and its whole tone became more Italianate, while the Puritan propaganda made its way "in shops, in stalls, in the tinker's budget." [21]

The young men at the universities and the Inns of Court saw the old Elizabethan order breaking up. Everything seemed uncertain. They themselves were not sure of getting the positions in the state and church for which they were being trained, as the number of graduates was too great to be absorbed. The satirists who inveighed against the degeneracy of the age expressed their feeling that the world was "mis-order'd" and the times "lawless."

3

The satirist who most fully expressed this steadily deepening current of feeling was John Marston. Marston went further than excoriating contemporary follies and vices. In his *Scourge of Villainy* he set the reality against the ideal and showed the incompatibility between the two.

Lust is the subject that haunts Marston's brain. For the presence of lust in mankind makes impossible the supremacy of reason, the self-possessed courtier, the well-ordered and virtuous society. In his third satire he describes the "damn'd vice" and "misshapen suit" of the gallant who thinks that sensuality is a mark of aristocracy and boasts of his giving himself up to his lusts. The extravagant conduct of this "inamorato" rouses the satirist's laughter till the tears come. His "inamorato" satire (Satire VIII) in the *Scourge of Villainy*, however, is quite different. It is neither scornful laughter nor merely a diatribe at a particular social type but sees lust as having corrupted mankind through and through. After passing in review several amorists, he finds "lust hath confounded all; /The bright gloss of our intellectual / Is foully soil'd." Reason, aided by the precepts of philosophy, had been wont to guide our actions. "But now affection, will, concupiscence, / Have got o'er reason chief eminence." Marston's explanation of the evilness of the time is expressive of his disgust and despair. Our body could not long retain its "stranger inmate," the soul, which was continually striving against the body's "dungy, brutish, sensual will." The intellectual part of our natures, scorning the "house of mortal clay" in which it was confined, silently departed, and with it whatever was good and beautiful and divine in man. Now the body is left to wallow in its own muddy filth, guided only by its unthinking appetites. It carries on as if nothing had happened, but its actions are purposeless, unanimated by any principle or reason. It raves, talks idly, adoring "female painted puppetry" as if divine,[22] and engages in childish pastimes, doting on baubles. The sacred synthesis is gone, and man is plunged in the slime of sensuality, in lethargy and brain-sick foolery.

Such a race of creatures cannot realize the dreams of the philosophers. In the light of reality Castiglione's ideal of the courtier is seen to be without substance. The courtier of real life resembles the ideal only externally. He is preoccupied exclusively with the outward signs of nobility, with the surface veneer of a decadent society. "Their richest time is wholly spent / In that which is but gentry's ornament." [23] As the soul of man has fled from his body, so the essential spirit of the courtier has departed, although the outward semblance remains. Marston's choice of name for the courtier whose portrait he draws [24] is highly ironic. For Castilio [25] is in appearance the complete courtier. He possesses all the social graces which Castiglione describes—and nothing else. His "substance" is but "ceremonious compliment."

Side by side with the figure of the courtier in Castiglione's dialogue appears the figure of the court lady, whose purity of mind, loveliness, and grace inspire him with a holy love. Marston also portrays a court lady,[26] and, like the courtier, she superficially resembles the ideal, but is really only painted show. Her beauty is not the reflection of goodness in the soul but the result of cosmetics on the skin. Seated in her coach, with its armorial bearings, she looks a "celestial angel"; having alighted, she is seen to be a "glazed puppet."

The feeling of contrast between appearance and actuality, between ideal and real, reaches its culmination in the seventh satire of the *Scourge of Villainy*, the "Cynic" satire. The streets are swarming with men, yet the Cynic cries: "A man, a man, a kingdom for a man!" For these are not really men. Circe's charm has overcome them, and the souls of swine now dwell in their breasts. They have the appearance of men, but the rational soul, the essence of man, is lacking in them. That gallant there looks resplendent in his gorgeous clothes, but his life is one of lewd viciousness. "Is this a man? Nay, an incarnate devil, / That struts in vice and glorieth in evil." He raises the cry again, "A man, a man!" and is answered, "Peace, Cynic, yon is one: / A complete soul of all perfection." This person seems to be a nobleman of high rank, for he "gapes for some grinding monopoly" and his lechery is "safe, secure under the shade of greatness." But beneath the external greatness of his exalted rank is filth and beastliness. In like manner, the Cynic dissects the other creatures purporting to be men. A shallow mind that is taken in by "seeming shadows" would swear that "yon same damask-coat" is a grave, sober magistrate. But this is mere illusion—"he's naught but budge, old gards, brown fox-fur face." That strutting soldier looks brave and heroic to outward show, but he is inwardly eaten up with the diseases of his vice-ridden life. All, all without exception, are only the shadows of men. Having lost his specific attribute in the order of nature, his rational faculty, man is no longer human.

4

If Marston, however, savagely exposed the reality beneath the appearance to contrast it with the humanist ideals, Donne placed these ideals under the hard light of his destructive skepticism, causing them to shrivel up. His satires are not bitterly critical of mankind, like Marston's. Rather are they coolly cynical in their observation of society. A foppish young man drags Donne out of his study to accompany him on a walk through the London streets, and Donne relates with amused detachment the fool's antics and chatter and his respectful attitude toward the effeminate courtiers and other grotesque types of humanity who pass by. Or he wittily describes how a person of strange aspect (of whose kind there are many in London) buttonholes him and recounts at great length the corruption prevailing in high places, while he, bored and fearful of apprehension, seeks in vain to escape. There is no passion or righteous indignation here, only cynicism.

Jack Donne was no penurious "university wit" writing for his living; he was a brilliant young man about town with promising connections and favorable prospects at court, "not dissolute but very neat, a great visitor of ladies, a great frequenter of plays, a great writer of conceited verses." His poems were circulated in manuscript among his friends, a group of fashionable young wits, most of whom he had met as a student at the aristocratic Lincoln's Inn. They were immensely popular, making their way into numerous commonplace books, for they expressed felicitously the mood of sophisticated cynicism current in this circle of advanced intellectuals.

In his early songs and sonnets and his early elegies Donne lightheartedly mocked and flouted the neo-Platonic and Calvinistic ideals of love. These poems were designed to startle with the frankness and unconventionality of their doctrines and to amuse with the cleverness with which these were stated. And they were intended to shock rather than to present a serious philosophy of love. Nevertheless, there was more than flippancy in these youthful productions. Donne was fascinated by the doctrines he advanced. He was preoccupied with the problems of love because love—the relationship between man and woman—involved the relationship between man and society, and man and God. The play of his wit mirrored his restless intellect searching beneath ideals and conventions.

Donne's wit undermined neo-Platonic idealism in every way: he described love in unromantic terms, as it seems to a sophisticated young libertine, depriving it of any trace or pretense of idealism; [27] he subtly parodied neo-Platonic theory; [28] he presented a doctrine in opposition to that of the Platonists which, although not advanced in all seriousness, was nonetheless destructive in the manner in which it stood conventional morality on its head. This doctrine, defended in "Community," "Confined Love," "Change," and "Variety," and taken for granted in such poems as "Woman's Constancy," "The Indifferent," "Love's Diet," and "The Primrose," states that love is simply a physical appetite which naturally seeks variety and change and that the conventions which seek to restrain it are the unnatural products of an artificial society.

The philosophical implications of the doctrine which Donne was presenting are most sharply brought out in "Variety." In it he contrasts the free love of a primitivistic golden age with the moral code of society:

How happy were our sires in ancient times,
Who held plurality of loves no crime!
With them it was accounted charity
To stir up race of all indifferently;
Kindreds were not exempted from the bands:
Which with the Persian still in usage stands.
Women were then no sooner asked than won,
And what they did was honest and well done.
But since this title honour hath been us'd,
Our weak credulity hath been abus'd;
The golden laws of nature are repeal'd,
Which our first Fathers in such reverence held;

Our liberty's revers'd, our Charter's gone,
And we're made servants to opinion,
A monster in no certain shape attir'd,
And whose original is much desired,
Formless at first, but growing on it fashions,
And doth prescribe manners and laws to nations. . . .
Only some few strong in themselves and free
Retain the seeds of ancient liberty,
Following that part of Love although deprest,
And make a throne for him within their breast,
In spite of modern censures him avowing
Their Sovereign, all service him allowing.

All of the humanist values are turned upside down here!
Political society is no longer the highest achievement of man
on earth, made possible and inevitable by the fact that man
is a rational, and, hence, a social and political being. On the
contrary, the lawlessness of uncivilized man is prior not only
in time but in nature. Mankind did not, in accordance with
its nature, grow up to civilization from the barbarism to
which it had been brought by the fall of Adam; it degenerated from its naturally free state to social bondage.

Instead of praising the harmony, the balance, the order
of Elizabeth's reign and its liquidation of the feudal dis-
orders, as Spenser had done in the fifth book of *The Faerie
Queene,* Donne deplores the "manners and laws" of the
state which have destroyed man's ancient freedom. "Our
liberty's revers'd, our Charter's gone"—these were strange
and startling words for Elizabethan readers. The state does
not guide men to virtue by means of its laws, says Donne,
for the good life consists of lawlessness, the free satisfaction
of all of one's desires. Any other concept of virtue is merely
"opinion"—social habit, custom. Each society has its own
laws and customs, prescribed by "opinion," which it believes
to represent true virtue. The Persians engage in practices

which are shocking to the English; the English engage in practices shocking to the Persians. There is no universal law of nature, no absolute and permanent good derived from reason—only the differing and changeable laws of the various nations based on "opinion."

Donne makes clever satirical use of this word. Plato had employed the word "opinion" to denote mere belief, as opposed to the knowledge derived from reason. Renaissance writers, consequently, used it to mean thoughts having their origin in the sensual appetite, which misleads and befuddles the mind. Skeptical philosophy, however, had also made the word familiar as referring to the moral code, which in this view is the product of a particular social environment.[29] When Donne wrote, therefore, "And we're made servants to opinion," he was repeating, with exquisite irony, the words of Elizabethan moral reformers,[30] but making them signify exactly the opposite thing—a plea for moral anarchy.

Similarly, his lament that "the golden laws of nature are repealed, / Which our first Fathers in such reverence held" had been made before, but to refer to a golden age, identified with the state of innocent purity of Adam and Eve, when man's natural reason was in complete control of his appetites and passions.[31] Since the fall of man, said the Calvinists, the glory of his reason had been tarnished, and only the elect, by virtue of the grace of God, were able to retain command over their sensual impulses. "Since this title honour hath been us'd" and the authority of social custom has grown, says Donne, "only some few strong in themselves and free / Retain the seeds of ancient liberty." These few persons—and here Donne uses the conventional image of Calvinist and neo-Platonist for the supremacy of reason within man [32]—"make a throne for [Love] within their breast." And love is synonymous with untrammeled sensual pleasure. Thus did Donne merrily demolish the ideal of the ordered control of man's inner nature and of human society.

5

Donne's corrosive cynicism and mocking skepticism, Marston's black pessimism, the other satirists' jaundiced view of contemporary society—these were the somewhat self-conscious expressions of an *avant-garde* literature which was outlawed by an absolutist government aware that it was a product of unrest. This literature, however, was merely the first territory touched by a current of thought and feeling which continued to flow, making its way through the drama, the great popular literary form of the period.

Chapter V

THE CHANGING SOCIAL CONDITIONS OF THE ELIZABETHAN THEATER

1

The great Elizabethan dramas belonged to the people of London, for whom they were a form of social divertisement, a means of historical and other information, and a source of aesthetic delight. The companies were formally under the patronage of some nobleman, but the dramatists addressed themselves to the popular audiences at the "public" theaters, whose tastes they knew intimately.

Harbage writes in his analytical study:

> We should distinguish among three Elizabethan audiences, recognizing that various occasions and various theatres would obscure our distinction: there was the genteel audience of the private theatres; there was the plebeian audience of such theatres as the Red Bull and perhaps the Fortune after the private houses had filched the gentry away; and then there was that audience both genteel and plebeian, or neither, of the nineties and, because of its peculiar prestige, of the Globe in the early decades of the seventeenth century. It was the audience for which nearly all the great Elizabethan plays were written. It was Shakespeare's audience. . . . Although the more leisured classes would have been better represented than by their pro rata of the population, it was predominately a

working-class audience because of the great numerical superiority of the working classes in the London area and because theatrical tariffs had been designed largely for them.[1]

By "working class" Harbage does not mean wage laborers but the craftsmen and their apprentices. These and the small shopkeepers far outnumbered the hired laborers and household servants. "In wealth," writes a contemporary London historian, "merchants and some of the chief retailers have the first place; the most part of retailers and all artificers the second or mean place; and hirelings the lowest room. But in number they of the mean place be first, and do far exceed both the rest; hirelings be next, and merchants be the last." [2]

Whereas many of the craftsmen of the decaying corporate towns were forced to take themselves to the country, London attracted to itself craftsmen to supply the needs of the court and the teeming metropolis. The craftsmen of London were sturdy, self-respecting, independent folk, the best craftsmen in England or anywhere else, says William Harrison, although in their desire for profit they do not pay so much care to their products as formerly. They were creators rather than slaves to machines and at the same time were freed of the restrictions of the medieval towns. Simon Eyre, the jolly shoemaker of Dekker's play, self-assured but respectful before the king, proud of his place but mindful of the distinction between classes, is an idealized hero of this class.

Likewise representative of the London petty bourgeoisie is Touchstone, the goldsmith of *Eastward Ho*. Unlike Security the usurer, he prides himself on not being a money shark, rising by other men's fall, but as having prospered through honest industry and thrift, avoiding immoderate speculation and bearing in mind the motto: "Light gains makes heavy purses." In the same spirit of conservatism and honest pride of station he objects to the marriage of his aspiring daughter with Sir Petronel Flash, an impecunious and improvident knight, because she is guided by "prouder hopes, which daringly o'erstrike / Their place and means." [3] Rather would he have "wealthy and honest matches, known good men." [4] His sober daughter, Mildred, the counterpart of her proud and ambitious sister, remarks, "These hasty advancements are not natural. Nature hath given us legs to go to our objects, not wings to fly to them." [5] Her bridegroom, Touchstone's industrious apprentice, Golding, promises her: "What increase of wealth and advancement the honest and orderly industry and skill of our trade will afford in any, I doubt not will be aspired by me." [6]

Golding is a model of apprentices. Although the younger son of a gentleman, he is proud of the trade to which he is apprenticed. Gentle birth was, in fact, quite common among the London apprentices, who, as numerous contemporary statements attest, formed an important part of the theater audience. The Statute of Artificers had restricted entrance into the skilled crafts and remunerative businesses to young men whose fathers could show certain property qualifications, and gentlemen, as well as citizens, were often glad to provide for a younger son in this way. A select body of single young men from seventeen to twenty-four, the London apprentices were full of *esprit de corps,* ever ready to voice their rallying cry of "Clubs!" Yet, except for some scapegraces such as Touchstone's other apprentice, Quicksilver, who, mindful of his gentle origin, scorns all trade, they served their masters obediently, knowing that they could rise to become members of the guild and perhaps even important city dignitaries. "I hope to see thee," Touchstone tells Golding, "one o' the monuments of our city, and reckoned among her worthies to be remembered the same day with the Lady Ramsey and grave Gresham, when the famous fable of Whittington and his puss shall be forgotten . . . and thy deeds played i' thy lifetime by the best companies of actors, and be called their get-penny." [7]

The London petty bourgeoisie and its apprentices, then, formed the bulk of the theater audience and set its tone. Other groups and classes, however, were also present, as Harbage shows, in the heterogeneous audience. The sharp young law students at the Inns of Court, like the apprentices, by whom, however, they were outnumbered ten to one, were accounted eager playgoers. Courtiers, gentlemen, soldiers, and professional men were also present, the wealthier ones sitting on the stage, while the lesser gentry and the poorer professional men must have shared the twopenny gallery with the wealthier craftsmen and shopkeepers. This section of the audience varied from the gallant caricatured in Dekker's *Gull's Hornbook* to Shakespeare's patron, the powerful Earl of Southampton, a confirmed theater lover. Finally, it seems that even the unskilled laborer would occasionally scrape up a holiday penny to go to this popular entertainment.

2

It is remarkable how this audience called forth its own kind of drama. Lyly, writing plays under the patronage of the Earl of Oxford for the boys' companies of Paul's and the Queen's Chapel to be presented before high-born audiences, had produced graceful, mannered comedies, supposedly portraying ancient times or mythological legends and full of classical references, but containing topical allusions to the contemporary court. Humanist authors of presentations at court had produced didactic dramas such as *Gorboduc*, with characters who were lifeless puppets in the hands of the author, following the tradition of intellectual edification of the early Tudor interludes by such humanists as Rastell. The writers for the students at the Inns of Court had produced scholarly tragedies such as *The Misfortunes of Arthur*, bloodless in their classical regularity. The later Jacobean playwrights, writing for a corrupt court and its hangers-on in the "private" theaters, produced frivolous comedies and shallow if sensational tragedies. On the other hand, playwrights such as Thomas Heywood, writing for the purely bourgeois audience at the Red Bull, produced bourgeois moral dramas, treating of middle-class life and preaching the prudential middle-class virtues.

The mixed audiences of the Elizabethan "public" theaters, however, called forth a drama which profited from the dramatic experiments and the intellectual content of the scholarly plays for courtly and academic audiences but had a full-blooded vigor of its own. "Give me life," cried the tanners, the masons, the innkeepers, the apprentices of all trades, as Falstaff had cried. Not for them were the automatons of *Gorboduc;* they would have a king who, although greater than life-size, "every inch a king," was also lifelike and could become "a very foolish fond old man." Stimulated by their residence in the commercial, political, and intellectual center of England (many of them, like Shakespeare, must have been quite fresh from the provinces, with the manifold activities of London still new and wonderful to them), where vessels would come sailing up the Thames with news of explorations and strange adventures, where the resplendent court of an idealized sovereign was close by, and where the open stalls were filled with inexpensive books which brought to readers all sorts of new information and entertainment, they were ready for something else than the peasant crudities of the morality plays, but they would not abide a drama whose characters were abstractions and whose action was stylized into a remoteness from life.

The companies of professional actors operating in commercial theaters, with dramatists writing for them who had absorbed the new learning and the new dramatic innovations drawn from the classics but who also knew the London in which they lived, were able to give them the drama they wished.

This drama was a romantic one. The London petty bourgeoisie had long delighted in prose romances of knightly adventure. The old chivalric romance had, in fact, become unfashionable among the sophisticated and had become the characteristic reading of the city. The romances satisfied the ordinary citizen's desire for vicarious adventure in strange and exotic climes and in aristocratic society, which had been stimulated by stories of far-off countries and of a glamorous court. This literary taste, which reflected the ideological subjection of the craftsmen and tradespeople, far from the incipient revolutionary sentiments of the capitalists engaged in banking and in industry, to the new aristocracy, was expressed in the drama in plays of heroic action by aristocratic heroes, in comedies of the romantic loves and adventures of lords and ladies sporting in delightful Arcadias, in chronicle plays of the glories of the kingdom in the reigns of strong kings and of its woes in the reigns of tyrants or weaklings. This drama was one which could be enjoyed by the aristocratic readers of *The Faerie Queene* and *Arcadia* as well as by the citizen readers of *Palmerin of England*. The world it presented was a glorification of aristocratic society and its ideology was the Christian humanist ideology of the new aristocracy, but it had a hearty plebeian spirit of its own. "Combine the message of the Gospels, the conception of 'laws and their several kinds' as codified in Hooker, the humane spirit of the circle of Colet, More, and Erasmus, and the moral emphasis of the Homilies, and one has the basic system of the popular drama in the time of

Shakespeare. Of primitive delight in action, combat, courage, and trickery there is ample evidence; but the heroes must conform with the system." [8]

3

A new element was interjected into Elizabethan drama with the migration of the satiric spirit to the theater after the banning of verse satires. This spirit was first manifested in the "private" theaters, whose higher fees insured a less plebeian audience. Jonson's *Poetaster,* presented by the Chapel Children at Blackfriars during the war between the theaters, satirizes the Globe by having one of its characters go there in search of ribaldry instead of to its rival, which plays "nothing but humors, revels and satires that gird and fart at the time." [9] It soon influenced, however, the plays presented at the Globe, not only the comedies but the tragedies.[10] Comedy took on a new kind of realism, anatomizing the class types of contemporary London, exposing to ridicule fools and knaves. Tragedy turned its attention from the contemplation of "the pomp of proud audacious deeds" [11] to the exploration of the murky depths of human nature. This conception of tragedy as the exposure of universal, affrighting evil was first voiced by Marston in his prologue to *Antonio's Revenge,* which marks a stage in Elizabethan drama as definite as the more famous prologues of Marlowe to *Tamburlaine* and of Jonson to *Every Man in His Humor:*

> If any spirit breathes within this round,
> Uncapable of weighty passion,
> (As from his birth being hugged in the arms,
> And nuzzled 'twixt the breasts of happiness)
> Who winks, and shuts his apprehension up
> From common sense of what men were and are,
> Who would not know what men must be—let such

77

Hurry amain from our black-visaged shows:
We shall affright their eyes.[12]

The conflict between the Christian humanist values and
the outlook on life represented by Marston and Donne—
the view of man as capable of ruling himself and society in
accordance with virtue and the view of man which either
bitterly or cynically rejected any possibilities of good in
him—furnished the emotional material for later Elizabethan
and Jacobean tragedy. Gradually, however, psychological
probing gave way to meretricious sensationalism, as the
drama became the exclusive property of a jaded, cynical
court. The moral tone, the emotional atmosphere, and the
philosophical sentiments of later Jacobean tragedy are
" 'Italianate' in the full derogatory sense in which Roger
Ascham employs the term, and to a much more harmful
degree than any literary force of Ascham's day could possibly have been." [13] In the drama of Shakespeare, however,
the soaring wings of the Renaissance are not clipped; he
retains his sense of the grandeur of man.

Part II

SHAKESPEAREAN TRAGEDY AND THE
ELIZABETHAN COMPROMISE

Chapter VI

THE SUBSTANCE OF SHAKESPEAREAN TRAGEDY AND THE ELIZABETHAN COMPROMISE

1

A tragic writer," says Joseph Wood Krutch, "does not have to believe in God, but he must believe in man." [1] This is well said and, I believe, correct: Christian humanism is not the only kind of humanism capable of producing tragedy. So in the appreciation of Shakespearean tragedy it is most important that we rise to Shakespeare's perception of the greatness of man. But in order to gain this perception most fully we have to understand the Christian humanist basis of Shakespearean tragedy, for it happens that his exalted view of man springs from his acceptance of this particular form of humanism. [2] We must look at the plays as perceptive Elizabethans looked at them if we are to apprehend most fully the Shakespearean vision of the potentialities and weaknesses of man and of the possibilities of chaos, with all of the significance this vision has for us today.

In this chapter I shall seek to present in summary form the essential characteristics of Shakespeare's tragic universe, using A. C. Bradley's remarkable analysis as a convenient point of departure, and to indicate in so doing how this uni-

Notes to this chapter begin on page 212.

verse is composed of the intellectual and emotional mate-
rials given to Shakespeare by his time. I shall, for the most
part, reserve the illustrative detail of my analysis for my
discussions of the individual tragedies, referring the reader
to the passages bearing out my general statements.

Bradley found that Shakespeare's tragic universe conveys
the impression of being a moral order that casts out evil by
the laws of its own nature but that mysteriously continues to
engender it and expels it only through a fearsome struggle
in which good as well as evil is destroyed. There are four
major alterations that have to be made in his picture of
Shakespearean tragedy: (1) Shakespearean tragedy conveys a
sense of divine providence; (2) this divine providence visits
a poetically appropriate retribution upon the guilty; (3)
characters and action suggest analogies with the Bible story;
(4) there are intimations of the heaven and hell of Christian
religion. In short, Bradley's analysis of the Shakespearean
tragic universe must be altered to make the order manifested
in the course of the tragedies explicitly Christian, its laws
the laws ordained by God, the evil within it the consequences
of man's fall constantly threatening to overthrow the entire
hierarchy of nature. Written when the challenge to Christian humanist values was felt most keenly, the tragedies
present most vividly the imperilment of the universal order
by man's evil passions, the legacy of his fall, reflecting in
doing so the dissolution of the Elizabethan compromise.

2

"A ghost comes from Purgatory," Bradley comments, "to
impart a secret out of the reach of its hearer—who presently
meditates on the question whether the sleep of death is
dreamless. Accidents once or twice remind us strangely of the
words, 'There's a divinity that shapes our ends.' . . . But

these faint and scattered intimations . . . avail nothing to interpret the mystery." [3] But what he does not see is that, while ghosts, prophecies, premonitory dreams, and portents are often doubted or disregarded, they are always vindicated. [4] Thus in *Richard III* the prophecies of divine vengeance of Margaret and of Richard's mother, the Duchess of York, are disregarded by the ironically skeptical, mocking Richard, only for him to find out that God is not to be mocked; in the destiny-haunted *Julius Caesar* Caesar, Calpurnia, and Cassius give up their skepticism under the pressure of the supernatural; in *Hamlet*, Horatio's doubts concerning the existence of ghosts are resolved.

The fact that they do not at first recognize the indications of the supernatural only contributes to the sense of man's blindness to the world of heavenly powers about him. Observing their ironic unawareness of the significance of prophecies and portents, the Elizabethan spectator would have had a certain godlike feeling of superiority, but he himself would have remained in the dark as to precisely how the prophecies and portents are to be realized. He would not have wondered whether a deity guides men's destinies but how it was to manifest itself.

Shakespeare, in keeping with the Christian humanist world view, shows man as part of a divine scheme of things the details of whose workings are beyond human ken but on whose general laws human beings may rely. The indications of divine providence used by Shakespeare would have been readily recognized by his audience, for they were commonly accepted as such. "One of the notions most useful to pamphleteers, writers of homiletic treatises, and playwrights," says Henry Hitch Adams,

was that Divine Providence intervened in the lives of men to assure the operation of divine justice. Divine Providence is a specific power of God which employs signs, portents, coincidences, seeming accidents, plagues, natural or unnatural phenomena, or minor miracles to dispense rewards and punishments according to His laws, either through His direct action or through His agents. The phrase "Divine Providence" was common enough in nondramatic literature, but was seldom employed by the playwrights. For this reason, providential operations have commonly gone unrecognized in investigations of the drama of the period.[5]

To find that Shakespeare, like the writers of bourgeois domestic "tragedy," uses the doctrine of divine providence without explicit reference to it is not, as has been contended,[6] to reduce his tragedy to homiletic drama. If one were to argue only on the basis of the use of the doctrine and not on how it is used, one could speak of Chaucer's "Pardoner's Tale" as just another homily on the text "Greed is the root of all evil." What matters is the depth and intensity of the writer's vision, whether he is reciting trite commonplaces or has made familiar doctrine come alive, whether he has shrunk life to fit a pattern or has presented the pattern as emerging from the contemplation of a work of art that seems to render the complexity of life.

Shakespearean tragedy, then, conveys an impression of an omnipotent power that is in command of the universe while somehow allowing man's will to be free to choose good or evil, a power whose operations, however, are shrouded in darkness, holding more things in itself than are dreamed of in the philosophy of Renaissance skeptics or in the metaphysical speculation of medieval scholastics. Even in *Romeo and Juliet* and the Roman tragedies, where Shakespeare relies upon his audience to free itself from conventional religious attitudes and regard the suicide of his heroes and heroines sympathetically as the noblest action that those guided by the attitudes and emotions of romantic love and by the philosophy of stoicism could take, there is a sense of providence at work. In *Romeo and Juliet* the adverse destiny of the lovers, pitiful and grievous as it is, is presented as part of the larger plan of divine providence. It is the means, the necessary means, by which their parents are punished in a manner that brings an end to the feud which had endangered the peace of the state. Throughout the Roman plays there is implicit a view of Roman history in which Rome was destined to become a great empire,[7] only, having become decadent and disunited, its plebeians ungrateful, its aristocracy arrogant, its emperors degenerate, to succumb at the height of its pride to barbarism, a view of history which invests the lives of the heroes with their country's grandeur and tragedy.

3

Although the ways of divine providence are dark, once its dictates have been achieved, they are seen to have been inevitable. The consequences of man's actions, which can only imperfectly be foreseen, seem in retrospect to follow so inexorably from their causes that a sense of natural law is conveyed, a natural law which the intimations of the supernatural indicate, however, is only part of a universal order. Retribution, in particular, appears in a form poetically appropriate to the crime. Bradley observed (p. 32) that in Shakespeare "villainy never remains victorious and prosperous at the last." What he did not notice—and it has been little noticed [8]—is the poetic fitness of the retribution that overtakes villainy. Such retribution is in accord with how Shakespeare's contemporaries thought God manifests Himself in this world.[9]

It is to be observed that the poetic justice of which I have been speaking is not the same as the poetic justice of the neo-classical critics. Sidney claimed that poetry is superior as a teacher to history, since history must frequently show the good dying in misfortune and the evil triumphing, while poetry can always—and should—show the good, having demonstrated their virtue in misfortune, come to prosperity, with the evil being punished. This became the credo of neo-classical criticism, a credo which, pressed to its logical conclusion, as was not generally done in practice, would make tragedy impossible, for only a villain, whose fall could excite neither pity nor fear, could come to misfortune. Samuel Johnson thus found Shakespeare's gravest defect to be his lack of a narrowly didactic poetic justice: "He makes no just distribution of good or evil." [10] There is indeed in Shakespeare no distribution of rewards and punishments so mathematical that all suffering is either shown to be warranted or made up for by subsequent happiness. A poetically appropriate retribution is, however, visited upon each of his villains.[11]

4

Shakespeare's villains, whose reason, while skillfully employed, has been perverted to serve their individualistic desires, blow themselves up in the explosion they themselves cause by their disregard of the law of nature. These desires, like the foibles and idiosyncrasies of the "humors" characters in the comedies, they make the be-all and end-all of their lives. In Twelfth Night the gracious living at Olivia's Tudor country seat would be destroyed if either the grim spirit of the "humorous" Malvolio, the aspiring puritanical steward of her estate,[12] or the loose conduct of the old feudal retainer Sir Toby Belch were the rule, just as the Elizabethan compromise was maintained only by bourgeois independent enterprise and feudal decentralization being held in check. In the tragedies it is ruthless individualism which threatens the natural order, whether the individualism is that of the feudal lords Richard and Macbeth striking at the rightful kings or that of the mercenary Iago, speaking the language of mercantile calculation,[13] and of the adventurer Edmund, whose words "Let me, if not by birth, have lands by wit" (*King Lear,* I, ii, 199) might have served as a motto for the acquisitive bourgeoisie.

Shakespeare's villains, then, embody values destructive to the ideal of Christian humanism. The conflict between different "passions, tendencies, ideas, principles, forces" animating opposing persons or groups that Bradley finds in the tragedies (p. 17) may be generalized as a conflict between Christian humanist values and anti-Christian humanist values.[14] And, as Bradley says (p. 18), the hero does not oppose "to a hostile force an undivided soul." In *Hamlet* the center of the struggle between these two conflicting values is within the prince; in *Othello* they are embodied in Desdemona and Iago, between whom Othello has to choose; in *Macbeth* the hero chooses values opposed to Christian humanism early in the play, but only at the end does he realize himself by the standard he has selected; in *King Lear* Edmund and the two sisters are arrayed on one side as against Edgar and Cordelia on the other, while Lear, in rejecting life before he is reclaimed by Cordelia, is opposing the values of Christian humanism in another way than do Edmund and the sisters.[15]

It may be added that Shakespeare gave this clash of values universal significance by placing the tragedies in the remote past or in distant countries while using contemporary character types and topical references.[16] Each tragedy, as H. B. Charlton has pointed out, has a lightly suggested cultural setting,[17] just as, contemporary illustrations indicate, the costumes of the actors, while predominantly Elizabethan, contained touches hinting of the historical period presented in the play, and this cultural setting contributes to giving each tragedy its own distinctive atmosphere. At the same time, however, each tragedy has features reminiscent of Elizabethan England, thus inviting the audience to think of the events of its own day as illustrating the eternal nature of man.[18]

5

The eternally tragic fact is that evil, in destroying itself, also destroys good. Yet it is important to note, as Bradley did (pp. 34–35), that the tragic hero also contributes to his own downfall. He is not merely the victim of evil, potent though it may be in this world, or of blind fortune, uncertain as this life is.[19] He has, Bradley found (p. 20), a "fatal tendency to identify the whole being with one interest, object, passion, or habit of mind." In doing so, it may be added, he becomes, to use the subtitle of Lily B. Campbell's *Shakespeare's Tragic Heroes,* a "slave of passion." The downfall of the Shakespearean tragic hero is brought about through some fatal defect in the armor of "solid virtue" with which he faces the "shot of accident" and the "dart of chance" (*Othello,* IV, i, 277–78), which can hurt his unconquerable mind only by using the opening provided by some passion. This is true not only of the guilty heroes Othello and Macbeth but of the comparatively innocent heroes Hamlet and Lear.

Concerned though Shakespeare's humanist drama is with the passions and struggles of human individuals rather than with the oppositions of allegorical figures, his characters, following the old patterns of temptation, sin, and retribution and of sin, repentance, and salvation, often are implicitly or explicitly compared with the biblical archetypes of erring humanity, diabolical evil, and divine goodness. In the Elizabethan homilies Adam's disobedience of God, Lucifer's rebellion against Him, and Christ's sacrifice for the sake of mankind were repeatedly presented as basic patterns which men followed in their conduct.[20] Writing for an audience accustomed to think in such terms of biblical analogy, Shakespeare was able through figurative language and allusions to suggest analogies in the course of his tragedies of human passion that gave them a deeper significance. The tragedies do not, however, contain within themselves elaborate and consistent systems of equivalences; Shakespeare's method, as in the history plays,[21] was like that of the Christian humanists in using the analogies between the various hierarchies of nature rather than allegorizing nature in detail.

The presence and significance of biblical analogies in Shakespearean drama are only just now being realized. Theobald, for instance, stumbled upon one of them in his observation that Othello's statement that Desdemona's death should have been accompanied by earthquakes and eclipses cannot but make us recall the earthquakes and eclipses at the time of the crucifixion, but he was shocked by what seemed to him a blasphemous comparison whose purpose he could not fathom.[22] By his time the Elizabethan audience's habit of thinking in terms of biblical analogy had been lost. Today, however, we understand that an allusion to the Christ story implying a comparison between a character and Christ would not at all have been regarded as blasphemous by the Elizabethans but would rather have been regarded as illustrating the idea that the best conduct is that which is most closely imitative of the conduct of Christ.

A character thus compared to Christ does not have to be inhumanly perfect or without any touch of earthiness. Desdemona, beguiling her anxiety for Othello by pretending to be merry, listens smilingly to Iago's double entendres and, frightened by Othello's violence, tells him a lie; she is, however, as we shall see, a Christ figure.[23] A character can even take on the aspect of a Christ figure for a moment although his conduct at other times is quite blameworthy. Thus Richard II, who has been a profligate and irresponsible monarch, in comparing himself to Christ is not merely engaged in self-dramatization but makes the audience regard him as one who through his deposition has become a martyr king.[24] Similarly, although Timon becomes an embittered misanthrope, there are allusions in the early part of the play, too clear and distinct to be merely fortuitous, which invite comparison between Timon's boundless generosity and Christ's overflowing love and between the duplicity of those who feed at Timon's expense and the duplicity of Judas at the Last Supper.[25] The analogies suggested in such scenes would have been recognized by the perceptive theatergoer of Shakespeare's day, just as the audience of Arthur Miller's *The Crucible* was able to recognize in it parallels to the stifling of intellectual freedom in its own day even though not a sentence explicitly related the Salem witch hunts to the happenings of the time. Such analogies are most prevalent in *Othello, Macbeth,* and *King Lear.*[26]

6

However, what most distinguishes these three tragedies and *Hamlet*—the four great tragedies which Bradley selected for extended discussion as having "one and the same substance" (p. 3)—is that the afterlife of Christian religion acts in them as an imposing but faintly painted and unobtrusive backdrop for the action. It is this backdrop which gives them what Bradley calls (p. 185) "the power of dilating the imagination by vague suggestions of huge universal powers working in the world of individual fate and passion." But, although there is suggested to the audience's imagination a heaven and a hell awaiting the outcome of the struggles of the characters, its attention is focused on this world, in which these struggles take place.

Christian humanism, ethical rather than theological in its emphasis, made possible Shakespearean tragedy, for tragedy must be concerned with this world, as the medieval moralities were not. I. A. Richards overstated what is essentially true when he wrote: "The least touch of any theology which has a compensating Heaven to offer the tragic hero is fatal [to the tragic effect]." [27] We can correct this overstatement by referring to Bradley, who, although misled by the mistaken notion of his time that Elizabethan thought and Elizabethan drama were "almost wholly secular" (p. 25), hovered on the brink of understanding the Christian implications of Shakespearean tragedy (p. 324): [28]

> The feeling I mean is the impression that the heroic being . . . is rather set free from life than deprived of it. . . . It accompanies the more prominent tragic impressions, and, regarded alone, could hardly be called tragic. It implies that the tragic world . . . is no final reality, but only a part of reality taken for the whole, and, when so taken, illusive; and that if we could see the whole, and the tragic facts in their true place in it, we should find them, not abolished, of course, but so transmuted that they had ceased to be strictly tragic. . . .

He adds in a footnote (p. 325): "It follows from the above that, if this idea were made explicit and accompanied our reading of a tragedy throughout, it would confuse or even destroy the tragic impression. So would the constant presence of Christian belief."

The intimation of an afterlife in Shakespearean tragedy does not become so dominant that the suffering of the good is made to seem unimportant in the light of eternity. There is no triumphant ascent to heaven, only a glimpse beyond the veil that contributes to the reconciliation essential to tragedy but does not nullify the suffering we have witnessed. We are left not amid the glories of heaven but with the survivors in this harsh world—a world, however, that, after doubts and perplexities, we have come to understand is ruled by a natural law through which is manifested its Creator. This understanding is no easy reassurance but a dearly acquired perception which has been attained only after we have been forced to look unblinkingly at man's situation here on earth and to accept it with all of its misery.

A resemblance with a difference between the ending of *Everyman* and that of *Hamlet* is significant. After Everyman has descended into his grave, Knowledge stands over it and says (ll. 892–94): "Methinketh that I hear angels sing, / And make great joy and melody, / Where Everyman's soul shall received be!" An angel's voice is then heard saying, in the final speech of the play, "Come, excellent elect spouse to Jesu! / . . . Now shalt thou in to the heavenly sphere." No angel's voice is heard after Horatio utters his farewell and prayerful wish (V, ii, 370–71), "Good night, sweet prince; / And flights of angels sing thee to thy rest!" Instead, there is a moment's silence, during which the audience may think back upon Hamlet's regeneration in the last act and may fancy that it hears what it will—and then its thoughts are brought back to this earth by the sound of Fortinbras's drum.

So, too, while Lear is accompanied and sustained at the end of his pilgrimage by the Cordelia whom he has shunted, as Everyman is accompanied and sustained by the Good Deeds whom he has neglected, there is only a shadowy intimation at the end of Shakespeare's play that Lear, in joining Cordelia in death, is following "the one companion who is willing to go with him through Death up to the throne of the Everlasting Judge," [29] but at the end of *Every-man* Knowledge proclaims (l. 890), "The Good Deeds shall make all sure." Both plays use Christian doctrine, but they use it differently. *King Lear,* with its tempest and its stormy human passions, its omnipresent animal imagery, and its vision of humanity finally devouring itself "like monsters of the deep" (IV, ii, 48–50), may be said to be a dramatization of the words of God in *Everyman,* which, since the play is concerned with the next world rather than with this one, remain undramatized in *Everyman* itself:

> For and I leave the people thus alone
> In their way of life and wicked tempests,
> Verily they will become much worse than beasts;
> For now one would by envy another up eat;
> Charity they all do clean forget. (lines 47–51) [30]

And after the *Lear* storm has worked its havoc, if order has been restored, it is an order that can be maintained only by the unremitting care of those to whom has been assigned the task to bear "the weight of this sad time" and "the gored state sustain" (V, iii, 322, 320) and that, we feel, must always be precarious as long as there remain in man the evil passions we have witnessed.

Just as the intimation of heaven does not obliterate the sense of tragic waste we feel in witnessing the suffering of the comparatively innocent heroes Hamlet and Lear, so the intimation of hell does not destroy our sympathy for the guilty heroes Othello and Macbeth. Dante's artistic breadth of sympathy made it possible for him to describe himself as fainting with pity for Paolo and Francesca when he saw in the second circle of Hell these two noble souls who had been overcome with passion. So, too, what makes *Othello* so painful is the fact that the audience is made to sympathize with the hero even as it is made to recognize that he has transgressed divine law and incurred damnation.[31] That he acts in accordance with his character, with its fierce passion lying deep beneath superb self-command, gives a sense of dramatic inevitability, but this sense of dramatic inevitability only strengthens the feeling of "he is proceeding to his damnation; the pity of it!" Similarly, the audience shudderingly accepts the justice of Macduff's epithet "hellhound" (V, viii, 3) for Macbeth, and yet underneath this response it retains some sympathy for him, a sympathy which has more of awed admiration intermingled with fear and less of pity than its sympathy for Othello.

> Such bravery and skill in war as win the enthusiasm of everyone about him; such an imagination as few but poets possess; a conscience so vivid that his deed is to him beforehand a thing of terror, and, once done, condemns him to that torture of the mind on which he lies in restless ecstasy; a determination so tremendous and a courage so appalling that, for all this torment, he never dreams of turning back, but, even when he has found that life is a tale full of sound and fury, signifying nothing, will tell it out to the end though earth and heaven and hell are leagued against him; are not these things, in themselves, good, and gloriously good? Do they not make you, for all your horror, admire Macbeth, sympathize with his agony, pity him, and see in him the waste of forces on which you place a spiritual value? [32]

7

Bradley's discussion of the admiration and sympathy we feel for the guilty hero brings us to the central paradox of Shakespearean tragedy. That paradox is expressed in his statement that the hero's tragic trait is also his greatness. The passion which brings about his downfall springs from a force of character that raises him above persons of ordinary clay. That force, that intensity, that Promethean fire, although it enlarges his capacity for suffering and brings it upon him, reveals the possibilities of existence, which we, dozing in our day-by-day routinism, forget. His vitality, the vitality of a Ralegh, of an Essex, and of all those other striking personalities of the new aristocracy who have made the word "Elizabethan" have such vibrant connotations, has potentialities for both good and bad, and the fact that it brings about his downfall does not destroy our awareness of this.

In giving his tragic hero the stature of a titan Shakespeare was making use of the Elizabethan concept of the king. A king, regarded as greater in every way than other men, was considered to have more occasion and capacity for intense feeling than they. "This jealousy," says Polixenes of Leontes (*The Winter's Tale*, I, ii, 451–54), "Is for a precious creature. As she's rare, / Must it be great; and as his person's mighty, / Must it be violent." The king was, in effect, a magnification of ordinary humanity, for, if his powers of reason were superior, his judgment was threatened by his greater intensity of emotion.[33] Thus, while the members of the audience regarded the king or other great person who was the tragic hero with respectful awe, they were also able to regard him as representative of themselves, to feel that

> the death of Antony
> Is not a single doom; in the name lay
> A moiety of the world. (*Antony and Cleopatra*, V, i, 1709)

The tragedy of the hero was their tragedy, his transgressions their transgressions, his suffering and death the payment every man has to make for them.

The Elizabethan audience's feeling toward the tragic hero would also have been influenced by the folk ceremonies in which its members participated, ceremonies that were survivals of pagan fertility cults in which a divine king or a god was presented as dying and being reborn in order to bring about through sympathetic magic the awakening of spring after the death of winter. The Londoner going to Paris Garden for his May games and mummers' plays may not have had the anthropologist's full knowledge of their significance (although the Puritan attacks show an awareness of their pagan origin), but, surrounded by the rural England from which he was often transplanted, he retained something of the peasant's sense of taking part in a vitally meaningful act. His feeling of everyone's fate being tied up with everyone else's, of communal life being renewed through the death of a powerful superhuman being, affected his response to tragedy. "Though the audience might not consciously equate the tragic hero and the god or king who suffers and dies for his people, the prevalence of the beliefs and habits of thought described must have served to increase the hero's dignity and to have gathered around him many associations of mystery and awe. . . ." [34]

Much more important in affecting the audience's response, however, must have been the Christian adaptation of the ancient myth and ritual pattern of which the folk ceremonies of the Elizabethans were remnants, the idea of the blessing wrought for mankind through the suffering and death of a man greater than other men. "Orthodox Christianity," writes Herbert Weisinger, "had at its disposal two versions of the paradox of the fortunate fall: the death and resurrection of Christ and the theme of Adam's fall and its subsequent benefits for mankind." [35] Each of these versions of the paradox cf the fortunate fall was associated with the idea of tragedy. "To call the Passion tragic," points out William Empson, "was a commonplace." [36] Christ's agony was conventionally presented to call forth pity as a supreme example of undeserved suffer-

ing. So, too, it was a commonplace to refer to the fall of
Adam as the first tragedy and the origin of all the rest.[37]
Adam's transgression was conventionally presented to call
forth terror as a momentous act resulting in the greatest
misfortune and performed in ironic ignorance of its consequences. Neither a divinely perfect Christ nor a more than
human Adam could become the subject of genuine tragedy,
but the association of each with the idea of tragedy must
have influenced powerfully the way in which the audience
regarded the tragic hero. The suffering and death of such
comparatively innocent Shakespearean heroes as Richard II,
Timon, Hamlet, and Lear bear some general resemblance
to the passion of Christ: the heroes seem to take on the
burden of the world's suffering, and at the conclusion of
their ordeal there is a sense of the renewal of life. The
transgressions of such guilty Shakespearean heroes as
Othello and Macbeth bear some general resemblance to the
fall of Adam: the heroes, noble men succumbing to temptation, bring to every man a new, deeper knowledge of the
nature of evil that is harrowing and terrifying, but they
bring also the inner paradise of a more profound faith in the
order of things which has been disturbed by their actions.
We need not suppose awareness of these general resem-
blances on the part of either the dramatist or the audience,
except at the moments of biblical allusion, when uncon-
scious associations were crystallized into conscious awareness, to say that they entered into the effect of the tragedy.

If the Shakespearean tragic hero, however, carried with
him associations of the suffering and dying god or god king
of the pagan fertility cults surviving in semi-feudal Elizabethan England and of the Adam and Christ of Christianity,
he also carried with him associations of the scapegoat who
embodied the forces of barrenness and evil and was, as Sir
James Frazer has shown, identified with or substituted for

the divine victim.[38] It is noteworthy that the comparatively innocent heroes Hamlet and Lear are malcontents, persons whose destructive cynicism good Elizabethans regarded with fear and shuddering. Hamlet, clothed in gloomy black, brooding morbidly, obsessed with thoughts of the body's decay and the foulness of sex, is a figure of death. Lear in his madness, seeing humanity as wholly evil, calls for the thunder to destroy all the seeds that produce men. Probing deeply into life and exposing that which the "normal" man would prefer to forget, they, like the guilty heroes, challenge the order of things. It is this challenge to the order of things which makes the Shakespearean tragedies not merely dramatic exempla that comfortably reassured their spectators concerning the rightness of their views but imaginative experiences that shook them up only to renew their basic faith and render it richer and deeper by having been forced to assimilate what Hamlet and Lear saw.

Chapter VII

HAMLET

1

In *Hamlet* the conflict between the acceptance of the Christian humanist outlook on life and a cynical disillusionment with it rages within the hero. Hamlet is depicted as having been before his father's death a prince who was a scholar, soldier, and the first courtier of the land. Ophelia exclaims brokenheartedly, as he leaves her, wild and ranting:

> O, what a noble mind is here o'erthrown!
> The courtier's, scholar's, soldier's eye, tongue, sword,
> The expectancy and rose of the fair state,
> The glass of fashion and the mould of form,
> Th' observ'd of all observers—quite, quite down! (III, i, 158–62)

Even in the depressed state in which we see him during the play there is evidence of what he was. He is an expert fencer, shows an intelligent interest in the drama, and possesses a philosophical and imaginative mind. Governed by the ideals of Castiglione, he had seen the universe in glowing colors and man as partaking of its beauty and reflecting with it the glory of his Creator. He reverts to this view of man— a skeptic struggling with his skepticism and a cynic contrasting ideals with reality, he voices, like Donne, the con-

Notes to this chapter begin on page 219.

flicting views of man, love, death, the universe—when he wishes to spur himself on:

> What is a man,
> If his chief good and market of his time
> Be but to sleep and feed? A beast, no more.
> Sure, He that made us with such large discourse,
> Looking before and after, gave us not
> That capability and godlike reason
> To fust in us unus'd. (IV, iv, 33–39)

The discovery of lust in human nature—for Hamlet's generalizing mind extends his sudden knowledge of his mother's true character to all mankind—has plunged him into the depths of melancholy,[1] and the revelation of his father's ghost and the burden it imposes on him prevent him from pulling himself out of it. From the perfect courtier he has become a malcontent, bitter, sneering, cynical. His "noble and most sovereign reason" is "like sweet bells jangled, out of tune and harsh" (III, i, 165–66). He even wears the recognized garb of the malcontent—"solemn black" (I, ii, 78), with unbraced doublet and ungartered stockings hanging down.[2] The court might have thought that he was wearing black out of deference for his father and that his apparel was disordered because he was a crazed lover, but the Elizabethan theater audience, to whom Hamlet had revealed the depths of his despair, knew differently and shuddered inwardly, even as it sympathized with him: he was a figure of death haunting the smugly mundane, corrupt court. The evil that he exposes to sight is seen actually to exist, yet he himself is opposed to life. The state of mind which he reveals in his raging at Ophelia is a public danger. The audience might sympathize with him in his suffering and his disillusionment, but this did not alter for it the fact that, as Laertes said (I, iii, 18), on him, the Prince of Denmark, depended "the safety and the health of the whole state" and that he himself was soul sick.

2

The audience's feeling toward Hamlet was, therefore, mixed, as it was toward the revenge to which he dedicates himself. "There is no question that the Elizabethans firmly believed the law of God to forbid private vengeance. . . . [Yet] there was a very real tradition existing in favor of revenge under certain circumstances, and especially of the heir's legal duty to revenge his father." [3] The Elizabethan tradition favoring revenge against a father's slayers may be compared to the "unwritten law" existing today in some parts of the United States which prompts juries to declare not guilty a husband who has killed his wife's lover caught in the act of adultery. Elizabethan public opinion, like public opinion in these American communities, sympathized with revenge committed in the heat of passion although this revenge was forbidden by the official moral, religious, and legal code. However, the contradiction between the official code and deep-lying tradition must have been much more sharply felt by the Elizabethans than by Americans, for it was continually being pointed up by preachers and political theorists, who, intent on defending the authority of the state against the continuing feudal tradition of personal action, constantly inveighed against revenge.

Dramatists played upon this contradiction, presenting revengers with whose situations the audience was called upon to sympathize but who, in carrying out their revenge, heaped crime upon crime to bring death and destruction to themselves as well as to their criminal victims.

The revenger of the drama started out with the sympathy of the audience if his cause were good. . . . It was only . . . when he turned to "Machiavellian" treacherous intrigues that the audience began to veer against him. . . . The audience sentimentally sympathized with the Kydian hero revenger and hoped for his success, but only on condition that he did not survive. Thus his death was accepted as expiation for the violent motives which had forced him to override the rules of God and, without awaiting the slow revenge of divine retribution, to carve out a bloody revenge for himself.[4]

Although Hamlet is not the ordinary Kydian hero revenger, Shakespeare, like the other writers of revenge drama, played upon his audience's mixed feelings about revenge. "There would be few Elizabethans," writes Bowers, "who would condemn the son's blood-revenge on a treacherous murderer whom the law could not apprehend for lack of proper evidence."[5] Hamlet, of course, is such a son. He has no legal proof of Claudius' guilt; the royal court, which has acquiesced in Claudius' incestuous marriage, is, moreover, made up of corrupt creatures of the king; and in any case a king, although he should be governed by the law of nature, cannot be tried by his subjects.[6] And yet, although the tradition of revenge would not permit Elizabethans to condemn wholeheartedly a son impelled by what he conceived of as his filial duty to kill his father's murderer, they could not readily forget what was being dinned into their ears by homilists and moralists: that revenge is criminal. That Claudius is the de facto king complicated matters even more, for it was a Tudor political axiom that regicide, even of a wicked sovereign, was rebellion against God's wishes.[7]

The Elizabethan audience was thus in a moral dilemma: it sympathized with Hamlet's desire for revenge but felt that its fulfillment would be wrong. Like Hamlet, it was divided within itself. Amid all of Hamlet's doubts, however

—the doubts of a melancholiac [8] searching desperately for what is right in a world of baffling uncertainties—he never questions the ethics of the code of revenge. The moral dilemma of the audience was not eased by being formulated and logically debated on the stage. Rather did it grow in intensity as it watched Hamlet flagellating himself for his inaction, for it realized that his inaction was caused by a sickness of soul, but that revenge, while bringing a merited retribution to Claudius, would bring the revenger's damnation.

The ghost from which Hamlet receives the injunction "Revenge!" is itself bathed in moral ambiguity. When Hamlet first sees it, he exclaims:

> Be thou a spirit of health or goblin damn'd,
> Bring with thee airs from heaven or blasts from hell,
> Be thy intents wicked or charitable,
> Thou comest in such a questionable shape
> That I will speak to thee. (I, iv, 40–44)

But when the ghost speaks, it reveals that it comes neither from heaven nor hell but from purgatory. It is not a devil, but neither is it "a spirit of health," for it was released from life uncleansed of its "foul deeds" (I, v, 12), the sins it had committed before death in its mortal frailty. The course of action Hamlet is urged by it to take with regard to Gertrude (I, v, 86–88)—"Leave her to heaven, / And to those thorns that in her bosom lodge / To prick and sting her"—is that of Christian forbearance and reliance upon divine justice; [9] Claudius, however, is not to be left to heaven and his conscience—the conscience which later torments him—but, instead, Hamlet is adjured by his love for his father to avenge him against his brother.[10] Love is to make Hamlet kill his uncle—yet the ghost itself describes murder as "most foul, as in the best it is" (I, v, 27).

103

When the ghost again appears, it is once more the eerie hour of midnight, "the very witching time of night / When churchyards yawn" (III, ii, 407–8). Hamlet exclaims when it appears (III, iv, 103–4), "Save me, and hover o'er me with your wings, / You heavenly guards!" as he had exclaimed "Angels and ministers of grace defend us" (I, iv, 39) when he first saw it. It remains a fear-inspiring visitor from a mysterious afterworld of "sulphurous and tormenting flames" (I, v, 3), even though Hamlet reveres it as his father's spirit and pities it for its suffering. And it remains a morally ambiguous figure. Hamlet says that its grim appearance and the reason for its visitation would rouse the lifeless stones to action, but he adds in the very next breath that it looks so piteous it stirs a compassion which washes away all thoughts of blood (III, iv, 125–30).

In accepting the awesome injunction of the ghost as a "dread command" (III, iv, 109), a fearful duty which he may not question, Hamlet had entered a world of moral twilight. To its words "Hamlet, remember me" he had exclaimed distractedly (I, v, 92–93): "O all you host of heaven! O earth! What else? / And shall I couple hell?" Should he call upon hell as well as upon heaven and earth to witness his oath to remember the ghost's command? He does not answer his question, but its very statement indicates that his resolution involves the jeopardizing of his soul. So, too, do his words, as he prepares to go to his mother, after his doubts concerning the ghost have been laid to rest, reveal the whirlpool of moral confusion in which he is caught:

'Tis now the very witching time of night,
When churchyards yawn, and hell itself breathes out
Contagion to this world. Now could I drink hot blood,
And do such bitter business as the day
Would quake to look on. (III, ii, 406–10)

With this we may compare the words of Macbeth about
the horror he is about to do as "o'er the one half-world /
Nature seems dead" (II, i, 49–50). Each feels murderous
impulses rise within him with the passage of midnight.[11]
Hamlet even fears he will be impelled to kill his own
mother. At this moment he seems to have become a Kydian
avenger, one who has become enveloped in moral darkness
in seeking to fulfill his mission.

But this is only the appearance of a moment, and Hamlet
never commits the crime that would have convinced the
Elizabethan audience that in prosecuting his revenge he
had irrevocably given himself over to the powers of darkness. In the scene with his mother his vengefulness gives
way to pity. At the beginning of the scene he is ferocious
with her and disregards her confession of a guilty conscience; at the end of the scene he speaks with a new gentleness as he entreats her to give up her sinfully incestuous
relations with Claudius, although, unpredictable as he is
in his oscillations of feeling, he indulges in another outburst
before he bids her a tender good night. Indeed he assumes
an almost priestly manner in addressing her:

> Confess yourself to heaven;
> Repent what's past; avoid what is to come;
> And do not spread the compost on the weeds,
> To make them ranker. (III, iv, 149–52)

This is a Hamlet of deep religious feeling, quite different
from the one who with a malevolent determination to obtain a richly meet revenge had forgone killing his uncle
when he supposed him to be purging his soul, like the
Italian revengers horrifiedly described by Gentillet: "According to the honour of his [Machiavelli's] nation venge-
ances and enmities are perpetual and irreconcilable. . . .

They seek in slaying the body to damn the soul if they could." [12]

Such waverings on the part of Hamlet must have been watched feverishly by the Elizabethan audience, as it saw him totter on the brink of moral destruction. It participated in his internal conflicts, sharing his sense of frustration but aware, as he was not aware, of the moral obstacles to revenge. Thus the castigation of himself as "muddy-mettled" (II, ii, 594), to which the actor's passion prompts him, while it would have made the audience feel more acutely the apathetic despondency from which he is attempting to pull himself, would have failed to convince it that he should be filled with passionate vengefulness. The actor in his worked-up emotion has turned pale, spoken brokenly, wept, and been so carried away that he has called attention from his speech to himself. This is quite contrary to Hamlet's advice to the actors (III, ii, 6–9): "In the very torrent, tempest, and, as I may say, the whirlwind of passion, you must acquire and beget a temperance that may give it smoothness." His praise of Horatio as a man who is not "passion's slave" (III, ii, 77) immediately afterward implies, in the light of this advice, a comparison between good acting and the proper conduct of life. Horatio does not "tear a passion to tatters" like a ranting actor; nor, his "blood and judgment," his emotion and reason, being "so well commingled," is he "too tame," as is an actor who is unable to rise to the occasion (III, ii, 11, 18, 74). He is "just," well-balanced, and therefore lets his "discretion" be his "tutor," suiting "the action to the word, the word to the action," that is, acting as is suitable to the situation (III, ii, 59, 19–20). The actor who has told the story of Priam's slaughter, on the other hand, "out-herods Herod" (III, ii, 15). To "drown the stage with tears / And cleave the general ear with horrid speech" (II, ii, 587–88)—or, in the words of Hamlet's discussion of the art of acting, "split the ears of the groundlings" (III, ii, 12)—is a poor performance, whether on the stage or in life. Horatio takes "fortune's buffets and rewards . . . with equal thanks" (III, ii, 72–73), as both Stoic fortitude and Christian patience demand (and here is the answer to Hamlet's question in the previous scene "whether 'tis nobler in the mind to suffer / The slings and arrows of outrageous fortune, / Or to take arms against a sea of troubles, / And by opposing end them") (III, i, 57–60); the actor, however—and he has entered into his role—cries out bitterly against fortune. Although Hamlet, therefore, is moved to shame by the actor's passion, feeling that it shows he himself is dull of mettle and would accept without answer any injury, the dramatic context indicates that this passion is not the proper criterion for his behavior. Hamlet himself, after working himself up into a rage in contemplating what he regards as his craven conduct, stops short and exclaims at himself in contempt that he, "like a whore," has unpacked his "heart with words" and fallen "a-cursing, like a very drab, / A scullion" (II, ii, 614–16).

The story of Priam's slaughter which the actor tells is, moreover, an indirect comment on passionate vengefulness. Pyrrhus, the son of the slain Achilles, is animated by "aroused vengeance" (II, ii, 510). His vengeance is presented as the epitome of horrible, unnatural cruelty. He is "like the Hyrcanian beast," the desert tiger which was the traditional example of savage fierceness; his "dread and black complexion," "horridly trick'd / With blood of fathers, mothers, daughters, sons," recalls the prevailing imagery of blood-spattered blackness of *Macbeth;* the blood with which he is covered is "baked and impasted" with the heat of the fire raging in Troy into a dough reminiscent of the pie in which Titus served Tamora the flesh and blood of her sons (II, ii, 477, 479–80, 481). The description of him, "roasted in wrath and fire, / And thus o'ersized with co-agulate gore, / With eyes like carbuncles," proceeding through the burning streets looking for "old grandsire Priam" by the lurid light of the flames, makes him resemble a devil deserving the adjective "hellish" that is applied to him (II, ii, 483–86). Contrasted with Pyrrhus's black, gore-clotted face is "the milky head / Of reverend Priam" (II, ii, 500–1), which has the gentleness and sanctity of old age. While the Elizabethan audience could sympathize with Hamlet's filial emotion aroused by the story of Priam's murder told by the actor representing his son-in-law Aeneas, it perceived in the revenge of Pyrrhus, hacking away with his bloody sword at the body of Priam lying before him, his blows echoing the "hideous crash" (II, ii, 498) of the down-fall of the Trojan citadel, the triumph of barbarism over civilization.

So, too, while it felt more strongly the oppressiveness of Hamlet's burden as it listened to his "to be or not to be" soliloquy and while it approved of his rejection of suicide, it felt that his response to his conclusion was wrong. The issue in this internal debate is between the Christian-Stoic idea of patience in enduring worldly affliction and the purely Stoic idea of suicide as the victory over the ills of life which the man of fortitude and self-discipline can al-ways achieve when his reason tells him that his situation has become such that death is desirable. Hamlet, unable any longer to be sure of anything at all—he would not con-template suicide before because of his acceptance of the injunction of religion that "the Everlasting had . . . fix'd / His canon 'gainst self-slaughter" (I, ii, 131–32)—longs for the obliteration of his consciousness but fears that consciousness and suffering will survive death. The sleep of death, which seems to bring peace, may bring dreams—

HAMLET

that is, consciousness may not be lost, and one may endure more anguish after death than he did in life. The conclusion he comes to is that "the dread of something after death . . . puzzles the will / And makes us rather bear those ills we have / Than fly to others that we know not of" (III, i, 78–82). We cannot act with skeptical disregard of another world but must think of the possibility of an afterlife and, implicitly, of the judgment in that afterlife preached by Christianity.[13] "Thus conscience," he comments on his conclusion, extending the generalization to all action,

> does make cowards of us all;
> And thus the native hue of resolution
> Is sicklied o'er with the pale cast of thought,
> And enterprises of great pitch and moment
> With this regard their currents turn awry,
> And lose the name of action. (III, i, 83–88)

"Conscience" means not only "reflection" but "concern for right and wrong," as in the grimly humorous words of the murderer in *Richard III* (I, iv, 137–38), which Hamlet's words almost echo, "It [conscience] is a dangerous thing: it makes a man a coward." There is no explicit reference to Hamlet's revenge; however, the audience could not help remembering that, after denouncing his own lack of resolution, he was still not doing that which he had accepted as his duty—but it would have felt that, while it was true that he was irresolute, the danger of damnation was not to be brushed aside with the statement that too much thought about moral rights and wrongs prevents one from taking bold action.

In his last soliloquy Hamlet castigates himself once more for his spiritlessness and concludes with a cry of desperation for the murderous vengefulness that he feels is lacking within him (IV, iv, 65–66): "O, from this time forth, / My thoughts be bloody, or be nothing worth!" What has provoked him is the sight of Fortinbras' men, who "go to their graves like beds" (IV, iv, 62), an instance of unthinking courage which he contrasts unfavorably with his own indecisiveness. These men have already been described, however, as "lawless resolutes" (I, i, 98), reckless adventurers, and Hamlet himself says of Fortinbras' aggressive military action to gain a worthless plot of land:

> This is the imposthume of much wealth and peace,
> That inward breaks, and shows no cause without
> Why the man dies. (IV, iv, 27–29)

A decadent prosperity has made the state sickly and incited the soldier prince to this senseless combat.[14] "Rightly to be great," comments Hamlet,

> Is not to stir without great argument,
> But greatly to find quarrel in a straw
> When honour's at the stake. (IV, iv, 53–56)

Truly noble conduct does not consist in fighting without cause, as these men do, but in fighting for honor even if that honor is involved in a trifle—and his honor is concerned with the avenging of "a father kill'd, a mother stain'd" (IV, iv, 57). The comment made the audience sympathize with Hamlet's feeling for the need of action on his part, but it did not serve to convince it that the recklessness of cutthroat desperadoes who have no need to call for bloody thoughts should be imitated by him.

This hotblooded recklessness is the dominant characteristic of Laertes, who, as has often been remarked, is a dramatic foil for Hamlet. His function as a dramatic foil would have had even more significance for the Elizabethan audience, which would have seen in him the courtier corrupted by his travels abroad, whom Spenser had contrasted with the true courtier. Laertes, a young nobleman sowing his wild oats abroad, has, like the Elizabethan Italianate noblemen, absorbed the Italian code of honor and Italian notions of revenge. His touchy sense of honor demands quick action—"That drop of blood that's calm proclaims me bastard," he shouts (IV, v, 117)—and he thinks neither of his conscience, his duty as a subject, nor of his soul's salvation in seeking revenge:

> To hell, allegiance! Vows, to the blackest devil!
> Conscience and grace, to the profoundest pit!
> I dare damnation. To this point I stand,
> That both the worlds I give to negligence,
> Let come what comes; only I'll be revenged
> Most thoroughly for my father. (IV, v, 131–36)

X foil for H

His blind wrath easily diverted by Claudius, he accepts his proposal of dueling Hamlet with an unblunted foil and even adds the idea of using poison, the traditional means of Italian revenge, to make any cut mortal. For the Italianate anything is permissible in avenging one's honor.

The contrast between Laertes and Hamlet would have attained almost emblematic expression for the Elizabethan audience in the duel scene. "I'll be your foil, Laertes," says Hamlet (V, ii, 266). It is Laertes who is his. "The bravery of his grief did put me / Into a towering passion," he says to Horatio concerning Laertes' ranting words by the grave of Ophelia (V, ii, 79–80). He, who had mourned his father with such somber intensity, had been repelled by Laertes' vaunting display of emotion, a display of emotion similar to the overacting which he had condemned as appealing to the groundlings. He regrets, however, his own loss of self-control and frankly and generously says to him (V, ii, 237–38), "Give me your pardon, sir; I've done you wrong; / But pardon 't, as you are a gentleman." Hamlet, however, is blinded by his generosity. Laertes is like Bertram, a "rash and unbridled boy" who has been misled by false fashions and has had his nobility corrupted.[15] Of noble birth, a traveled man and an accomplished duelist, he is the new model of gentility followed by the members of the court where Hamlet was once "the glass of fashion and the mould of form" (III, i, 161)—the silly fop Osric, "spacious in the possession of dirt" (V, ii, 90), but with more land than brains, looks up to him as "the card or calendar of gentry" (V, ii, 114–45)—but his are only the superficial qualities of the gentleman.

To Hamlet's openhearted offer of friendship, a friendship to be given ceremonial expression in the fencing match, in which they are to "frankly play" a "brother's wager" (V, ii, 264), to engage in sportive competition as members of the brotherhood of gentlemen, Laertes replies that he is "satisfied in nature" but is not sure whether he is satisfied in "terms of honour" (V, ii, 255–57). He withholds formal reconciliation until experts in the punctilios of the code of honor will tell him that he can do so with reputation unsullied. In the meantime, however, he professes to accept Hamlet's friendship while nursing his secret rancor and planning to take his revenge in the Italian way, as he regards himself honor bound to do. Although he says in an aside (V, ii, 307), "And yet 'tis almost 'gainst my conscience," incensed by what he takes to be a taunt at his fencing skill, he pushes aside conscience and abides by his conception of honor, which permits treachery.

Hamlet, on the other hand, would have been taken by the audience as representative of the true gentleman, who, "most generous and free from all contriving" (IV, vii, 136), takes Laertes' profession of friendship without question and does not examine the foils. For Hamlet's ocean voyage has made him undergo a sea change. From a malcontent he has become again the ideal prince he once was. Telling Horatio what had happened to him, he describes the fighting within his heart, "worse than the mutines in the bilboes" (V, ii, 6), as he lay aboard the ship. But then, he goes on, his doubts and hesitations were suddenly resolved, and he acted without further thought, as though under compulsion. He had previously met cunning with cunning, seeking to lay bare Claudius' secret as Claudius sought to pluck the heart of his mystery, and, like other malcontent revenger heroes,[16] had taken delight in scheming and in laying hidden mines for his enemy. Now he acted without thinking to contrive "deep plots" (V, ii, 9). In doing so he felt himself to be in the hands of a "divinity that shapes our ends" (V, ii, 10), a divinity that was sculpting smooth the rough-hewn results of his own ineffectual efforts to set the time right. The new commission that he drew up to have Rosencrantz and Guildenstern put to death he was able to seal because he had his father's signet, the model of the state seal, with him—"even in that was heaven ordinant" (V, ii, 48). Moreover, although he does not mention it, his return to Denmark through the strange chance of his capture by pirates who deal with him like "thieves of mercy" (IV, vii, 21–22) gives the impression of providential intervention.

For the Elizabethan audience, accustomed to the standard revenge tragedy with its passionately vengeful criminal hero, the change in Hamlet was a significant departure. Its sympathy for the hero was confirmed, not alienated, for Hamlet has struggled out of the debilitating depression of the malcontent not to the desperate resolution of the criminal avenger but to a firm reliance upon divine providence. It will be only a short time before Claudius learns from England of the death of Rosencrantz and Guildenstern and consequently of Hamlet's knowledge of his murderous plans, but Hamlet is sure that he will have accomplished his task before then. He has misgivings about the duel but cheerfully accepts the dictates of providence, echoing the Bible on God's constant supervision of the universe and the need for man to be ready at all times to leave this world, whose goods can only temporarily be possessed by him (V, ii, 230–35): "We defy augury. There's a special providence in the fall of a sparrow. If it be now, 'tis not to come; if it be not to come, it will be now; if it be not now, yet it will come; the readiness is all. Since no man has aught of what he leaves, what is't to leave betimes?" [17]

The conclusion justifies his confidence in providence. Not only does he kill Claudius but he does so in a way whose poetic justice would have been recognized by the Elizabethans as divine judgment.[18] Claudius is exposed before all by the dying Laertes, even though it seemed as if he had made assurance doubly sure in his plot to dispatch Hamlet. His tool is turned against him in more senses than one, for the poisoned foil of Laertes is thrust through his body by Hamlet, the weapon of treachery being transformed into the sword of justice. The chalice with whose poisoned wine he had planned to kill Hamlet is forced between his own lips, a dramatic enactment of Macbeth's image:

> This even-handed justice
> Commends the ingredients of our poisoned chalice
> To our own lips. (I, vii, 10–12)

"He is justly served," comments Laertes (V, ii, 337). "It is a poison temper'd by himself." The chalice has touched Gertrude's lips, as it touches Claudius', the two being united as if in a ritual that damns them in death as their marriage rites had united them in sinful incest. Hamlet, punning bitterly on the word "union" which Claudius had used to refer to the pearl he supposedly threw into the wine, acts

as the minister of God who completes the ritual and sends
Claudius to join Gertrude in damnation:

> Here, thou incestuous, murderous, damnèd Dane,
> Drink off this potion. Is thy union here?
> Follow my mother. (V, ii, 336–38)

The death of Claudius, like that of Polonius, Rosencrantz,
Guildenstern, and Laertes, is not murder. It is virtually
self-defense, the answering thrust of Hamlet to the mortal
thrust he has received in the duel which Claudius has waged
against him by proxy. By waiting for the time allotted by
God, he has done his work as His instrument without having incurred His wrath. His death is not an expiation of sin,
as it is with the Kydian hero revenger, but the necessary
sacrifice that he must make in purging Denmark of the
rottenness at its heart without subjecting it to the toxic
effects of the counter-poison of criminal revenge. Exchang-
ing forgiveness with the dying Laertes in the spirit of charity
of the Christian gentleman, he is cleared by him of any
guilt in the death of Polonius,[19] for which he has already
expressed his repentance:

> Exchange forgiveness with me, noble Hamlet:
> Mine and my father's death come not upon thee,
> Nor thine on me! (V, ii, 340–42)

The "Good night, sweet prince; / And flights of angels sing
thee to thy rest!" which Horatio utters over him (V, ii,
370–71) as he dies echoes the traditional idea of angelic
choirs convoying the soul to heaven.[20] For the Elizabethan
audience these words were a farewell that expressed its
regret for the death of Hamlet and its gratification at his
passing beyond the bourn of this world with his nobility
shining unobscured by the black clouds of misanthropy
and with his soul saved. And mixed with these feelings was

a sense of relief at having been freed from the conflicting emotions of distress at the hero's inaction and of repugnance toward the murder which had seemed the only positive action he could take.

3

Not only is Hamlet regenerated but Denmark is also. Fortinbras, newly arrived in martial array from the Polish wars, puts in his claim to the crown, and, since he was the choice of the dying Hamlet and there are no other claimants, we are assured that he will be the new king. His are the last words of the play. He orders that Hamlet be borne off "like a soldier" and that, to mark his passing, "the soldiers' music and the rites of war / Speak loudly for him." The sound of the cannon as the dead bodies are being carried off is an ironic echo of the cannon which had fired as Claudius had drunk to Hamlet's health in the first act and during the dueling scene in the last act. Claudius' carousing to the accompaniment of the firing of cannon had set the tone for the state; the "heavy-headed revel" (I, i, 17) had caused Denmark to lose its honor among nations. The cannon roar at the close of the play marks the accession of a king who, tested and matured, will toughen the fiber of the state without plunging it into senseless adventures, a military commander like Alciabides, who was transformed from a figure of destruction to a soldier statesman whose mission it will be to regenerate a decadent Athens:

> Bring me into your city,
> And I will use the olive with my sword,
> Make war breed peace, make peace stint war, make each
> Prescribe to other as each other's leech.
> Let our drums strike. (*Timon of Athens*, V, iv, 81–85)

HAMLET

The cultural setting of *Hamlet,* no doubt derived from the no longer existing older play which was Shakespeare's immediate source, is the corrupt foreign court of Marston's *Antonio's Revenge,* a setting which was to become popular in Jacobean drama. The hypocritical, time-serving Rosencrantz and Guildenstern, the Italianate Laertes, and the foppish Osric are instances of the corruption of an effete society. Hamlet speaks of "the fatness of these pursy times" (III, iv, 153), a phrase which Kittredge glosses (pp. 1078–79): "Hamlet compares the corrupt times to a body that is unhealthily corpulent (*pursy*)." Cf. Heywood, *Apology for Actors,* 1612, sig. B r°: In the fatness and rankness of a peaceable commonwealth; Chapman, *Byron's Conspiracy,* i, 1 (Pearson ed., II, 191):

> Peace must not make men cowards, nor keep calm
> Her pursy regiment [i.e., government] with men's smother'd breaths.

Hamlet's words refer to a doctrine that had been voiced by Sidney, Ralegh, and Nashe and used by many popular dramatists, the doctrine that "a long peace is dangerous to the health of the state both internally and externally and both through the danger of malcontents and the weakening effects of luxury and idleness; and a just foreign war is a normal and healthful activity." [21] Thus under Claudius, a subtle diplomat, wily and intriguing, who is a far cry from his older brother, a chivalric warrior king, Denmark is a state which Fortinbras thinks he can challenge with impunity and to which England neglects to pay the tribute that the old Hamlet had exacted from it. Moreover, the disease imagery, particularly the image of the hidden ulcer, that Caroline Spurgeon has noted runs throughout *Hamlet,*[22] is a familiar part of this doctrine.

The peace-bred imperfections of a state were described in morbid imagery by so many Elizabethan writers that peace itself became almost synonymous with disease. Thus Fulke Greville in "A Treatise of Monarchy":

> So doth the War and her impiety
> Purge the imposthum'd humors of a peace,
> Which oft else makes good government decrease.

Churchyard visualizes peace as "a swelling sore, that festers soundest mind and so bursts out in boils, in botch or ulcers great." There is an important tendency to select a hidden type of disease to describe the sinister workings of peace. John Norden, asking why England must fear aggression in the apparently peaceful year 1596, answers that "the body may be most sick when it feeleth no grief at all. . . . And therefore saith the wise man, *A disease known is in manner cured.*" [23]

Shakespeare's picture of Denmark may be said, then, to be a reflection of warlike middle-class opinion at the ascendancy of the cautious foreign policy of Cecil over the war policy that had been espoused first by Sidney and then by Essex and perhaps also a reflection of the feeling that court life had degenerated under the aged Elizabeth.

Chapter VIII

OTHELLO

1

In *Othello* a noble soul is caught in the toils of one who, although diabolically cunning, is base of spirit. Iago, in contrast to the royal-blooded Othello and the courtly Cassio, is a man of low birth, who, passed over for the post he had aspired to in favor of one who is his social superior and a friend of the commander, is a malcontent resentful of his position. He has a reputation as a plain, blunt-spoken soldier, a good fellow who can be depended upon to speak the truth without ceremony, but he is not regarded as a gentleman with a gentleman's humanistic as well as militaristic virtues. "You may relish him more in the soldier," Cassio tells Desdemona (II, ii, 166–68), "than in the scholar." As he is saying this to Desdemona, Iago is watching them and commenting caustically in his coarse-spoken manner on Cassio's social graces, which he proposes to use to ruin him (II, i, 172–79): "Ay, smile upon her, do; I will gyve thee in thine own courtship. You say true; 'tis so, indeed; if such tricks as these strip you out of your lieutenancy, it had been better you had not kissed your three fingers so oft, which now again you are most apt to play the sir in. Very good; well kissed! an excellent courtesy! 'tis so, indeed. Yet again your fingers to your lips? would they were clysterpipes for your sake!" The wish that the fingers which Cassio

Notes to this chapter begin on page 225.

is kissing be enema-tubes suits the lips of him who had presented bizarrely obscene pictures to the mind of Brabantio with such malicious relish in informing him of his daughter's elopement. Contemptuous though he is of Cassio's gentlemanly manners, Iago has an obscure but gnawing sense of inferiority. "He hath a daily beauty in his life / That makes me ugly," he says of Cassio in one of his soliloquies (V, i, 19–20). "Let it not gall your patience, good Iago," says Cassio, as he kisses Iago's wife with the self-assurance of a gentleman permitted such liberties by social custom (II, i, 98–100), "That I extend my manners; 'tis my breeding / That gives me this bold show of courtesy." He does not know that the seeming complacency with which Iago accepts this kiss hides a cankered envy which finds expression in the jealous suspicion that Cassio is having an affair with Emilia.

Iago's psychology is that of the servant who hides his hate behind his obsequiousness. When Roderigo, having been told by Iago how much he hates Othello, says (I, i, 40), "I would not follow him then," Iago replies, "I follow him to serve my turn upon him: / We cannot all be masters, nor all masters / Cannot be truly follow'd." "Truly follow'd" by Iago's values means being deceived by "shows of service" by timeservers who, "when they have lined their coats," desert their masters (I, i, 52–53). He who lacks the soul of the true follower, however, "wears out his time, much like his master's ass, / For nought but provender, and when he's old, cashier'd" (I, i, 47–48). "Lined their coats," "cashier'd"—the expressions come naturally to the professional soldier who, oblivious to the ideal that the "pride, pomp and circumstance of glorious war" (III, iii, 354) represent for Othello and guided solely by the mercenary considerations of the man for whom money talks, says of himself (I, i, 11), "I know my price," speaks of the "trade of war"

(I, ii, 1), and advises his dupe Roderigo (I, iii, 344–45), "Put money in thy purse; follow thou the wars," using money as his weapon in besieging Desdemona.[1] It is ironic that the devoted Cassio, not a true follower by Iago's inverted scale of values, is in fact dismissed from his office and that Iago gets it. "I will be hang'd," says Emilia to Desdemona (IV, ii, 130–33), unaware that she is describing her own husband, "if some eternal villain, / Some busy and insinuating rogue, / Some cogging, cozening slave, to get some office, / Have not devised this slander." And when Iago is at length revealed for what he is, Montano speaks of him (V, ii, 239, 243) as a "notorious villain" and a "damned slave." The mark of the bondsman, the villein, is upon Iago, even as he secretly dominates his noble victim.

2

But Iago is no mere knave.[2] He is, at least symbolically, a devil who asserts his service to the Prince of Darkness to the foolishly blind Roderigo and, above all, in his soliloquies. "Sanctimony and a frail vow betwixt an erring barbarian and a super-subtle Venetian," he vows to Roderigo (I, iii, 361–65), will not be "too hard for my wits and all the tribe of hell." As he hatches his plot in the dark depths of his mind, he exclaims (I, iii, 409–10), "I have 't. It is engender'd. Hell and night / Must bring this monstrous birth to the world's light." When the ugly spawn of his brain takes shape and Cassio is persuaded to request Desdemona to urge his suit to Othello, he comments with diabolical glee on the speciousness of his advice (II, iii, 356–59): "Divinity of hell! When devils will the blackest sins put on, / They do suggest at first with heavenly shows, / As I do now." Othello, when Iago's evil is revealed, regards him as a devil and looks down upon his feet to see if they are cloven like those of the devils in the morality plays. They are not, but Othello rejects this literal view of a devil's appearance as a fable and, thrusting his sword at Iago, exclaims (V, ii, 287), "If that thou be'st a devil, I cannot kill thee." "I bleed, sir; but not kill'd" is Iago's triumphant reply. In his final moments he remains true to his diabolical self and seems indeed no mortal man. When Othello asks that it be demanded of "that demi-devil" why he performed his evil, he replies, "Demand me nothing: what you know, you know: From this time forth I never will speak word." "What, not to pray?" exclaims Lodovico, horrified by this unrepentant malevolence in the face of death. But they are indeed Iago's last words, and as he is led away, fixing no doubt a petrifying glare upon Othello in leaving, we are sure that torture will not make him speak and that the secret of his evil being will remain locked within him.

Iago is the devil of cynicism who makes men doubt the genuineness of their ideals and turns them away from virtue. "Who has a breast so pure, / But some uncleanly apprehensions / Keep leets and law-days, and in session sit / With meditations lawful?" he says (III, iii, 138–41), pretending to attempt to dissuade himself of his suspicions in order to provoke Othello into inquiring about them. But it is upon such "uncleanly apprehensions," "foul things" that intrude even into a "palace," that he in fact plays.

Although himself a passionless rationalist, a Machiavellian who says of himself (I, i, 65), "I am not what I am," Iago sees lust as at the bottom of human nature. "Very nature will instruct her in it and compel her to some second choice," he tells Roderigo (II, ii, 237–39)—it is a view which he reiterates in a soliloquy—arguing that Desdemona's love for Othello is a temporary passion which must be succeeded by an extramarital affair. It is therefore easy for him to persuade himself that Emilia has had an affair with Othello,

"The thought whereof," he says (II, i, 305–6), "doth, like a poisonous mineral, gnaw my inwards." Iago's cynicism is a consuming poison which he seeks to transfer to others. "I'll pour this pestilence into his ear," he says of his plan to persuade Othello that Desdemona speaks in behalf of Cassio "for her body's lust" (II, ii, 362). "The Moor already changes with my poison," he comments after, spiderlike, he has injected his venom into his ensnared victim.

> Dangerous conceits are, in their natures, poisons,
> Which at the first are scarce found to distaste,
> But with a little act upon the blood
> Burn like the mines of sulphur. (III, iii, 325–59)

When Othello announces his intention to avenge himself on Cassio, as Iago had announced his intention to avenge himself on him, he, who had been "of a constant, loving, noble nature" (II, i, 301), exclaims (III, iii, 449–50), "Swell, bosom, with thy fraught, / For 'tis of aspics' tongues!" Hate has replaced love in his heart, and it is now full of asps' venom. And when, overcome by the poisonous thoughts and loathsome images by which he has become obsessed, Othello falls down in a faint, Iago stands over him, exulting fiendishly (IV, i, 45–46), "Work on, / My medicine, work!"

Iago's poisonous cynicism discolors his victims' view, making them see the blackness of hell where there is the radiance of heaven. In the first act, where the tragic catastrophe of the last act is foreshadowed, he makes Othello's love for Desdemona seem to Brabantio something foul and abhorrent and Othello himself a devil. "Awake the snorting citizens with the bell," he calls (I, i, 90–91), "Or else the Devil will make a grandsire of you." The irony of the characterization of Othello as the devil by this mocking demon is emphasized by his words (I, i, 108–9), "Zounds, sir, you are one of those that will not serve God, if the devil bid you."

It is indeed a devil who is speaking to Brabantio, but he is not bidding him to serve God. Brabantio accepts Iago's picture of Othello, seeing him as the devil that Iago is and addressing him in words that apply to Iago:

> Damn'd as thou art, thou hast enchanted her . . .
> Judge me the world, if 'tis not gross in sense
> That thou hast practised on her with foul charms,
> Abused her delicate youth with drugs or minerals
> That weaken motion: I'll have't disputed on;
> 'Tis probable, and palpable to thinking.
> I therefore apprehend and do attach thee
> For an abuser of the world, a practiser
> Of arts inhibited and out of warrant. (I, ii, 63–79)

Later he speaks of Desdemona as having been "corrupted / By spells and medicines" (I, iii, 60–61) and worked upon by "practices of cunning hell" (I, iii, 102). It is Iago who works upon Othello with diabolic arts, "the practice of a damnèd slave" (V, ii, 292), and who, on the metaphorical level, with "drugs" and "minerals" that "weaken motion" impairs his mental faculties. It is he who should be apprehended as an "abuser of the world," a dissembling corrupter of society at large who has at this very moment endangered the state by raising the alarm and disrupting the proceedings of the council, which has met to consider the Turkish threat.

Iago, who knows how well the Senate regards Othello and how much it needs him, does not hope in rousing Brabantio to have the marriage annulled. He seeks only to "poison" Othello's "delight," to "plague him with flies" (I, i, 68, 71). The shouts in the streets, as when "the fire / Is spied in populous cities" (I, i, 76–77), and the armed bands with torches and drawn swords in the night are an ominous stormy accompaniment to Othello's marriage. The consummation of the marriage takes place only when Othello and Desdemona are reunited on Cyprus after the Turkish threat has been dispelled and the tempest surmounted—and the consummation of the marriage is also disturbed by the sounding of the alarm bell, "that dreadful bell" (II, iii, 175) which, "in a town of war, / Yet wild, the people's hearts brimful of war" (II, iii, 213–14), reverberates frighteningly. Cassio and Montano, says Iago in explaining to Othello the clash between them that evoked the alarm (II, iii, 179–84), were "friends all but now, even now, / In quarter, and in terms like bride and groom / Devesting them for bed; and then, but now, / As if some planet had unwitted men, / Swords out, and tilting one at other's breast, / In opposition bloody" —and we think of Desdemona and Othello, the bride and groom who had only just now actually divested themselves for the nuptial bed, and fear a similar rapid transformation under the same evil influence, a transformation that will "unwit" one of them and bring the marriage to a bloody end.

Just as Brabantio has been made to see the marriage in a false light and Cassio has been robbed of his senses, Othello is "unwitted" and made to see Desdemona as a "fair devil" (III, iii, 478). In a deception worthy of Satan, "the father of lies," Iago contrives for him a drama of a wicked, deceitful Italy, in which Desdemona plays the part to be played by Vittoria Corombona, "the white devil," in Webster's drama of a world dominated by evil. She, who appears "like one of heaven" (IV, ii, 36), has a "young and sweating devil" (III, iv, 42) in her moist palm, the sign of her sensuality. "Devil!" he exclaims as he strikes her (IV, i, 251). Emilia, whom he treats as the madam of the house where Desdemona prostitutes herself, he addresses (IV, ii, 90–92), "You, mistress, / That have the office opposite to Saint Peter, / And keep the gate of hell!"

In seeing the heavenly Desdemona as a fair devil, Othello

gives himself over to the devil of cynicism. He accepts Iago as an authority on human nature, one who is able to anatomize humanity and who speaks forthrightly about his findings (III, iii, 258–60): "This fellow's of exceeding honesty, / And knows all qualities, with a learned spirit, / Of human dealings." "Good sir, be a man," Iago adjures him (IV, i, 66). Manhood consists of the knowledge and the cynical acceptance that married men are bound to be cuckolded: "No, let me know; / And knowing what I am, I know what she shall be." "O, thou art wise; 'tis certain," responds Othello (IV, i, 73–75). He accepts the picture of Desdemona as a "super-subtle Venetian," one of the Venetian ladies who had acquired a reputation for marital deceptions, and, in doing so, takes the role of the Italian husband, who was notorious for avenging himself by such means as the hiring of bravoes to kill the gallant and by secret wife murder. He does not realize that when Iago says, "O, 'tis the spite of hell, the fiend's arch-mock, / To lip a wanton in a secure couch, / And to suppose her chaste" (IV, i, 71–73), the reverse is true, that it is his fiend's mocking way of stating that hell laughs at the murder of an innocent woman in her marriage bed by a husband who believes her false.

In giving himself over to the devil of cynicism, Othello, like Adam, who was made to question the justice of God's injunction, is made to question Desdemona, who is "heavenly true" (V, ii, 135), and, like Adam, he loses an earthly paradise. After a storm at sea he had come to the island of Cyprus to find Desdemona miraculously waiting for him. The island citadel of which he was to be governor with Desdemona at his side was his harbor, the blissful end of his life's voyage as the soldier of a maritime state. But there was a serpent in his Eden.[3] There was truly need for the "grace of heaven" (II, i, 85) which Cassio had called upon to encircle Desdemona when she landed on Cyprus. Even as

Othello and Desdemona are voicing the exquisite harmony of their ecstatic love, Iago is expressing with satanic malice at the sight of the happy pair his intention of destroying that harmony (II, ii, 202–4): "O, you are well tuned now! / But I'll set down the pegs that make this music, / As honest as I am." [4]

The loss of his paradise makes Othello, like Adam, the prey of his passion. He had been a commanding personage, grand, self-contained, dignified, "the noble Moor whom our full senate / Call all in all sufficient . . . the nature / Whom passion could not shake" (IV, i, 275–77). His acceptance of Iago's view wrenches him apart and looses the passions which gush forth from within him. A man from a southern nation, whose inhabitants, wrote John Davies of Hereford, are "if good, most good, if bad exceeding bad," [5] Othello contained within himself the utmost potentialities for good and evil. In his greatness and his weakness he showed the possibilities of human nature. That a man of his nobility could fall as he did was a terrifying reminder of the fall of Adam, the noblest of men, and of man's subsequent proneness to soul-destroying sin.

The moment of his kneeling to vow revenge is the moment of Othello's giving himself over to Iago. "Do not rise yet," commands Iago (III, iii, 461). He kneels side by side with Othello and vows to be at his service in "what bloody business ever." The oaths that the two exchange are horrifying in their solemnity: it is a pact with the devil that Othello has made. "Now art thou my lieutenant," says Othello. "I am your own for ever," replies Iago in the last words of the scene. Iago becomes Othello's Mephistopheles, and in making the devil his servant Othello gives himself up into his power.

Like Faustus, however, Othello cannot rest easily in his pact. As he thinks of Desdemona's sweetness, his vengefulness gives way to poignant regret. Each time he voices this regret, however, Iago reminds him of his dedication to revenge—"Nay, you must forget that," "Nay, that's not your way" (IV, i, 190, 197)—and each time Othello is called back to his purpose, only to lapse once more into tender reminiscence. "O! she will sing the savageness out of a bear," he exclaims, and for a moment it seems that Desdemona's divine virtues will triumph, that the sweet harmony of her nature will quell the storm within Othello. But Iago overcomes the influence of Desdemona, as the bad angel overcomes the influence of the good angel in the moralities; he rouses Othello's jealousy and sense of outraged honor so that, accepting the drama of Iago's contriving as reality, he goes through with his assigned role as the Italian husband. His promise to abide by his vow, "Ay, let her rot, and perish, and be damned tonight; for she shall not live," is a reaffirmation of his pact with the devil which brings him closer to his doom: he himself will be damned that night in the murder of Desdemona.

When Othello comes to kill Desdemona, he does so in the exalted mood of being about to render divine justice, not to perform revenge.[6] And this justice is to include clemency. Desdemona is to be given the opportunity to pray and ask for heaven's forgiveness (V, ii, 31–32): "I would not kill thy unprepared spirit; / No; heaven forfend! I would not kill thy soul." But the soul that he is about to kill, the divine light that he is about to quench, is his own. The mercy that he offers Desdemona and the mood of elevated pity in which he offers it are Othello's last hope of escaping damnation. When he says "amen" in reply to Desdemona's "Then Lord have mercy on me!" Desdemona exclaims, "And have you mercy too!" (57–58) But Othello cannot call up from within him the forgiveness of Christ and, forgetting the Lord's Prayer, loses his own claim to God's mercy. When Desde-

mona denies having been unfaithful to him, Othello's rage is
rekindled: "O perjured woman! thou dost stone my heart, /
And makest me call what I intend to do / A murder, which
I thought a sacrifice" (63–65). In his oscillation of feeling
he is back to the vengeful spirit in which he had told Iago
(IV, i, 193–94), "My heart is turned to stone; / I strike it,
and it hurts my hand." No more does he speak of "justice"
but of his "great revenge" (17, 74). Desdemona is now not
"sweet soul" but "strumpet" (50, 77). When Desdemona
entreats, "But while I say one prayer," he refuses her the opportunity for salvation which he had previously offered her
and stifles her, saying, "It is too late" (83). At this moment
Emilia pounds on the locked door to tell Othello of the
attempted assassination of Cassio, who, escaped from death,
can help the truth to be revealed, but it is indeed too late:
the noise only makes him hurry the killing of Desdemona.

An old tradition of the stage has it that at this point he
stabs her, a form of death which would make Desdemona's
regaining of consciousness more plausible than death by
strangling. This would further dramatize the contrast between the reverential mood in which he entered and the
revengeful manner in which he commits the murder, for he
had said (V, ii, 3–5), "Yet I'll not shed her blood; / Nor scar
that whiter skin of hers than snow, / And smooth as monu-
mental alabaster." His cry (III, iii, 451), "O, blood, blood,
blood," made when he had given himself over to revenge,
and his statement after he thinks Cassio has been killed
(V, i, 34–36), "Strumpet, I come. . . . Thy bed, lust-
stain'd, shall with lust's blood be spotted," would then be
fulfilled.

Othello kills Desdemona, as Granville-Barker says, with
a "cold deliberate anger" so that "the abrupt knocking at
the door and Emilia's insistent voice can set his wits alertly
on the defensive even while the fully sentient man barely

yet comprehends what he has done." [7] His mind continues to work with swift defensiveness, concerned with whether or not the murder has been truly completed and, if it has, whether it is safest to admit Emilia—"Shall she come in? Were 't good? / I think she stirs again. No" (V, ii, 94–95)—as Emilia's pounding resounds with the reverberations of Macduff's on the gates of Macbeth's castle, for his thinking is undisturbed by any flow of normal feeling. His heart made "stone," it is only with the utterance of the word "wife" (V, ii, 96) that his frozen, blocked-up emotion is pierced, and a torrent of agonized grief is released. His earlier "I that am cruel am yet merciful; / I would not have thee linger in thy pain" Granville-Barker rightly characterizes (p. 80) as "hangman humanity." The paradox of the mercifulness of his cruelty in slaying her forthwith, voiced with a kind of grim irony as he proceeds to dispatch her, is the expression of his benumbed feeling, which causes him to regard the struggling Desdemona with the detachedly "humanitarian" consideration of an executioner who seeks to kill with but one stroke of his ax.

The moment he gets his revenge it turns sour. Emilia enters to inform him that Cassio is alive, and Othello exclaims (115–16): "Not Cassio kill'd! then murder's out of tune, / And sweet revenge turns harsh." As if to emphasize his words comes Desdemona's cry: "O, falsely, falsely murder'd!" (117) When she takes upon herself, however, the guilt for her death, Othello, in his bitterness at what he believes to be her final lie, asserts that he killed her and, defending himself against Emilia's charge that Desdemona was "heavenly true" and that he is "a devil" (135, 133), affirms his certitude in terms that confirm his damnation (137–39): "O, I were damn'd beneath all depth in hell, / But that I did proceed upon just grounds / To this extremity." And when the truth is finally revealed to him, he is overwhelmed by the feeling that he is indeed damned. "Will you, I pray, demand that demi-devil / Why he hath thus ensnared my soul and body?" he asks (301–2).

Crushed by the sight of her lying pale on the white marriage sheets, the symbol of her purity, he calls to be transported to hell at once. His words are expressive of what the "Homily of Repentance" calls "Judas' repentance,"[8] that is, the overwhelming sense of guilt without faith in the mercy of God which is the heinous sin of despair. The sight of his victim blasts any hope of salvation in him (V, ii, 273–75): "When we shall meet at compt, / This look of thine will hurl my soul from heaven, / And fiends will snatch at it." When he continues, "Whip me, ye devils, / From the possession of this heavenly sight," he is not only expressing his despair but is already entering upon the punishments of hell in this life.[9]

In committing self-murder at the conclusion he is continuing to follow Judas' example. His behavior in his last moments, therefore, would have confirmed Elizabethans in the impression that his soul is lost which they gained from observing the dramatic irony of his offering Desdemona an opportunity, as he supposes, for salvation and then withdrawing it in a rage, not realizing that his own salvation is at issue and forgetting that those who do not forgive will not be forgiven.

In killing Desdemona he had rejected her divine goodness and cast away, he says in his final speech, a pearl worth more than all the world, losing his soul.[10] His last words, however, are not those of heartbreak or of self-torture. They are spoken with the resolution of one who knows his irrevocable fate and the regret of one who knows the preciousness of what he has lost and act as a valediction summing up for us the pathos of the ensnarement of this noble nature.

3

The painfulness of this conclusion is mitigated by the fact that, although Iago triumphs over Othello, it is at the same time demonstrated that his values cannot triumph over Othello's. His view of reality is false: Desdemona is pure. She remains heavenly true to Othello, although the worldly cynical Emilia lightheartedly suggests that she avenge herself by cuckolding her husband, as the devilishly cynical Iago had counseled revenge to Othello. "Wouldst thou do such a deed for all the world?" asks Desdemona (IV, iii, 67). We are reminded of Christ's rejection of the temptation to possess the world. "Marry, I would not do such a thing for a joint-ring," Emilia replies (73–79), "nor for measures of lawn, nor for gowns, petticoats, nor caps, nor any petty exhibition; but, for the whole world,—why, who would not make her husband a cuckold to make him a monarch? I should venture purgatory for 't." Although she is speaking jestingly to divert her mistress, it is clear that Christ's words (Mark, viii, 36) "What shall it profit a man to gain the whole world and lose his soul?" have no great significance for her.

This is Desdemona's temptation scene, the counterpart of Othello's temptation scene, as Bradley calls it. Of course, Desdemona's scene does not have the long-drawn-out dramatic intensity of Othello's, as the Christlike Desdemona is immune to the temptation offered her. It does, however, parallel it and contrast with it significantly. Unlike Othello, she does not follow her preceptor's ethic of revenge; she obeys the vow she had made, kneeling in the presence of Iago as Othello had kneeled to vow hatred and revenge, that she would continue in her love and devotion for Othello no matter what he does to her. In doing so she follows the

Christian ethic of returning good for evil, accepting ill-treatment as a discipline enabling her to grow in virtue: "Good night, good night: heaven me such uses send, / Not to pick bad from bad, but by bad mend!" (107–8) What makes her deeply painful suffering tolerable is that as a result of this suffering she is able to reach heights of love and sacrifice that enable her to transcend it. The words in which she accepts her misfortune echo the centuries-long praise of adversity as a teacher of Christian patience and as a means by which we attain the "felicity or perfect good which is God" and are guided by "the love of God," which "keepeth the world in due order and good accord" and "knitteth together the sacrament of wedlock with chaste love between man and wife." [11] They help to reconcile the audience to her suffering and death, as through her Griselda-like patience and devotion she becomes a saint and a martyr in her love, dying with a divine lie upon her lips, ironically committing the deathbed perjury against which Othello had warned her, but a perjury which makes her, as Emilia says (V, ii, 130), "the more angel."

Although Emilia attends Desdemona as Iago does Othello, instead of her corrupting Desdemona as Iago corrupts Othello, Desdemona summons forth the best in Emilia's nature. In her easy-going tolerance of her husband, the depths of whose iniquity she does not realize, in her theft of the handkerchief at his behest, she plays a part in her mistress's calamity, but she redeems herself by her loyalty. "I durst, my lord, to wager she is honest," she tells Othello (IV, ii, 12–13), "Lay down my soul at stake." She does indeed stake her soul on the purity of Desdemona. "Moor, she was chaste," she says (V, ii, 249–50) as she lies dying, "she loved thee, cruel Moor; / So come my soul to bliss, as I speak true." These words, at the supreme moment of death, carry the assurance that in losing her life by heroically defying Iago and revealing the truth she has won her soul. They also carry the assurance that there are virtues in ordinary humanity unsuspected by a cynical Iago.

Desdemona raises and redeems such earthly souls as Emilia. Belief in her, the symbolic equivalent in the play of belief in Christ, is a means of salvation for Cassio as well as for Emilia. Cassio, like Othello, is deceived by Iago, but he makes no pact with him, as Othello does, and his worship of Desdemona, expressed in his rapturous description of the storm miraculously permitting "the divine Desdemona" to come to Cyprus (II, i, 68–73), is constant. He rejects Iago's insinuating "What an eye she has! methinks it sounds a parley of provocation" with "an inviting eye; and yet methinks right modest" (II, iii, 22–25). If in Othello Shakespeare's audience had a terrifying reminder of the possibility of even the noblest of men succumbing to the wiles of the devil, in Cassio it had a hopeful reminder of the possibility of the ordinary man—one who, like each of them, was subject to mortal frailty—achieving salvation through faith and repentance.

Cassio has the conventional weaknesses of the gentleman just as Emilia has the conventional weaknesses of the servant-confidante, and Iago makes use of these weaknesses, just as he makes use of the weaknesses of Emilia in having her steal the handkerchief. One of Cassio's vulnerable points is his false sense of honor, which Iago uses to get him drunk by inviting "a brace of Cyprus gallants that would fain have a measure to the health of black Othello" (II, iii, 31–33). His courtliness then becomes a narrowly constricting social code that obligates him to drink with them: "I have very poor and unhappy brains for drinking: I could well wish courtesy would invent some other custom of entertainment." The gallants, moreover, swaggering, quarrelsome in their cups, sensitive about points of honor, "noble swelling spirits, / That hold their honours in a wary distance, / The very elements of this warlike isle," have also been befuddled with drink by Iago. Cassio, in consorting with them, disregards the words of "A Sermon against Contention and Brawling" in denouncing the extreme touchiness of spirit demanded by the feudalistic code (*Certain Sermons,* p. 145): "And the wise King Solomon saith, *Honour is due to a man that keepeth himself from contention; and all that mingle themselves therewith be fools.*" In following the forms of courtesy, in obeying the punctilios of the code of honor, by which "a cross word is ground enough for a challenge, . . . not to pledge a health is cause enough to lose health and life too," [12] Cassio, driven by "the devil drunkenness" (II, iii, 297) and forgetting "Christian shame," engages in a "barbarous brawl" (II, iii, 172), losing, ironically, his honorable reputation as a trustworthy officer.[13]

Iago also makes use of Cassio's sexual laxity, guying him about Bianca while Othello goes mad thinking that Cassio's lightheartedly contemptuous laughter is directed at Desdemona. "Did you perceive how he laughed at his vice?" Iago asks Othello (IV, i, 181). It is a laughter for which all pay dear. Cassio himself is set upon and wounded as he comes home from Bianca's house in a night scene of fighting in the streets, of calls for help, and of lights making the darkness visible that acts as the final peal of thunder and flash of lightning, the culmination of the ominous reverberations of the previous street-fighting scenes, before the awful quietness in which Othello looks upon Desdemona lying asleep in her bedchamber. "This is the fruit of whoring," says Iago over the wounded Cassio (V, i, 116). He is trying to attach the blame for the attempted assassination to Bianca, but there is a sense in which the words are true. Cassio's dalliance with Bianca was one point around which Iago spun his web, and in order to assure himself that the web would not be broken Iago had to try to kill him. From our weaknesses the devil derives his strength; from our blind spots comes his attack upon us.

But Cassio's sins are venial, not mortal. Having atoned for his weaknesses with his shame and his blood, he is worthy of the position that Othello, a greater man than he, has lost. "I hold him to be unworthy of his place that does those things," he says (II, iii, 102–3), attempting to regain his dignity when he has got drunk on his watch. Unworthy indeed, but repentance wipes out the stains of misdoing. In his realization that he has done wrong he exclaims, albeit with drunken piety, "Forgive us our sins!" His contrition when he comes to himself is deep. "Confess yourself freely to [Desdemona]," Iago advises him (II, ii, 323–28). "Importune her help to put you in your place again: she is of so free, so kind, so apt, so blessed a disposition, she holds it a vice in her goodness not to do more than she is requested." The blessed Desdemona, to whom Cassio dedicates himself as her "true servant" (III, iii, 9), in a feeling of gratitude for her bounteous goodness akin to the Mariolatry which affected the language of chivalric devotion in which he speaks, does intercede for him after he has confessed himself to her. Her intercession brings martyrdom for herself, a martyrdom prefigured by her words "thy solicitor shall rather die / Than give thy cause away" (III, iii, 27–28), which remind us of the steadfastness of Christ in sacrificing Himself for mankind. At the conclusion, however, Cassio gains an even higher place than the one he had lost, as all sons of Adam who repent their sins gain a higher place than they lost when they sinned in Adam. "I hope to be saved," he had said in his drunken religiousness, which, though ludicrous, had serious overtones. He was.

Roderigo, on the other hand, is the ordinary weak man led on by his sensual desires to damnation. He at first

OTHELLO

regards Desdemona as highly as does Cassio, speaking of her
as "blessed" (II, ii, 255) in a scene that immediately pre-
cedes and contrasts with the one in which Cassio rejects
Iago's cynical insinuations. His damnation parallels that of
Othello in a subplot which has something of the flavor of
Jonsonian comedy. Roderigo is the degenerate gentleman
gulled by a knave. Effeminate, shallow, stupid, weak, at the
mercy of his sensual desires, he is controlled by a contemptuous wave of the hand by the boldly clever, coldly emotion-
less Iago, who uses him for his "sport and profit" (I, iii, 392).
"I will incontinently drown myself," he whimpers when
Othello's marriage has been ratified (I, iii, 306), but after
Iago has forcefully told him that if he does not foolishly
do away with himself in his passion but pursues Desdemona
with bribes he will get his desires, he agrees to talk no more
of drowning (I, iii, 388): "I am changed: I'll go sell all
my land." Sell his ancestral land he does, bit by bit, making
himself bankrupt to buy jewels which supposedly go to
Desdemona. Each time he weakly protests that Iago has not
delivered the goods, Iago convinces him that he should wait
or sends him on a new enterprise, hustling him off before
he has time to think. In this way, goaded by his passion,
propelled by Iago, he engages, even though he has no stom-
ach for fighting, in a brawl with Cassio, in which he is
soundly thrashed.

But Roderigo is being gulled by no ordinary parasite who
merely swindles him of his money and tricks him into being
beaten but by a devil. It is his soul that is at stake. "If thou
wilt needs damn thyself," Iago had told him (I, iii, 359–61),
"do it a more delicate way than drowning." The words are
spoken in the lightly jesting manner of the man of the
world, but they are the temptation of the fiend. Damned
Roderigo is, but he is cheated even of the luxurious manner
of damning himself in Desdemona's arms that has been

promised. For a moment he has a chance to save himself. Complaining petulantly that Iago has given him false promises, he announces his readiness to give up a fruitless chase (IV, ii, 199–202): "I will make myself known to Desdemona: if she will return me my jewels, I will give over my suit and repent my unlawful solicitation." In his expressed intention to repent lies his hope for salvation. But, flattered by Iago, who commends his dim-witted suspicion of him as perspicacity and his petulance as spirit, and urged by him to show his courage and determination in a valiant action that will prevent Desdemona from leaving Cyprus, he permits himself to be persuaded to participate in the assassination attempt on Cassio. " 'Tis but a man gone," he says to himself (V, i, 10), as he stands concealed behind a building, ready to fall upon his intended victim. The words seal his own doom: Iago attacks him in the confusion created by his assault upon Cassio and kills him. "Kill men i' the dark!" Iago cries in self-righteous incredulity. It is ironic that these words be spoken by this Machiavellian arch-intriguer, but they indicate, nevertheless, the retribution that overtakes Roderigo in dying in the manner in which he had planned to kill Cassio: the devil has his part to play in bringing punishment to vicious men.

This element of dramatic justice helps to make the conclusion of *Othello* tolerable. Iago himself, who has put Othello "on the rack" (III, iii, 335), is sentenced to torture. "If thou the next night following enjoy not Desdemona," he had told Roderigo, knowing this was not to be, "take me from this world with treachery and devise engines for my life." He is indeed betrayed by the treachery of Emilia, who had been devoted to him, a treachery that is in reality a higher loyalty—as she says (V, ii, 196), " 'Tis proper I obey him, but not now"—and has "engines," instruments of torture, ingeniously contrived "cunning cruelty / That can

OTHELLO

torment him much and hold him long," (V, ii, 333–34) devised for him. These torments are merely the temporal prelude to the eternal torments of hell, to which he returns. "I hate him," he had said of Othello early in the play (I, i, 155), "as I do hell-pains," speaking as if of something with which he is familiar. They are also merely the extreme continuation of the torments he had suffered in life, where his thoughts did "like a poisonous mineral, gnaw [his] inwards," as hell in Emilia's imprecation upon the unknown villain who is her husband is to "gnaw his bones" (IV, ii, 136). Iago, the spirit of negation, is self-consuming and self-destructive.

And Othello himself, having voiced the pathos of his loss, in killing himself as he had killed "a malignant and a turban'd Turk" who "beat a Venetian and traduced the state" (V, ii, 353–54), visits justice upon himself. The Turk is symbolic in *Othello* of the evil in human nature destructive of order. "Are we turn'd Turks, and to ourselves do that / Which heaven hath forbid the Ottomites?" exclaims Othello at the sight of the fighting which has disturbed Cyprus (II, iii, 170–72). "For Christian shame, put by this barbarous brawl." The threat of the Turks to Cyprus had been dispelled by the destruction of their fleet by a storm. But this was merely the visible threat from without; the invisible threat from within the island, the evil passions within men which leads to civil strife, still remained. Even as Othello is being waited for on the quay after the destruction of the Turkish fleet, Iago, laughingly affirming the validity of his cynical statements about women (II, i, 115), says, "Nay, it is true, or else I am a Turk." It is not true: his statements are the inventions of the Turk inciting to chaos, of Satan seeking to extend the domain of negation. When Othello thrusts his sword into his breast, he is stabbing the Turk, the evil, within himself which Iago, evil incarnate, had

139

OTHELLO

aroused. "Good, good: the justice of it pleases: very good," he had said when Iago had suggested, "Do it not with poison, strangle her in her bed, even the bed she hath contaminated" (IV, i, 220–23). He had sought to execute poetic justice in avenging himself and in doing so had laid himself open to such justice at the hands of God. "Going about to revenge evil, we show ourselves to be evil" (*Certain Sermons*, p. 138). He falls upon the bed upon which he himself has done foul murder. To him, if we take "lust" in the general sense of "passion," apply his words, "Thy bed, lust-stain'd, shall with lust's blood be spotted" (V, i, 36). His fate is the inevitable consequence of his action. "Perdition catch my soul," he had said (III, iii, 90–92), "But I do love thee! and when I love thee not, / Chaos is come again." He has indeed brought chaos to his moral being and perdition to his soul, having traduced divine goodness and violated the law of God.

4

The world in which this drama of passion and damnation is played out is the world of sixteenth-century Venice engaged in warfare with the Turks. In the situation of the commercial city-state, fighting for its freedom,[14] there is perhaps a reflection of the situation of England. The Spanish Armada had been destroyed by a storm at sea, as was the Turkish fleet threatening Cyprus. Now England, "this scepter'd isle, / This earth of majesty, this seat of Mars, / This other Eden, demi-paradise," [15] a garrisoned garden of Eden like Cyprus, was also faced with the threat of the Turk within.

Venice, however, is not only the image of a free and independent state; it is the image of a highly sophisticated society which shows signs in the sexual laxity of Cassio, Roderigo, and Emilia and in the cynicism of Iago of a decadence that renders it liable to enslavement. In this image there is, also, a reflection of some features of Elizabethan England. The paradoxes and epigrams in Iago's raillery of women, with which he beguiles Desdemona's anxiety as she waits on the harbor for Othello, as well as his more obscene humor in addressing Brabantio in the first scene, are spoken in the very language of the Elizabethan satirists. Neither Desdemona nor Cassio takes Iago's raillery seriously, but his flippant jibes, it is implied, contain a poison capable of dissolving the moral fabric of society.

Chapter IX

MACBETH

1

In *Macbeth* we are shown evil as frighteningly present in all of us, ready at all times, given the favorable circumstances and the relaxation of our will, to drag us down to our doom. At the beginning of the play Macbeth is highly esteemed for his valiant and honorable service to the state. Sinister suggestion, unique opportunity, the goading of a superior will, and his own lack of self-knowledge contribute to make all that is bad within him stifle his better nature, which speaks to him through his imagination. In his fall we see the latent possibilities for evil in the murky depths of human nature.

The witches, whose prophecy immediately suggests the murder of Duncan to Macbeth, have, as agents of the devil, a mysterious knowledge of the future, but they are not masters over it. Macbeth himself is responsible for his crime and its consequences. Banquo, who is counterposed to him as being met with by the witches in the same way but responding in the proper fashion, tells him (I, iii, 123–26): "Oftentimes, to win us to our harm, / The instruments of darkness tell us truths, / Win us with honest trifles, to betray 's / In deepest consequence." So is Macbeth betrayed, while Banquo, resisting their solicitations, is ultimately triumphant although murdered by Macbeth, being the

Notes to this chapter begin on page 229.

father of kings. However, although Banquo rejects the solicitations of the instruments of darkness, he is tempted by them and has to struggle to overcome them. Following Macbeth's allowing himself to be convinced by his wife to murder Duncan, Banquo is shown walking in the night, afraid of the thoughts that come to him in the stillness of his bed (II, i, 7–9): "Merciful powers, / Restrain in me the cursed thoughts that nature / Gives way to in repose!" The struggle between good and evil takes place in all of us, and all of us have need of the grace of God.

The pervasiveness and omnipresence of evil is suggested throughout the play. It begins with an account of a rebellion defeated by Macbeth and of an attack by a foreign power secretly assisted by a traitor that follows it and is also defeated by him. But although Macbeth beats down these two threats to Scotland's order, he succumbs to the third one, the one within himself. We cannot tell where the forces of disorder will strike next. "There's no art / To find the mind's construction in the face: / He was a gentleman on whom I built / An absolute trust," says Duncan of the traitor Cawdor (I, iv, 11–14)—and Macbeth, the new thane of Cawdor, already harboring murderous thoughts, enters, to be greeted with expressions of praise and gratitude. He has fixed the head of the rebel Macdonwald upon the battlements; at the end his own head is thus held up for display. Such repetition and duplication takes place, it is implied, because the evil passions of men constantly impel them to violate the natural order.

Perceptive Elizabethans, for whom the Bible furnished the great truths and basic situations of history, would have heard in the play distant echoes of the Bible story that would have strengthened this feeling. Lady Macbeth, urging her husband to sin, appealing to his love for her with the words "from this time / Such I account thy love"

(I, vii, 38–39), fatally unaware of the momentousness of the act and of the repercussions it will bring for them and their entire people, is like the mother of mankind. The words "a little water clears us of this deed" (II, ii, 67) not only convict Lady Macbeth of an Eve-like lightness of thought but remind us of Pontius Pilate. Duncan, who "hath borne his faculties so meek, hath been / So clear in his great office" (I, vii, 17–18), is a Christlike figure, overflowing with love, beneficence, and graciousness, giving to all his "graces" (I, vi, 30), the royal favors which are the sign of his love.[1] "Yet nought thou ask'st in lieu of all this love," said Spenser of Christ ("An Hymn of Heavenly Love," lines 176–77), "But loue of vs for guerdon of thy paine." So does Duncan say to Lady Macbeth with graciously playful logic (I, vi, 11–14): "The love that follows us sometime is our trouble, / Which still we thank as love. Herein I teach you / How you shall bid God 'ild us for your pains, / And thank us for your trouble"—that is, he is grateful for the love which attends him even though it is sometimes troublesome; and in like manner she should be grateful for his love, evidenced by his visit, even though it has put her to an inconvenience. "We rest your hermits," we remain your grateful beadsmen, giving ourselves up to the prayers, the expressions of gratitude to God, you ask of us, Lady Macbeth makes the proper reply, adding that everything they have is really his, to be accounted for whenever it so pleases him to call for it. The words have a further significance than the ceremonious statement of feudal vassalage: Macbeth and Lady Macbeth disregard their debt to the One to Whom they owe everything and forget the great accounting they must make at their death. Macbeth, welcoming Duncan to the banquet in his castle, plays the part of Judas at the Last Supper; the murder of Duncan is accompanied by an eclipse of the sun and an earthquake, as was the crucifixion.

Macbeth, the first of the Scotch nobles, the brilliant commander of the king's legions, is also like Lucifer, who fell
because of his ambitious desire to assume the kingship of
heaven, setting the pattern for future sin, and his internal
dismay when Duncan proclaims Malcolm the Prince of
Cumberland is like Lucifer's dismay when God announces
the begetting of His Son.[2] In making his proclamation Duncan states (I, iv, 40–41) that when the Prince is formally
invested with his new title "signs of nobleness, like stars,
shall shine / On all deservers." The foremost of the shining deservers, as Lucifer, the morning star, was the brightest of the angels before his glory was darkened by his fall,
is Macbeth, but, as a result of his sinful ambition, he becomes "black Macbeth," than whom "in the legions of horrid hell" is no "devil more damn'd / In evils" (IV, iii, 52–
57). Malcolm carries on the Christ-Satan analogy when he
speaks of himself (IV, iii, 15–16) as "a weak, poor, innocent
lamb" whom Macduff may think wise to offer up to "ap-
pease an angry god," that is, the devil who has taken the
form of a pagan god. Going on to excuse his suspicion that
Macduff is of Macbeth's party in spite of his appearance of
virtue, he makes another implied comparison between Macbeth, the "tyrant . . . once thought honest" (12–13), and
Satan: "Angels are bright still, though the brightest fell:
/ Though all things foul would wear the brows of grace, /
Yet grace must still look so" (22–24). Good remains good,
although in this world, where Satan, "the father of lies," is
constantly at work, evil deceptively takes on the appearance
of good.

In the world of *Macbeth* the masked omnipresence of evil
brings doubt and confusion. With the discovery of the
murder of Duncan consternation and suspicion become rife.
Malcolm and Donalbain suspect everybody, not knowing
who or how many are involved, but fearing most the nobles

who are most closely related to them (II, iii, 146–47): "There's daggers in men's smiles: the near in blood, / The nearer bloody." They flee, putting upon themselves suspicion of the deed. The election thus lights on Macbeth, but Macduff has vague doubts about him. He does not go to Scone to see Macbeth crowned and expresses some fear of his accession to the throne (II, iv, 37–38): "Well, may you see things well done there: adieu! / Lest our old robes sit easier than our new!" The old man who discusses the recent events and Macbeth's assumption of the kingship with him and Ross recognizes with the wisdom and insight of age the terrible mistake that the Scotch nobility has made in electing Macbeth king, but he can speak of it only in soliloquy. Banquo fears that Macbeth has played foully for the kingship, but he, too, must keep his fear to himself.

Yet murder will out. The ugliness of evil's visage is revealed, and men of good will, although they must first make sure of each other, since they are suspicious and fearful of everyone in the dark world in which they are living, proceed together against it. For, although evil is present throughout nature, it is monstrous, unnatural. It comes unbidden into men's thoughts, but in doing so is immediately and intuitively perceived and proclaimed by the heart as contrary to nature. "If good," says Macbeth of the witches' tempting prophecy (I, iii, 134–37), "why do I yield to that suggestion / Whose horrid image doth unfix my hair / And make my seated heart knock at my ribs, / Against the use of nature?"

But Macbeth and Lady Macbeth cast out nature from within them. "Yet do I fear thy nature," says she of him in her soliloquy (I, v, 17–19). "It is too full o' the milk of human kindness / To catch the nearest way." "Human kindness" here means both "those qualities peculiar to mankind" and "compassion," compassion being precisely

one of those qualities which human beings absorb with
their mother's milk so that it is a part of their very being.
Macbeth has too much of ordinary human nature in him
to resort to crime without external stimulus, although, like
ordinary weak human beings, he may think longingly of
the death of the man who stands in his way and hope that
his crime be done for him. Lady Macbeth, however, teaches
him to suppress his natural inclinations. She herself calls
upon the "spirits / That tend on mortal thoughts," the
evil spirits whose business it is to foster thoughts which are
"mortal," deadly, murderous—"mortal," too, because they
are all too characteristic of men, frail as they are in their
mortality—she calls upon them to take her milk for gall
so that "no compunctious visitings of nature," no instinctive
feelings of pity, may prevent her from fulfilling her purpose.
"Milk" here, as in "milk of human kindness," signifies the
gentle qualities in human nature, the tender, womanly feelings she describes herself as having had when she says (I, vii,
54–55), "I have given suck, and know / How tender 'tis to
love the babe that milks me," and "gall" signifies black,
inhuman cruelty, the unnatural feeling that makes it possible for her, now possessed with the spirit of evil, to go
on to say that she would rather have dashed her infant's
brains out than to have failed to perform a vow to murder.

2

Although in her invocation to the powers of darkness,
where she calls upon evil to be her good, she impliedly
recognizes that the social feelings are natural to man, she
acts upon a different view of man, a view in which intrepid
and conscienceless ambition, ready to dare all and disregard
ordinary morality to fulfill itself, replaces these feelings as
the highest quality of man. She exhorts Macbeth to practice

the Machiavellian virtues of craftiness and courage, to dis-
simulate, play the part of the welcoming host, "look like
the innocent flower, / But be the serpent under 't" (I, v, 66–
67), and to seize boldly his supreme opportunity to gain
that "which thou esteem'st the ornament of life" (I, vii, 42),
the crown. In this view of man the conventional virtues are
reasons for reproach. "Milk of human kindness," as far
as Lady Macbeth—if not the audience—is concerned, is a
contemptuous phrase alluding to the proverb that milk is a
food for infants as against meat for grown men, as in
Goneril's scorn for the "milky gentleness" of Albany (*King
Lear,* I, iv, 364) and Richard's scorn for the "milksop"
Richmond (*Richard III,* V, iii, 325). For Lady Macbeth
"milk of human kindness" is a symbol for the weakness of
ordinary men incapable of greatness. "Thou wouldst be
great," she goes on,

> Art not without ambition, but without
> The illness should attend it: what thou wouldst highly,
> That wouldst thou holily; would not play false,
> And yet wouldst wrongly win. (I, v, 19–23)

Ambition, and with it the ruthlessness necessary for its
achievement, is represented as the supreme virtue; moral
scruples standing in its way, the desire to act "holily," like
a saint ignorant of practical affairs, is represented as shame-
ful.

The clash between the Christian humanist and the
"Machiavellian" views as to what is proper to man forms a
kind of running debate in *Macbeth* and is part of its dramatic texture. The Machiavellian villain of Elizabethan
drama is distinguished by the fact that he gleefully boasts to
the audience of the crimes of which the other characters do
not suspect him. Macbeth is not at all this melodramatic ster-
eotype. However, the principles by which he seeks to guide

himself are those of the Machiavellian villain, and this would have been recognized by the perceptive members of Shakespeare's audience.

The Machiavellian villain regards himself as a superman and the vast majority of mankind as children, lacking in courage and energy and stupidly beguiled by religious superstitions. "Nil mediôcre placet: sublimia sola voluto," says Machiavelli in Gabriel Harvey's "Epigramma in effigiem Machiavelli." "Lac pueris cibus est: sanguine vescor ego." In its expression of a drive for power and its statement that milk is food for children, unlike the blood on which he feeds, this is echoed by Lady Macbeth's soliloquy. So, too, Machiavelli's "I count religion but a childish toy" in the Prologue to Marlowe's *Jew of Malta* is echoed by her " 'Tis the eye of childhood / That fears a painted devil" (II, ii, 54–55). Her statement that Macbeth is too weak to "catch the nearest way," to proceed by the most direct course regardless of the human lives blocking it, is reminiscent of Richard's speech in which he proclaims that he will "set the murderous Machiavell to school" (*Henry VI, Part III*, III, ii, 193)—that is, reduce even the progenitor of the superman idea to the level of a schoolboy. He is, he says, as one "lost in a thorny wood" and "seeking a way . . . to catch the English crown" who will "hew [his] way out with a bloody axe." Blood, the image which pervades *Macbeth*, was associated with the name of Machiavelli, who had observed at one point in his *Discourses* that Christian forbearance and submission had done away with the valor of the pagans, whose religious ceremonies, unlike the Christian ceremonies, "were sacrificial acts in which there was much shedding of blood and much ferocity. . . ." [3] This passage became notorious, being taken up by Primaudaye,[4] by the Huguenot Innocent Gentillet in his immensely influential reply to Machiavelli,[5] and by Donne, who in his satiric *Ignatius His Conclave* has Machiavelli say, as he is seeking to supersede Ignatius Loyola in Lucifer's favor while flatteringly affirming that all he himself has done is "childish" compared to the accomplishments of the Jesuits: "For I myself went always that way of blood, and therefore I did ever prefer the sacrifices of the Gentiles . . . before the soft and wanton sacrifices of Christians." [6] Macbeth takes the "Machiavellian" way of blood and guile, performing, although in a far different spirit, the actions which Richard boasts he will perform (*Henry VI, Part III*, III, ii, 182–85).

> Why, I can smile, and murder whiles I smile,
> And cry "Content" to that which grieves my heart,
> And wet my cheeks with artificial tears,
> And frame my face to all occasions.

But unlike the orthodox Machiavellian villain Macbeth takes this way in a kind of hypnotized fascination that breaks down his will and continues along it with a weary desperation. "I dare do all that may become a man. / Who dares do more is none," he replies to his wife's taunt of cowardice (I, vii, 46–47), affirming that murder is inhuman and that boldness shown in performing it is not a proof of manliness. Lady Macbeth retorts fiercely and with scornful logic that, if this is so, then he must have been ruled by the spirit of a beast when he broached the enterprise to her, rejecting this idea immediately: "When you durst do it, then you were a man" (49). If he would only do now what he had before resolved to do, he would be still more a man. Instead, the opportunity for which he had longed has only served to "unmake" (54) him, undo his manhood. She prevails over him, and he exclaims in admiration: "Bring forth men-children only; / For thy undaunted mettle should compose / Nothing but males" (72–74). She is all the more praiseworthy, he thinks, for having the hardiness of a proper man in that she is a woman, who would be expected to have the weakness women ordinarily have, a view of womanliness which stands in contrast to that implied in the dramatically ironic words of Macduff to Lady Macbeth shortly after, when he has discovered the murder of Duncan (II, iii, 88–91): "O gentle lady, / 'Tis not fit for you to hear what I can speak: / The repetition, in a woman's ear, / Would murder as it fell."

When Macbeth speaks to those who are to murder Banquo, ruined gentlemen turned malcontent, disgusted with life and desperately ready to do anything "to spite the world" (III, i, 111) and advance their fortunes, he urges them, if they are "not i' the worst rank of manhood" (103), to revenge themselves on Banquo, to whom he falsely ascribes their broken careers, and incidentally to gain his favor. He thus implies that men can be marshaled according to an order of manliness and that in this order those filled with murderous vengefulness stand in the front ranks. Christian forgiveness and the endurance of worldly misfortune in the reliance on the justice of God he disposes of by implication with the same rhetorical scorn that Lady Macbeth had used in sweeping aside his moral objections:

> Do you find
> Your patience so predominant in your nature
> That you can let this go? Are you so gospell'd
> To pray for this good man and for his issue,
> Whose heavy hand hath bow'd you to the grave
> And beggar'd yours for ever? (86–91)

There is no direct attack on the Christian ethic, but the first question implies: do you have the despicable patience of a saint or the spirit of a true man? In the second question "gospell'd" is used in the general sense of "taught"—is *this* what you have accepted as your guiding principle?—

but it recalls that what is being contemptuously rejected is indeed the injunction of the Gospel (Matt. v, 44) to "pray for them which despitefully use you." "We are men, my liege," replies the first murderer, speaking for both, accepting the view implied by Macbeth's rhetorical questions that men with the passions of men and not the listlessness of weaklings can respond in but one way: bloody revenge.[7]

When Lady Macbeth seeks to impel Macbeth to conquer his fear of Banquo's ghost so that he may cease betraying himself before the nobles assembled as his guests, it is to his manhood that she appeals (III, iv, 58, 73): "Are you a man? . . . What, quite unmann'd in folly?" It is folly that unmans him because the visions that he sees she, in her skeptical rationalism, can believe only to be delusions rising from the womanish credulity that accepts old wives' tales: "O, these flaws and starts, / Imposters to true fear, would well become / A woman's story at a winter's fire, / Authorized by her grandam" (63–66). Macbeth defends his courage in terms similar to those he used before: "What man dare, I dare" (99). If he tremble before any natural danger, he asserts, "protest me / The baby of a girl" (105–6), the weakling infant of an immature mother, but such supernatural visitations must rob any man of his courage. The vanishing of the ghost, however, brings back the resolution in crime which he thinks of as his manhood: "Why, so: being gone, I am a man again" (107–8). Further crime, he thinks, will harden him against fear and obliterate the horrible visions which by the end of the scene he has come around to believing are imagined by him: "My strange and self-abuse / Is the initiate fear that wants hard use: / We are yet but young in deed" (142–44). "We are yet but young in deed"—he will cease to be a fearful novice and will become mature, a man, in crime, ridding himself of the bogeyman terrors of the child. In spite of the evidence to the contrary, he has taken to himself the rationalism of Lady Macbeth, who had said (II, ii, 53–55), "The sleeping and the dead / Are but as pictures: 'tis the eye of childhood / That fears a painted devil."

At the turning point of the play Macduff is likewise urged to act in a manner becoming a man. "Dispute it like a man," says Malcolm (IV, iii, 220), telling him to ease his grief at the news of the murder of his wife and children by taking action against the outrage. "I shall do so," replies Macduff. "But I must also feel it as a man" (220–21). The gentler feelings of pity, grief, and love are as much a part of manhood as anger and courage. Macduff has both, but he neither gives way to tears nor makes a mettlesome display of spirit, rather controlling his emotion and tempering it to a righteous anger and resolution:

> O, I could play the woman with mine eyes
> And braggart with my tongue! But, gentle heavens,
> Cut short all intermission; front to front
> Bring thou this fiend of Scotland and myself;
> Within my sword's length set him; if he 'scape,
> Heaven forgive him too! (230–35)

He, like the murderers of Banquo, is seeking revenge, but his is a revenge on the field of battle by one whom the murder of his wife and children—a murder in which "no mind that's honest / But . . . shares some woe" (IV, iii, 197 –98)—has made the symbol of outraged Scotland and an agent of divine justice against the tyrant Macbeth. His words "if he 'scape, Heaven forgive him too"—if Macbeth escapes him after heaven has put him in his reach, let heaven forgive Macbeth, as he hopes it will forgive him for having left his wife and children in danger—express his certitude of his role as divine avenger and his determination not to fail in it.

At the conclusion, when Macduff meets Macbeth, Macbeth, old and weary in crime, has become inured to horror, a man at last, according to the standard he has accepted. The sudden shriek of women does not disturb him (V, v, 14–15): "Direness, familiar to my slaughterous thoughts, / Cannot once start me." But this indifference to horror is the apathy of one who has been drained of human feeling and for whom life has lost all significance. Informed that the shrieks were caused by the death of his wife, who had once been so close to him, he does not even inquire concerning the manner or the cause, but receives the news with the statement that she had to die sometime or other and that it makes no difference just when, life being meaningless and futile.

But now that he has become dead to all social feeling and that the horror of the invisible and the supernatural holds no terror for him, now that he exists merely in the immediate moment, a thing unto himself, fear of a natural danger, the end of his life in single combat, comes to him. When Macduff tells him that he is a man not born of woman, he exclaims (V, viii, 16–17), "Accursed be that tongue that tells me so, / For it hath cow'd my better part of man!" Nature, the order of God whose creative processes Macbeth has disturbed, revenges itself against him through one who, as if to meet the harsh needs of the time, was "from his mother's womb / Untimely ripp'd" (V, viii, 15–16), a bloody prodigy of nature in travail. He now momentarily feels fear not in the presence of a supernatural visitation but of a man, for in this man he sees the bloody child of the witches' prophecy who is fated to put an end to him and also that other bloody child, the one he has had slain, no longer pitifully weak but terrifyingly invincible. Daunted, he refuses to fight, but, on learning that he must either do so or yield "to be baited with the rabble's curse" (29) and continue to suffer that wearisome harassment to which, bearlike, he has been subjected, he opposes Macduff with satanic defiance in the face of the inevitable. Terrible in his desperation and in his sense of isolation from humanity, he nevertheless does not, in the courage of his despair (which recalls his former valor while contrasting with it) and in his weary yearning of a few moments ago for "the honour, love, obedience, troops of friends" which he once had had, permit us to see him depart forever without some sense of loss for the extinguished glory of this figure of darkness.

His death is in contrast to that of young Siward, one of "many unrough youths that even now / Protest their first of manhood" (V, ii, 10–11), the beardless boys, the earnest of the future Macbeth has endeavored to suppress, who give evidence of their attainment of manhood by taking arms against him. "Thou liest, abhorrèd tyrant," cries Siward when Macbeth charges him with being afraid of his dread name. "With my sword I'll prove the lie thou speak'st" (V, vii, 10–11). "He only lived but till he was a man," says Ross of him (V, viii, 40–42), "The which no sooner had his prowess confirm'd / In the unshrinking station where he fought, / But like a man he died."

Human nature and nature generally, which have been violated by Macbeth, triumph over him. The youth of Scotland, grown to be men, and the greenery of Burnam Wood rise against him. Before nature violently expels Macbeth from herself, however, he, as part of nature, is caught up in her convulsions. Like the tyrant that he is, he brings an ever-deepening anarchic chaos to his "single state of man" (I, iii, 140), the kingdom of his own being, as well as to the kingdom of Scotland. The unnatural thought of murder unfixes his hair and makes his heart beat against his ribs; his will weakening before this thought, he calls upon his "eye" to "wink at the hand" (I, iv, 52); his body resists that which his will commands, and he has to "bend up / Each corporal agent to this terrible feat" (I, vii, 79–80); he cannot say "amen" to the chamberlains' "God bless us," although he desires desperately to do so (II, ii, 28–29); his bloody hands "pluck out mine eyes" (II, ii, 59); he cannot keep the "natural ruby" of his cheek at the sight of Banquo's ghost (III, v, 115). As one of the Scotch lords says of him at the end (v, ii, 22–25), "Who then shall blame / His pester'd senses to recoil and start, / When all that is within him does condemn / Itself for being there?"

3

This internal chaos is the natural analogue to the hell to which, Macbeth recognizes in his despair, he has given his soul to no avail (III, i, 65–69): "For Banquo's issue have I filed my mind . . . and mine eternal jewel / Given to the common enemy of man." If he could be sure, he had said in his soliloquy, that the blow he struck would have no repercussions here in this life, he would risk the life to come. The irony is that he loses peace and contentment in both worlds. The crown he gains brings him no satisfaction, and "on the torture of the mind" he lies "in restless ecstasy" (III, ii, 21–22), suffering the torments of the damned.

The retribution that comes to him, like the punishment of the lost souls in the hell of Christian tradition, is poetically appropriate in its details. As he himself says (I, vii, 10–12), anticipating what will happen, "This even-handed justice / Commends the ingredients of our poison'd chalice / To our own lips." Like Lady Macbeth in her sleepwalking, his hell on earth is to continue to relive the horror he has committed and to have his own words and actions turn against him. He has refused to listen to the knocking of his heart warning him against murder, and Macduff's knocking at the gate resounds ominously in his ears. He has feasted

Duncan and then killed him in his sleep, and he is condemned to "eat our meal in fear, and sleep / In the affliction of these terrible dreams / That shake us nightly" (III, ii, 17–19). He has played the hypocritical host, and he must continue to do so, flattering Banquo and dissimulating before the nobles of the kingdom, all of the time feeling "unsafe the while, that we / Must lave our honours in these flattering streams, / And make our faces visards to our hearts, / Disguising what they are" (III, ii, 32–35). He has committed regicide, and he imagines Banquo will do the same—"Our fears in Banquo / Stick deep / . . . 'Tis much he dares" (III, i, 49–51)—afraid that his crime, as he had said before he was prevailed on to go through with it (I, vii, 9–10), will teach "bloody instructions, which, being taught, return / To plague the inventor."

Like one of the new landowners evicting tenants unprotected by a perpetual lease, he seeks to take the place of nature and "cancel and tear to pieces that great bond," that temporary lease on life, of Banquo, for whom, as for all mortals, "nature's copy's not eterne" (III, ii, 49, 38), and he himself, despite the hope he derives from the witches' prophecy that he will "live the lease of nature" (IV, i, 99), the time allotted to him if he were to die a natural death, dies at the point of the sword of divine justice. He cannot rest after the murder of Banquo any more than he could after the murder of Duncan but must keep on wearily adding horror to horror, unable to "trammel up the consequence" (I, vii, 3) of his original assassination (III, iv, 136–38): "I am in blood / Stepp'd in so far that, should I wade no more, / Returning were as tedious as go o'er." He has sought what, like Tamburlaine, he regarded as the sweet fruition of an earthly crown, and he finds "a barren sceptre in my gripe" (III, i, 62). Sterile evil is opposed to the creativity of nature: Lady Macbeth has called upon the powers of darkness to unsex her and change her milk to gall, and Macbeth cannot be "father to a line of kings" but has made "the seed of Banquo kings" (III, i, 60, 70). And at the conclusion the revolts springing up all about him remind him, as one of his nobles says, of his own breach of faith in murdering Duncan.

4

For having violated the laws of nature Macbeth suffers the penalty of nature. A usurping tyrant, in seeking peace of mind for himself, he can only devastate his country, which shares the "fitful fever" (III, ii, 23) that life has become for him, a fever in which he continually passes back and forth from the mad frenzy to which he is stimulated by his desperately held belief in his invulnerability to the despairing apathy into which he is sunk by the recognition of the futility of any effort to bring him contentment. Malcolm, the instrument of "the powers above" (IV, iii, 238), is "the medicine of the sickly weal" who will "purge it to a sound and pristine health" by ridding it of the "mind diseased" that rules it (V, ii, 27; V, iii, 52, 40). Having defeated Macbeth, he stands amid his nobles on the field of battle in a closing tableau, "compass'd," as Macduff says (V, viii, 56), "with thy kingdom's pearl," like the sun surrounded by its planets. He acknowledges his debt of gratitude as Duncan had done after the quelling of the rebellion at the beginning of the play, using the same imagery suggesting nature's bounty (I, iv, 28–29; V, viii, 65), proclaims his thanes and kinsmen earls, the first of that title in Scotland, promises to perform whatever rectifications and reforms are necessary "in measure, time, and place"—observing the propriety and order violated by Macbeth—and announces his forthcoming coronation at Scone. We think back to Duncan's promise that when Malcolm is invested with his title "signs of noble-

ness, like stars, shall shine / On all deservers" (I, iv, 40–41).
The promise is fulfilled. Macbeth and Lady Macbeth had in
their adjurations, "Stars, hide your fires; / Let not light see
my black and deep desires" (I, iv, 50–51), and "Come, thick
night, / And pall thee in the dunnest smoke of hell . . .
Nor heaven peep through the blanket of the dark" (I, v,
51–54), given themselves and Scotland over to darkness.
Now the stars shine once more.

More than a return to normality, however, is implied.
The world of *Macbeth* is one of gloomy castles whose mas-
sive strength and outlying walls and fortifications "laugh a
siege to scorn" (V, v, 3), with boding ravens croaking
hoarsely in their battlements, barred gates, and alarum bells
to call to arms; of barren heaths and uninhabited spaces
where "spurs the lated traveller apace / To gain the timely
inn" (III, iii, 6–7), and murder takes place unobserved less
than a mile from the king's residence; of savage hand-to-
hand conflicts in which the brandished steel rips the foe
from the jaws to the navel. It is a world of a vaguely suggested early feudalism that has established a social order
after the bloody chaos of presocial communism but that is
still struggling to maintain it:

> Blood hath been shed ere now, i' the olden time,
> Ere humane statute purged the gentle weal;
> Ay, and since too, murders have been perform'd
> Too terrible for the ear. (III, iv, 75–78)

In the coronation of Malcolm and the proclamation of thanes
and kinsmen as earls is indicated the dawn of a new epoch,
with hereditary succession of the monarchy and a more
sharply defined and stable social hierarchy.

But while indicating the beginning of a new epoch for
Scotland and giving promise, in the pageant seen by Macbeth and in the joining of the English and Scottish forces

against him, of the union of Scotland and England, the play would also have brought forcefully before its Elizabethan audience, both that at the court and at the Glove Theatre, before both of which it was probably presented in 1606, the dangers which had only recently threatened the achievements of the past and the prospects of the future. Macbeth's and Lady Macbeth's Machiavellian plotting of Duncan's murder and the enormity of the crime—which includes in itself violation of the family blood tie and of feudal hospitality, "most sacrilegious murder" breaking open "the Lord's anointed temple" (II, iii, 72-73), and the parricide of one to whom his subjects owe the duties of "children and servants" (I, iv, 25)—must have called to their minds the Gunpowder Plot of November 1605, which so terrified the king and excited the people of London.[8] The plot, by which the king, the nobility, Parliament, and part of London were to be wiped out, was regarded as exhibiting to broad daylight the devilish Machiavellianism of the Catholics, which was further illustrated by the confession of the plotter Garnet to the use of equivocation, the swearing to statements made with mental reservations or deceptive ambiguities which Jesuit doctrine permitted before questioners whose authority the Pope did not recognize. "Faith, here's an equivocator . . . who committed treason enough for God's sake, yet could not equivocate to heaven," says the drunken porter (II, iii, 8-12), welcoming him with grim irony to hell and reminding the audience of the Machiavellian wickedness of regicide in the present as in the past. Disguise itself in the habiliments of religion though it might, assume whatever form it would, evil remained evil, and the struggle between it and good went on everlastingly, in their time as before.

Chapter X

KING LEAR

1

Why have bastards best fortune?" asked Donne in the first problem of his *Paradoxes and Problems,* and he gave the reply that "the Church having removed them from all place in the public service of God, they have better means than others to be wicked and so fortunate." He was cynically taking for granted the very opposite of the Elizabethan article of faith that the wicked come to a bad end. In *King Lear* Shakespeare seriously examines the point which Donne had frivolously made. Edmund is a bastard. He is outside of the recognized structure of society and, being outside, he has no regard for its laws. In the soliloquy in which he reveals himself he, like Donne, sets nature in opposition to civilization. The various bonds which society imposes—kinship, friendship, allegiance—he regards as alien to nature, whose only law is that of complete egoism. "The younger rises when the old doth fall" (III, iii, 28)—this, and not the love of son for father, is the primal law. All the rest is "custom" and "the curiosity of nations" (I, ii, 3, 4), the artificial legal distinctions of each country, all of which are in opposition to this primal law. In proceeding upon this philosophy, he seems to prosper, flouting the moral order without any immediate effects and, as the prospect widens, even casting his eye on the crown. So, too, do Goneril and Regan, who act

Notes to this chapter begin on page 230.

upon this philosophy without explicitly formulating it, seem to prosper. The question pressed upon the minds of the audience as it watches their actions is: does divine justice exist?

This question is made all the more insistent by the questionings of the good persons in the play and by their appeals to the gods of the pagan age in which they are living. The divine powers seem equally indifferent to their questions and entreaties and to the words of pious hypocrisy of the wicked. But, although divine justice moves in its own mysterious fashion and with agonizing slowness, at the end it reveals itself and prevails. The wicked, deluded by their seeming security, grow in wickedness and eventually destroy themselves. The good are tested by affliction or else, in undergoing a purgatory of suffering, have their sins redeemed. In either case they exhibit or come to exhibit a sense of the true meaning of life that makes the adversity they have experienced worth the pain.

2

In its depiction of Goneril, Regan, Cornwall, and Edmund, and of the fate that overtakes them *King Lear* might almost be said to be a dramatization of the words which Greene, embracing orthodoxy on his deathbed, addressed to Marlowe:

Is it pestilent Machiavellian policy that thou hast studied? O, punish folly! What are his rules but mere confused mockeries able to extirpate in small time the generation of mankind? For if "Sic volo, sic iubeo" hold in those that are able to command and if it be lawful, "Fas and nefas," to do anything that is beneficial, only tyrants should possess the earth, and they, striving to exceed in tyranny, should each to other be a

slaughter-man till, the mightiest outliving all, one stroke were
left for Death, that in one age man's life should end.[1]

It is, however, not a glib refutation of Machiavellianism but
a terrifying vision of man's appetite tearing away from the
bonds of social organization and, become a ravening, hydro-
phobic beast, almost destroying all of humanity in its madness.

For, although the evil characters of the play are so cold-
bloodedly rational, their behavior is actually a kind of "reason in madness" (IV, v, 179) which, unlike that of Lear,
blinds them to reality. Their reason, through which they
should apprehend the moral imperatives of natural law, is,
as Hamlet says, made pander to their will, their selfish desires. They are full of practical good reasons for their inhuman behavior. Goneril's sharp, savagely spontaneous attack on Albany, by which she seeks to justify the sisters' exposure of Lear to the elements, reduces their previous
specious rationalizations, however, to mad absurdity:

> Milk-liver'd man!
> That bear'st a cheek for blows, a head for wrongs;
> Who hast not in thy brows an eye discerning
> Thine honour from thy suffering; that not know'st
> Fools do those villains pity who are punish'd
> Ere they have done their mischief. (IV, ii, 50–55)

In one breath she says that Albany is cowardly and impracti-
cally Christlike in turning the other cheek—to the blows
which Lear, of all persons, has presumably struck at him!—
and cannot distinguish between what he can and what he
cannot bear with honor; in the next breath she implies
that while Lear has done them no harm he is a villain who
was planning to do so and Albany is a fool for pitying him
for having suffered punishment before he has committed a
villainy. So, too, Edmund's excuse for his betrayal of his

father, his statement that his loyalty to the state came first, is made absurd by Regan's statement to Gloucester that Edmund "is too good to pity thee" (III, vii, 90) and by her statement to Oswald—the culmination of crazy rationalization—that Edmund has gone to dispatch Gloucester of his life "in pity of his misery" (IV, v, 12).

The fierce, overwhelming desires ministered to by the sisters' rationality is typified by their lust for Edmund, a lust which violates the marriage bond of Goneril and makes her plot the death of her husband and which, it surely should be indicated on the stage, was felt by Regan before the death of Cornwall, the "most speaking looks" which she refers to (IV, v, 25) as having been directed by her sister to Edmund being duplicated by herself in accordance with the parallelism of the play. Edmund himself exalts the "lusty stealth of nature," the animal passion of illicit love, as against the "dull, stale, tired bed of marriage" (I, ii, 11–12). He rejects contemptuously the idea that it is because of the position of the stars at the time of his conception that he is "rough and lecherous," a tacit admission that, although he claims free will, he is bound to be what he is regardless of the stars, being ruled by his appetites.

It is the individualistic pursuit of their appetites that brings the wicked to their destruction. In a game in which each engages in double-dealing against the others, all are bound to lose. Although Goneril and Regan join against their father, in the rumor of war between Albany and Cornwall (II, i, 11–15) the clash between the two is early foreshadowed. The clash is for the moment averted by the necessity of uniting forces against the army that has come to England to take up Lear's cause. The fascination that Edmund holds for both of the sisters, however, indicates that this is only temporary.

The collaboration of all of these single-mindedly individ-

ualistic persons has an element of irony. "I will lay trust
upon thee," says Cornwall to Edmund (III, v, 25–26), who
has betrayed his own father, "and thou shalt find a dearer
father in my love." In taking the place of Edmund's father,
he can scarcely expect anything but to be betrayed by him,
and such a betrayal would be indicated to the audience by
the glances exchanged by Edmund and Regan. Edmund is
also false to both Goneril and Regan. "To both these sisters
have I sworn my love. / Which of them shall I take? / Both?
One? Or neither?" (V, i, 55–58) he meditates with characteristic amused cynicism. He decides that Albany stands in
his path in attaining the throne and that he will therefore
hold Regan off and encourage Goneril to do away with her
husband, continuing to play each along. So, too, does Oswald,
the ape of his social superiors, refuse to be bribed by Regan
to show Goneril's letter to Edmund but accepts the delivery
of a love token from her. The two sisters are suspiciously
afraid of each other, as "the stung / Are of the adder" (V, i,
56–57). At the end Regan, who has sought to "loosen"
Edmund from her sister, with whom, she suspects, he has
been "conjunct / And bosom'd" (V, i, 12–13); Goneril, who
has poisoned Regan; and Edmund, who has deceived both
—all are united in death, like venomous reptiles—"adder" (V, i, 57), "gilded serpent" (V, iii, 84), and "toad-spotted
traitor" (V, iii, 138)—locked simultaneously in fatal embrace
and death grapple, from which they are unable to extricate
themselves. "I was contracted to them both," says Edmund
(V, iii, 228–29). "All three / Now marry in an instant." His
words to Goneril (IV, ii, 25), "Yours in the ranks of death,"
delivered with the flourish of an adventurer conscious of his
debonair grace, prove true, not only as far as Goneril but
as far as Regan is concerned.

Edmund's death, like that of Cornwall and Oswald, is a
punishment inflicted by nature, which he has violated.

Cornwall, in passing summary judgment and punishment upon Gloucester, disregarded the recognized social obligation and duty that he owes to his host, of which Gloucester reminds him, and uses his absolute power in a manner out of accord with the law of nature. To Gloucester's appeal (III, vii, 72–73), "He that will think to live till he be old, / Give me some help," there comes, suddenly, unexpectedly, as if by a miracle, an answer. The servants had been obeying Cornwall's commands, although reluctantly (Cornwall had to command them twice to blind Gloucester), and, our attention riveted on the central figures of the drama, we had tended, with Cornwall and Regan, to regard them as depersonalized automatons. The intervention now of one of the servants comes as a complete surprise both to ourselves and the actors of the drama. Cornwall, who had been served by this man ever since the latter's boyhood without even suspecting that the goodness in his heart would cause him to react in this way, cries out in mingled anger and amazement, "My villain!" and Regan exclaims, "A peasant stand up thus!" (III, vii, 83) It is unheard of. Albany, when he learns that Cornwall received his deathblow from a servant he had bred who, horrified by what he was witnessing, had dared to remonstrate with the master of one half of Britain, says with awed piety (IV, ii, 78–80), "This shows you are above, / You justicers, that these our nether crimes / So speedily can venge!" It does indeed seem in the context of the play a miracle of divine justice, even though our imaginative faith in it is disturbed by the completion of Gloucester's blinding, we, like the characters of the play, not being able to see as yet the purpose of his suffering.

The servant who kills Cornwall is only one of a number of characters who speak with the voice of nature, simple and unspoiled, against the corrupt representatives of a sophisticated civilization. The old man who, at the risk of his

KING LEAR

life, leads Gloucester to Poor Tom and brings his best apparel to clothe the naked mad beggar for "ancient love" (IV, i, 45) of his master, typifies the feudal loyalties which are being swept away by this civilization (IV, i, 13–15): "O, my good lord, I have been your tenant, and your father's tenant, these fourscore years." In this feeble old man and Cornwall's servant, vigorous in the prime of life, we see common humanity, rooted in nature and enduring through the generations. So, too, the servants who are left on the stage after Regan leads off Cornwall reassure us about humanity. Their simple, kindly speech, with its natural, prosaic style and reference to homely household remedies, comes as a relief, like the gentle rain of heaven, after the feverish nightmare of the preceding part of the scene, and brings us back to ordinary, everyday life after we have been transported to a den of horrors. They express the awe and fear that simple minds feel in the presence of evil, which is too terrible for them to understand. "I'll never care what wickedness I do, / If this man come to good," says one (III, vii, 99–100). "If she live long," replies the other (III, vii, 100–1), "And in the end meet the old course of death, / Women will all turn monsters." But justice is indeed visited upon the wrongdoers: the wound Cornwall has received is mortal, and Regan is shortly to die an unnatural death.

Cornwall is struck down by outraged humanity rising up against him in the form of a servant; Oswald, the base-born foppish steward of Goneril, who has pretentiously assumed the airs and dress of a gentleman and, as Kent says, wears a sword without possessing a sense of honor, is fittingly struck down by the cudgel of Edgar, son of an earl disguised as a peasant. The ironic reversal of roles, made possible by an effete civilization in which servile acquiescence flourishes and honorable gentility is forced to hide, is emphasized: Oswald addresses Edgar as "bold peasant," "dunghill," "slave," and "villain" (IV, vi, 235, 241, 249, 252); Edgar addresses Oswald as "good gentleman" (IV, vi, 242). Their true nature shines out, however, in their behavior. Oswald swaggeringly attempts to thrust Edgar aside; Edgar stands boldly against him, undismayed by Oswald's vaunting words and fancy sword thrusts. The cudgel of the gentleman triumphs over the sword of the steward, and Oswald, ignobly knocked over the head, gets a just valediction from Edgar, which restores the two to their proper places:

> I know thee well: a serviceable villain;
> As duteous to the vices of thy mistress
> As badness would desire. (IV, vi, 257-59)

So, too, in Edgar's combat with Edmund is there a reversal of roles which is at the end redressed. It is Edgar who says (V, iii, 121), "My name is lost"; Edmund, the bastard, has name, place, and eminence. Edmund is at the height of his fortune, a victorious leader who had shared the command of the British army, contended for by two queens and speaking with proud assurance to the king of one half of Britain. In a moment he loses everything—his ill-gotten gains, his reputation, and his life. Slowly, surely, unknown to him, retribution against him has been gathering force. When the blast of Edgar's trumpet, tensely waited for and late in coming, sounds out in answer to the third and final blast of his own, it is as the trumpet announcing the last judgment. The duel in which he engages is the medieval trial by combat, in which God was thought to indicate the right. In his arraignment of human justice Lear, speaking with the insight he had gained in his madness, had said (IV, vi, 169-70): "Plate sin with gold, / And the strong lance of justice hurtless breaks." In this trial by combat, in which divine justice manifests itself, Edmund's "fire-new fortune" (V, iii, 132), his recently acquired coat of arms as an earl, just off the fires of the smith's forge, as it were, and shining brilliantly, is no protection for him. As he lies vanquished, he is confronted with the letter to him from Goneril, which convicts him, as Edgar was falsely convicted by the forged letter he had used. When Edgar reveals himself and affirms the justice of the gods, Edmund, crushed at a blow, assents.

3

The suffering that Gloucester and Lear undergo has in it elements of poetic justice of the kind which the evil characters meet. Gloucester, blindly credulous—his credulity is related to his readiness to accept the easiest way, regardless of morality—is punished by being made actually blind. He accepts as Edgar's the idea, in reality Edmund's, that "sons at perfect age, and fathers declining, the father should be as ward to the son, and the son manage his revenue" (I, ii, 77–79). As a result it is Edmund who acquires his revenue, and he, ironically, becomes dependent on Edgar. His blindness, an impairment of one of his senses, is also a form of retribution for his sensual indulgence. At the final reckoning, when Edgar stands over the fallen body of Edmund, Edgar explicitly states the connection between Gloucester's blindness and his self-indulgent sensuality:

> The gods are just, and of our pleasant vices
> Make instruments to plague us:
> The dark and vicious place where thee he got
> Cost him his eyes. (V, iii, 170–72)

The grimly moral words about our "pleasant vices" act as a comment on Gloucester's man-of-the-world observation at the beginning of the play (I, i, 23), "There was good sport at his making."

Lear acted with insane anger in disinheriting Cordelia and dividing the kingdom between Cornwall and Albany, so much so that Kent, who, although a plain-spoken man, is ordinarily respectfully ceremonious in his speech to his sovereign, had to address him roundly (I, i, 147–48): "Be Kent unmannerly, / When Lear is mad." He becomes indeed mad. He sought to have his daughters go beyond natural affection in their love, to vie with nature, promising to give the most generous dowry "where nature doth with merit challenge" (I, i, 54), and rejecting Cordelia because she will only promise to love "according to my bond" (I, i, 95). Goneril's and Regan's conduct toward him proves unnatural, as unnatural as their strained words of love and his own conduct toward Cordelia, but the love which Cordelia has for her husband—the love which she had stated she would not give up to him—does not lessen her devotion to him and enables her to bring the forces of France to his aid. He made a show of adding up the amount of each daughter's love and rewarding her accordingly, measuring the weight of rhetoric each is able to put in the scales without looking at the value each attached to her words. Goneril and Regan in return take away from the number of his retainers without regard for the symbolic value he attaches to them. He turned out Cordelia without a dowry and went to live with Goneril and Regan; they turn him out with nothing, and, although he hides for shame of his former treatment of her, he is called for by Cordelia, who sends a "century" (IV, iv, 6), a troop of a hundred men—we are reminded of the hundred knights which his other daughters have refused him—to attend him with the homage due a king.

The suffering of Gloucester and Lear is, however, more than punishment; it is a purgatory which burns away their previous selfishness. Adversity brings for the good the miracle of love, a heightening of their humanity, the humanity whose lack is so unnatural in the wicked. The theme is stated by secondary characters whose words act as universalizing comment applicable to Gloucester and Lear. "Gods, gods!" exclaims France (I, i, 257–59), sounding the theme at the very beginning, as he sees Cordelia poor, forsaken, and despised, " 'tis strange that from their cold'st neglect / My love should kindle to inflamed respect." The coldness of ill fortune miraculously brings the warmth of love. Lear had indeed, as the Fool says later (I, iv, 115–16), given Cordelia "a blessing against his will," the blessing of France's love. So, too, does Kent, suffering the ignominy of being placed in the stocks, read the letter from Cordelia, whose love promises to redress the situation of the king and his devoted follower, by the "comfortable beams" (II, ii, 171), the comforting and warming rays, of the rising sun, saying (II, ii, 172–73), "Nothing almost sees miracles / But misery." And Edgar, in reply to his father's question, identifies himself as one who by the "art," the magic, "of known and feeling sorrows, / Am pregnant to good pity" (IV, vi, 226–27).

This is the miracle that happens to Gloucester. He has been a man who, although having good intentions, has been yielding before power wrongly used, heeding his ease rather than his duty and loving himself more than humanity. Unlike Kent, he has not spoken out against Lear's division of the kingdom between his two daughters and their husbands. When Kent is placed in the stocks, he stays behind and tells him,

> I am sorry for thee, friend; 'tis the duke's pleasure,
> Whose disposition, all the world well knows,
> Will not be rubb'd nor stopp'd: I'll entreat for thee.
> (II, ii, 159–61)

Everyone knows that the duke, his "worthy arch and patron"
(II, i, 61), will not be diverted from whatever he is pleased
to do, and no practical person would therefore think of
standing in his path—this is his implied defense of his com-
pliance, although he tries to salve his conscience by saying
that he will entreat Cornwall to release Kent, an entreaty
he has already fruitlessly made. It is the way of the world
to tread warily in the presence of the powerful and to
compromise with principle. When he goes to aid Lear, it is
a delicate question whether political prudence or compassion and duty are the main motivating forces in his
mind (III, iii, 12-20): "These injuries the king now bears
will be revenged home; there's part of a power already
footed: we must incline to the king . . . Though I die
for it, as no less is threatened me, the king my old master
must be relieved." Although our doubt as to which motive
is stronger enables Gloucester to retain our sympathy, it
is clear that devotion gets a push it badly needs from ex-
pediency.

It is only after he is blinded that Gloucester sees right
and wrong clearly. Adversity has proved to be a boon. As
he says,

> I stumbled when I saw: full oft 'tis seen,
> Our means secure us, and our mere defects
> Prove our commodities. (IV, i, 21-23)

He is referring specifically to his acquired knowledge that
Edgar is faithful to him, but his words have a wider mean-
ing, for he has learned more than this. Giving his purse to
Poor Tom, he says,

> That I am wretched
> Makes thee the happier. Heavens, deal so still!
> Let the superfluous and lust-dieted man,
> That slaves your ordinance, that will not see
> Because he doth not feel, feel your power quickly;

So distribution should undo excess,
And each man have enough. (IV, i, 68–74)

He realizes that he has abused his prosperity in gratifying his sensual desires, making heaven's will in appointing him a lord subservient to his own by paying insufficient attention to the obligations as well as the privileges of his position and failing to care for such beggars and vagabonds as the one on whom he is now forced to rely. He is now, for the first time, able to see what hardship is because, having felt the power of the gods, he is able to sympathize with those suffering privation. He sees what the uncertain world, whose ways he has followed, is. As he says to Lear, in response to Lear's "Yet you see how this world goes," "I see it feelingly" (IV, vi, 151–52).

But Gloucester's purgatorial progress is not yet ended. Having renounced the world, he still takes the easier way— that of seeking to commit suicide in despair—instead of fulfilling the will of heaven by accepting life in this world while remaining uncorrupted by it. Edmund's comment on his father's belief in the effect of the stars on the lives of men has relevance for his submission to despair, which elicits from him the words (IV, i, 38–39), "As flies to wanton boys, are we to the gods. / They kill us for their sport." "This is the excellent foppery of the world," says Edmund (I, ii, 128–32), "that when we are sick in fortune—often the surfeit of our own behaviour—we make guilty of our disasters the sun, the moon, and the stars . . ." Gloucester, "the superfluous and lust-dieted man," "sick in fortune" as a result of the "surfeit" of his own behavior, does not realize fully the relation between his past conduct and his disaster. Edmund, in rejecting all correspondences between the interrelated hierarchies of nature, is rejecting the cardinal principle of order, but Gloucester, in regarding the gods as arbitrary in their malicious sportiveness, is also rejecting the concept of the ordered universe. He cannot endure his pain any longer, he says (IV, vi, 37–38), "and not fall / To quarrel" with the gods' "great opposeless wills." But he has already quarreled with their wills in regarding them as unjust. and suicide is itself a rebellion against the gods, who have placed man on earth to fulfill their own design.

His statement of despair contrasts with his address to the "ever-gentle gods" (IV, vi, 221) after Edgar has made him realize that it was a fiend which had tempted him to suicide and after he has learned that the love of Cordelia has come to succor and relieve Lear from the greatest affliction imaginable. Now he prays to them,

> Let not my worser spirit tempt me again
> To die before you please! (IV, vi, 221–22)

for he has faith that the pain they inflict has ultimately a beneficent purpose.

He does not, however, remain firm in his faith even now. It is Edgar who continually raises his faith when it languishes. Edgar has learned to understand the meaning of life as a result of the adversity he has faced—Lear is right in a way no one realizes when he calls Poor Tom a philosopher—and is a guide to his father not only in a physical but a spiritual sense. His saving of him from suicide in despair is presented as a kind of miracle, a miracle which significantly follows Gloucester's blessing of his son, who, unknown to him, stands beside him. Gloucester's words (IV, vi, 40), "If Edgar lives, O, bless him," are addressed to the gods as he is kneeling to them in prayer, and it is as if he is blessed from on high in answer. He falls, as he thinks, from a tremendous height and wakes up not to death but to life. "Thy life's a miracle," Edgar tells him (IV, vi, 55). The idea of suicide had indeed been a dizzying and terrifying prospect before which, his brain reeling, he had succumbed to the temptation of a fiend, not in the form of Poor Tom but his own "worser spirit." That he was saved after this fall as a result of the surveillance of the son whom he had cast out and reduced to a beggar and to whom he had just given "a jewel / Well worth a poor man's taking" (a jewel valuable monetarily but more valuable as the precious gift of heartfelt gratitude that is his last possession)—that he was saved in this manner is one of the miracles of love in *King Lear,* where love and benediction are, like the mercy of which Portia speaks, twice blessed, blessing him that gives and him that takes.

So, too, is he saved by his unrecognized son, now in the guise of a peasant, from death at the hands of Oswald immediately after he has asked for him "the bounty and the benison of heaven" (IV, vi, 229) for having offered to lead him to a resting place, a blessing which also, it would seem, is made on his knees, as he has just addressed to the gods the words of acceptance of their wills which brings from Edgar the comment "Well pray you, father" (IV, vi, 223). Oswald, entering and seeing Gloucester as he is blessing his son, tells him to repent his sins, for he is about to die, and the words would have greater dramatic significance if Gloucester is still kneeling. This attitude of prayer he no doubt maintains during the course of the fighting.

Gloucester finally dies blessing Edgar. The conflict of emotions within him as he listens to his son's account of how he "became his guide, / Led him, begg'd for him, saved him from despair" (V, iii, 190–91) is a concentration in a few minutes of the previous struggle within him between serene faith and dark hopelessness. "I asked his blessing," relates Edgar,

and from first to last
Told him my pilgrimage: but his flaw'd heart,
Alack, too weak the conflict to support!
'Twixt two extremes of passion, joy and grief,
Burst smilingly. (V, iii, 195–99)

The words "burst smilingly," the final words of the seven-teen-line sentence that comprises Edgar's account of his pilgrimage, a sentence that mounts in intensity as it reaches the climax of how Edgar related his story to his father—the words "burst smilingly" come as a discharge of emotion that brings relief and peace. It is joy which is finally victorious in Gloucester's conflict of emotions, for his own and his son's sufferings have become meaningful by their reunion in a love which has brought them closer together than ever before. "O dear son Edgar," he had said at the beginning of his purgatorial ascent to bliss,

The food of thy abusèd father's wrath!
Might I but live to see thee in my touch,
I'ld say I had eyes again! (IV, i, 23–26)

He does live until then, and what he sees in that moment makes his agony become an ecstasy that life cannot sustain.

The same miracle happens to Lear. He had been so impressed by the pomp and power of his position as king that he had forgotten his responsibilities. To gratify his own ego and minister to his comfort he had put on a public spectacle in which his daughters were to compete in expressions of love with fragments of the kingdom as reward, he himself retaining his title and all of the regal splendor connected with it while giving up his duty to rule. The pride which he had accused his truthfully sincere daughter and his plain-speaking counselor of possessing had been his to an over-weening degree—the willfulness of a king whose passions have been pampered and judgment flattered all of his life

176

so that now in his old age he never stops to question himself. His purgatorial experience teaches him his human limitations. The elements which he had so readily invoked, he has discovered, were not his to command like the servile courtiers who had flattered him. "When the rain came to wet me once and the wind to make me chatter; when the thunder would not peace at my bidding: there I found 'em, there I smelt 'em out. Go to, they are not men o' their words: they told me I was every thing: 'tis a lie, I am not ague-proof" (IV, vi, 102–7). Grandiose diction and imperial pomp have given way to homely colloquialism and the humility of wisdom. In his next words he proclaims himself "every inch a king," and so, in the grandeur of his suffering, he is, but he is a king who realizes his kinship with other men. "Let me wipe it first," he replies when Gloucester begs to kiss his hand (IV, vi, 136). "It smells of mortality."

Like Gloucester, Lear in his suffering awakens to a new feeling of sympathy for his fellow man.

> Poor naked wretches, whereso'er you are,
> That bide the pelting of this pitiless storm,

he comments before the hovel to which Kent has brought him and the Fool in the storm,

> How shall your houseless heads and unfed sides,
> Your loop'd and window'd raggedness, defend you
> From seasons such as these? O, I have ta'en
> Too little care of this! Take physic, pomp;
> Expose thyself to feel what wretches feel,
> That thou mayst shake the superflux to them,
> And show the heavens more just. (III, iv, 28–36)

Just as Gloucester becomes aware of the selfishness of his sensual indulgence, the vice of the nobleman, Lear becomes aware of the selfishness of his proud willfulness, the vice of the king.

But Lear does not hold on to his new compassion for humanity. "I'll pray, and then I'll sleep," he says (III, iv, 27), but before he can pray in behalf of the "poor naked wretches" whose suffering he has learned to feel, a prayer that would have been succeeded by peace of mind and health-giving rest, Poor Tom, the very lowest of such wretches, is brought out of the hovel by the Fool's terrified cries and ironically drives Lear over the brink of insanity. "Hast thou given all to thy two daughters? / And art thou come to this?" he exclaims (III, iv, 49–50). Henceforth his mind can keep only on the way along which madness lies. Compassion is supplanted by revulsion. He sees mankind as conceived in lust and dedicated to evil. Like Gloucester he rejects life, but, in accordance with his character, not with passive despair but with passionate denunciation. His view is shown to have truth in it—have we not seen the evil and the social injustice which he excoriates?—but not the whole truth. As he is crying (IV, vi, 191) "Kill, kill, kill, kill, kill, kill," he is apprehended with the words "lay hand upon him," but, although the man who speaks them is acting for his daughter, he does so to receive him not as a prisoner but as a king. If Goneril and Regan exist in the world, so does Cordelia.

When Lear sees Cordelia, it is after an artificially induced slumber prescribed by her physician that acts as a restorative, as the disturbance to his sleep by the need to flee from the plot against his life of Goneril and Regan had prevented his recovery. He is, according to the Folio stage direction, brought in on a chair, and we are told in the dialogue that fresh garments have been put on him. Royally arrayed, he is as if enthroned again. The music played as he wakes contrasts with the storm of the night he sought sleep in the farmhouse on Gloucester's estate. He awakes to a new reality. Like Gloucester regaining consciousness after his supposed fall, he does so as if he is returning from death to a life which he is at first loath to resume. "You do me wrong to take me out o' the grave," he says (IV, vii, 45). But Cordelia, standing before him, is as an angel of mercy whose kind words are balm to his hurts. "O, look upon me, sir," she urges him gently,

> And hold your hands in benediction o'er me:
> No, sir, you must not kneel. (IV, vii, 57–59)

Lear has descended from the throne of his chair to kneel to her, as she has knelt to him in asking him for his blessing. The act, reminiscent of the manner in which Gloucester blessed Edgar, is one that has long been prepared for. Lear in his rage had imperiously sent Cordelia away "without our grace, our love, our benison" (I, i, 268). He had withheld his love and his blessing because she had been reticent in the expression of her feeling for him. "Nothing will come of nothing" (I, i, 92)—this had been his motto. Of the love that asks for nothing in return, of the forgiveness for injuries that is freely given, he had been ignorant. When Goneril had disappointed him, he had gone to Regan, seeking the love that he was to find in Cordelia, but this love he envisaged as finding expression in *lex talionis:*

> Yet have I left a daughter,
> Who, I am sure, is kind and comfortable:
> When she shall hear this of thee, with her nails
> She'll flay thy wolfish visage. (I, iv, 327–30)

When Regan had coldly counseled him to apologize to Goneril, he had replied, kneeling with bitter mockery to demonstrate the utter ridiculousness of the father begging forgiveness of the child,

> Ask her forgiveness?
> Do you but mark how this becomes the house:
> "Dear daughter, I confess that I am old;

Age is unnecessary: on my knees I beg
That you'll vouchsafe me raiment, bed, and food."
(II, iv, 154–58)

But he does now kneel before his child, to whom he owes raiment, bed, and food, asking her forgiveness and begging pathetically not to be ridiculed in words that remind us of his previous derision of what he is at this moment doing:

Pray, do not mock me:
I am a very foolish fond old man . . .
All the skill I have
Remembers not these garments; nor I know not
Where I did lodge last night. Do not laugh at me;
For, as I am a man, I think this lady
To be my child Cordelia. (IV, vii, 59–70)

His abdication to his daughters while retaining the empty pomp of kingship had been a subversion of order; his kneeling to Cordelia, in a sense unnatural, is a miracle accompanying the restoration of order: Cordelia speaks to "this child-changèd father" (IV, vii, 17)—this father who has been changed to a child by his children—not with the authority of a parent but with the deference of a daughter and a subject.

In Cordelia's love, which finds no cause for ceasing in the injury he has done her, Lear has found the perfect pattern of love, which he is now able to see and follow. His education and redemption are now complete. But it is for heaven that Lear has been redeemed, not for earth. The purgatory through which he has gone has not fitted him for life in this world. He could not possibly resume the kingship, which Albany announces at the end he will return to him, even if Cordelia were alive, for he is beyond thought of the things of this world in his blissful bathing in the radiant light of Cordelia's "heavenly eyes" (IV, iii, 32), a light that, as he had mistakenly said of the light of Regan's eyes, does "comfort and not burn" (II, iv, 176). When he is captured, he welcomes prison, for prison with her will be a heaven:

> Come, let's away to prison:
> We two alone will sing like birds i' the cage:
> When thou dost ask me blessing, I'll kneel down
> And ask of thee forgiveness: so we'll live,
> And pray, and sing, and tell old tales, and laugh
> At gilded butterflies, and hear poor rogues
> Talk of court news; and we'll talk with them too,
> Who loses and who wins; who's in, who's out;
> And take upon 's the mystery of things,
> As if we were God's spies: and we'll wear out,
> In a wall'd prison, packs and sects of great ones
> That ebb and flow by the moon. (V, iii, 8–19)

The greatest blessedness will be that kneeling for forgiveness which calls down divine benediction. They will pray and sing like the angels of heaven and tell each other old tales, legendary stories with miraculously happy endings such as that of *The Winter's Tale*, the report of which had caused the wonder-stricken teller of it to remark (V, ii, 30–32), "This news which is called true is so like an old tale that the verity of it is in strong suspicion." From the height of their serene contentment they will look down with amused condescension upon the creatures of this world and their concern with ephemeral things such as the latest political gossip of the court. They will engage in conversations with these creatures but will speak as those not of their world, regarding their assumed political omniscience as if they in turn had the omniscience of angels acting as God's observers. And, so doing, they will outlive, as if they existed in eternity, whole generations of political lives subject to all the vicissitudes of factional strife on this mutable sublunary planet.

But as we listen to Lear, we have more than an inkling

that this is not to be. Edmund, who has already told us his intention of dispatching Lear and Cordelia in anticipation of Albany's releasing them, is standing by him as he is speaking. Cordelia, knowing, it would seem, what to expect from their captor, weeps for the fate she sees in store for her father. Edmund is inflexible. "Take them away," he orders (V, iii, 19), and then instructs the captain to put them to death. To expect a heaven in this world of evil seems to be a delusion.

When Lear comes on the scene again, it is, like Gloucester in listening to Edgar's story, to relive in concentrated form all of the grief and joy he has hitherto experienced. Gloucester's last moments, however, had been described, not enacted, in order that the feelings evoked by Lear's death may not be weakened by the repetition. In the last scene of *King Lear* the audience's emotions are stretched to the breaking point. It had been reminded by Edmund's words (V, iii, 199–200), "This speech of yours hath moved me, / And shall perchance do good," of his having sent his captain to kill Lear and Cordelia, if it had forgotten it. As Edgar told the story of the disclosure of Kent's identity, it had listened sympathetically but with uneasy impatience. When a gentleman with a bloody knife had burst upon the stage, crying (V, iii, 222), "Help, help, O, help," it had remained suspended in fearful doubt—a suspense prolonged by the horror-stricken inarticulateness of the gentleman, which for a moment permitted him only to exclaim "It came even from the heart of—O, she's dead" in reply to the excited queries. When its fears had been relieved by the announcement that the knife came from the heart of Goneril, its tension had once more been keyed up by Albany's question concerning the whereabouts of Lear and Cordelia and the interruption of Edmund's reply caused by the bringing in of the bodies of Goneril and Regan, the fast-succeeding events holding its interest but not driving out of its mind the knowledge that Edmund's captain was on his way to execute his order. Finally, after Edmund, overwhelmed by his downfall, by the story he has heard Edgar relate, and by the sight of the dead sisters, tells, "despite," as he says (V, iii, 244), "of mine own nature," what he has commanded and after Edgar, who has already acted as the agent of divine justice, has gone to rescue Cordelia and Lear, it had had its hopes dashed by the entrance of Lear with Cordelia dead in his arms.

It seems the cruelest of ironies. Albany has just exclaimed (V, iii, 256), "The gods defend her!"—and this seems to be the answer. A moment or two earlier, and she would have been saved; now she is dead. Lear, who had been reclaimed from insanity, is mad once more, this time surely with no hope of recovery. In the mighty grief of his loss he is indifferent to the news of the death of Goneril and Regan. Albany, in consideration of these happenings, replies to the announcement of Edmund's death (V, iii, 295), "That's but a trifle here." Cordelia's death seems to have deprived the others' of all significance.

But Lear refuses to accept the reality of Cordelia's death. He calls for a looking glass to see if she is breathing, seizes a stray feather, and applies it to her lips. "This feather stirs," he exclaims exultantly (V, iii, 265). "She lives!" But then he immediately lapses into doubt and is diverted by the words of the others. "A plague upon you, murderers, traitors all!" he flashes, with a return to his old wrath, and then turns again to Cordelia:

Cordelia, Cordelia! stay a little. Ha!
What is 't thou say'st? Her voice was ever soft,
Gentle and low, an excellent thing in woman.

(V, iii, 269–73)

It is Cordelia's voice that he fancies he hears, speaking so softly that it can barely be heard, that gentle voice whose "low sound" (I, i, 155) he had once thought indicated her empty heart. The repeated self-deception is not only highly pathetic but, as the scene proceeded with the denouement evidently still to be completed, probably awakened a faint hope in the Elizabethan audience, many or most of whom must have known of the triumph of Cordelia and Lear's resumption of the kingship in Holinshed, *A Mirror for Magistrates,* Spenser, and an earlier play, that she would in fact revive, such revival scenes having been used in previous dramas of the day. As Lear's mind, benumbed by its agony and incapable of continued concentration, strays once more to the kindly faces about him, now dimly recognizing the faithful Kent through his dazedness, the tension is slackened but not relieved. He is absorbed in apparently vacant contemplation, Albany and Edgar having agreed that it is useless to attempt to waken him from his torpor, as Albany states that he will hand over the power to him and promises that rewards and punishments will be distributed, seemingly the conventional close of the play. Suddenly, however, his agony bursts forth:

> And my poor fool is hang'd! No, no, no life!
> Why should a dog, a horse, a rat, have life,
> And thou no breath at all? Thou'lt come no more,
> Never, never, never, never, never! (V, iii, 305–8)

Then, his clothes hampering the anguished heaving of his chest, in a return to the tone of entreaty of the scene in which he awoke to find Cordelia, he requests, "Pray you, undo this button: thank you, sir"—and in that moment gains the certitude that she is not dead in a blinding flash that transfigures him with joy and makes his heart burst in an ecstasy such as Gloucester died in:

Do you see this? Look on her, look, her lips,
Look there, look there! (V, iii, 310–11)

For that which would make everything all right—if Cordelia
is alive, he had said (V, iii, 266–67), "it is a chance which
does redeem all sorrows / That ever I have felt"—has come
true for him, as it did for Gloucester.

His death, which puts an end to his agony, comes as a
relief to the tension of the scene, a relief that Kent, who in
the storm scene had told his royal master that he had rather
break his own heart than Lear's, voices when he says (V, iii,
312), "Break, heart; I prithee, break!" But an Elizabethan
audience, at least its most sensitive members, with their
strong religious assumptions, would have felt more than such
relief; they would also have experienced a greater measure
of reconciliation in their perception of a deeper meaning.
Lear's final conviction that Cordelia is alive might be regarded as the mysterious insight believed to be granted a
man on the point of death,[2] the last blessing conferred upon
him as he is kneeling by the corpse of his daughter.[3] The
heaven that he had seen would be his and Cordelia's in
prison, while ironically false as a picture of what awaited
them there, was thus given an aspect of prophetic vision.
The intimation of an afterlife would also have been
strengthened by the memory of the scene in which he awoke
to the sight of Cordelia. "Thou art a soul in bliss," he had
said,

but I am bound
Upon a wheel of fire, that mine own tears
Do scald like molten lead. (IV, vii, 46–48)

It was as if from purgatory he had heard the celestial music
and seen the angelic radiance that he was at last about to
attain, a vision of what he would experience after death. For
the Elizabethans, with their penchant for regarding what

happens in this world as an analogue of what will happen in the next world, this would have had a deep significance.[4]

There is, then, hinted to the poetic imagination a miracle greater than all the other miracles in the drama that has been wrought by the "love, dear love" (IV, iv, 28) which has brought Cordelia from her high place in another country to suffer in gentle fortitude for the sake of Lear. This miracle is the redemption of Lear for heaven, a redemption analogous to the redemption of mankind, for which the Son of God had come down to earth. The analogy between Cordelia and Christ, who redeemed human nature from the curse brought on it by Adam and Eve, is made unmistakable, although not crudely explicit, by the choric comment of her gentleman:

> Thou hast one daughter,
> Who redeems nature from the general curse
> Which twain have brought her to. (IV, vi, 210–11)

The Elizabethans, who were constantly being adjured in the homilies to follow the pattern of conduct established by Christ, would have more readily apprehended than we do that Cordelia's ignominious death completes the analogy between her and Christ. "Upon such sacrifices, my Cordelia," Lear said (V, iii, 20–21), "The gods themselves throw incense." The sacrifice Cordelia's love renders, made complete by her death, is indeed blessed. The "brand of heaven" (V, iii, 22) that has temporarily parted her and Lear has, in releasing their souls from the prison of their bodies, enabled them to become reunited in eternal bliss.

4

But if *King Lear* concludes with a poetic suggestion of what was flatly presented in the morality plays,[5] it remains firmly rooted in this world. Albany, who has learned during the course of the action to recognize the monstrous visage of evil despite the fair coloring with which rationalization paints it, is left to rule as king of Britain in accordance with justice and mercy. Edgar, a philosopher who knows the divine order that lies behind the mutability of the things of this world and, in the final scene, a knight of Christian chivalry who exchanges charity with his brother—Edgar is fittingly to be his counselor. Kent, it is indicated, will shortly join Lear in death. It is the task of the new generation to bear "the weight of this sad time" and "the gored state sustain" (V, iii, 322, 320). The storm has broken the giants of the forest and left the young saplings. We are left with the impression of life continuing after great waste, fragile but capable of further existence.

How long it is to continue is, however, left in doubt. "The oldest hath borne most," says Albany in the last lines of the play (V, iii, 325–26). "We that are young / Shall never see so much, nor live so long." The lines may mean that future generations, less hardy but more humane, will not witness such sufferings as that of Lear, whose primitive vigor enabled him to attain a remarkable longevity and to endure the hammer blows of an iron age which had seen just the beginnings of a civilization capable of subduing the animal passions of men. They may also mean that with the passing of Lear the shadows are drawing close about mankind and that those who remain are a pygmy race dwindling away in the twilight of life, which they must face unflinchingly, doing the tasks that have been allotted to them.

The first interpretation agrees with the idea that imperfect commonwealths which only gradually acquired the stability of the Tudor and Stuart regimes were established on mankind's emergence from primitive communism. The second interpretation is strengthened by the frequent references to the decay of nature and the end of the world and by the darkness of the play's atmosphere. The ambiguity seems to be purposeful. For while the world of *King Lear* is a primitive one, abounding in references to the pagan gods, to nature, and to animals, it is also, with its unscrupulous Machiavellian adventurers, its foppish pretended gentlemen, and its homeless vagabonds, a mirror of the contemporary world—and in this, the grimmest of his tragedies, Shakespeare leaves unresolved whether the darkness of the time will gradually give place to light, as did the darkness of ancient Britain, or whether it will steadily deepen, the ruthless individualism of the Edmunds and the cold, unfeeling calculation of the Gonerils and Regans [6] being the storm clouds warning of the total darkness of the extinction of humanity.

NOTES

CHAPTER I

1. By "old aristocracy" I mean those peers who held titles conferred before the accession of Henry VIII (there were twenty-five of them out of sixty-two peers in 1560) and the untitled members of their powerful families. By "new aristocracy" I mean those peers who held titles conferred since the accession of Henry VIII, the untitled members of their families, and the court gentry who were not members of old aristocratic families, the Sidneys, Raleghs, Cecils, Bacons, Walsinghams, Dyers, and Grevilles, the most dynamic element of the new aristocracy.

2. R. H. Tawney, "The Rise of the Gentry," *Essays in Economic History,* ed. E. M. Carus-Wilson (London, 1954), p. 189. This article was first printed in *Economic History Review,* XI (1941), 1–38.

3. Sir Robert Naunton, *Fragmenta Regalia,* ed. Edward Arber (Westminster, 1895), p. 16. I have modernized the spelling and punctuation of all Elizabethan quotations for the convenience of readers who are not Elizabethan specialists.

4. Mr. Gilbert Talbot to his father, the Earl of Shrewsbury, May 11, 1573. Quoted by Sir Harris Nicolas, *Memoirs of the Life and Times of Sir Christopher Hatton* (London, 1847), pp. 22–24.

5. Naunton, pp. 45–46.

6. Sir Fulke Greville, *Life of Sir Philip Sidney* (Oxford University Press, 1907), p. 189.

7. Tawney, "The Rise of the Gentry," p. 180.

8. *Ibid.,* p. 181.

9. This does not mean that some of them did not try and even

succeed. The Earl of Northumberland in his "Advice to His Son" describes how he was brought up in ignorance of his estate, was robbed by his officers and servants right and left, gave himself up to "hawks, hounds, horses, dice, cards, apparel, mistresses," ran heavily into debt, sold woods, leased land at unfavorable terms for cash—and how then, having resolved to take heroic measures, he practiced rigorous economy and good husbandry and brought his estate into good condition. Cf. Henry Percy, *Advice to His Son*, ed. G. B. Harrison, pp. 80–84, quoted by A. L. Rowse, *The England of Elizabeth* (New York, 1951), pp. 258–59.

10. Lawrence Stone, "The Anatomy of the Elizabethan Aristocracy," *Economic History Review*, XVIII (1948), 19.

11. Rowse, p. 231.

12. Tawney, "The Rise of the Gentry," pp. 195–96 and 196–97; Rowse, p. 225; S. B. Liljegren, *The Fall of the Monasteries and the Social Changes in England Leading up to the Great Revolution* (Lund, 1924), pp. 123–24.

13. Tawney, *Religion and the Rise of Capitalism* (New York, 1947), p. 119.

14. Henry Brinklow, *Complaint of Roderick Mors*, c. 1542, Early English Text Society ed. (London, 1874), p. 9.

15. Thomas Becon, "The Fortress of the Faithful," 1550, *The Catechism and Other Pieces*, Parker Society Publications (Cambridge University Press, 1844), pp. 598–99.

16. In the second half of the sixteenth century such capitalist farming, which meant that the land could be given over to the crop best adapted to it, raised the productivity of agriculture. The soil of England, says an Elizabethan social observer, "is even now in these our days grown to be much more fruitful than it hath been in times past. The cause is for that our countrymen are grown to be more painful, skillful and careful through recompense of gain than heretofore they have been. . . ." William Harrison, *Elizabethan England*, ed. Lothrop Withington (London, 1902), p. 133.

17. Tawney, *The Agrarian Problem in the Sixteenth Century* (New York, 1912), pp. 189–91.

18. H. R. Trevor-Roper, "The Gentry, 1540–1640," *Supplement to the Economic History Review*, April 1953, p. 30.

19. Trevor-Roper, "The Elizabethan Aristocracy: An Anatomy Anatomized," *Economic History Review*, III (1951), 294–95.

20. Tawney, "The Rise of the Gentry," pp. 185–86.

21. Rowse, pp. 79–80. Since I have quoted from each of the participants of a controversy that has become celebrated among students of economic history, it is perhaps incumbent upon me to explain my basis of selection—that is, to make some statement on their positions, diffident as I am about venturing outside of my own field to arbitrate in a battle of titans. At first glance it may seem that they are far apart: Tawney finds that the gentry, because of its superior estate management, rose at the expense of the nobility; Stone finds that the nobility declined primarily because of its extravagant spending habits; Trevor-Roper denies that the gentry made greater profits of agriculture than the nobility, that it had relatively less wasteful spending habits, and indeed that it rose as a class. On closer inspection, however, it seems to me that it becomes evident that the differences are mostly those of emphasis rather than of substance, with Tawney and Stone modifying their emphases in the course of the controversy as a result of Trevor-Roper's searching though often unbalanced criticism. Tawney concludes his "Postscript" (*Essays in Economic History*, pp. 206–14) with the statement that "the crude classifications" of "aristocracy" and "gentry" should be "broken up" by "an analysis sufficiently refined to bring to light the variety of species, economic, regional and cultural, within the groups concerned. . . ." In his article itself, as we have seen (pp. 6 and 7 above), he at one point differentiates between the older and the newer families among the aristocracy, asserting that the organization of the older families' estates tended to be more obsolescent, and at another point states that within the gentry itself there was the same difference in types of economy. So, too, Stone, in the midst of treating the nobility as an entity, admits ("Anatomy of the Elizabethan Aristocracy," 39), "It is perhaps misleading, though convenient, to describe the Tudor aristocracy at the end of the

reign of Elizabeth as a class," citing the "diversity of wealth, political ideas and heredity" within it. In his attack on Stone, Trevor-Roper also finds that both the aristocracy and the gentry were not homogeneous classes, asserting ("The Elizabethan Aristocracy: An Anatomy Anatomized," 294–95) that "the older gentry" was in the same financial straits as "the older aristocracy" but going on to say that, with "the new economic energy" brought to it by its recruits from merchants and yeomen, the gentry as a whole "rose relatively to the nobility." In his reply Stone, admitting that "a great many of the older landed gentry were going under," reformulates the concept of "the rise of the gentry" ("The Elizabethan Aristocracy—A Restatement," *Economic History Review*, IV [1952], 320) so that his statement of it is much the same as Trevor-Roper's. However, in his attack on Tawney, Trevor-Roper, mistakenly, as it seems to me, goes beyond his previous position to state that the gentry as a whole did not rise relatively to the nobility but that there was a rise within the gentry of families which derived their fortune primarily from their official positions or from trade. (Stone had pointed out the economic importance for the gentry as well as for the nobility of offices and Tawney of trade ["The Anatomy of the Elizabethan Aristocracy," 26–37, and "The Rise of the Gentry," pp. 187–88], though no doubt with insufficient emphasis.) But at the conclusion of his article ("The Gentry, 1540–1640," 51–52) he unexpectedly makes a new and complicating distinction in addition to the distinction between "mere gentry" and "court gentry" which he has been propounding. It is the distinction between two different types of economy of which Tawney spoke, between, in Trevor-Roper's words, the "improving gentry" and the "unenterprising country gentry." The members of the "improving gentry," "the solid substance of rural society," were not the "signal profiteers" of "the secular change" and were "generally unobtrusive in national affairs"; the "unenterprising country gentry" was "a depressed, declining class"; "the greater gentry, the rising gentry," the bulk of whose wealth "came directly or indirectly, from offices or trade—those offices and that trade which, in the preceding century, had been continually centralized in the ever-growing capital," "directed political history." There is much to be commended in this tripartite distinction. Trevor-Roper's discussion of the politics of the "declining gentry" thus helps to explain the Essex Rebellion and the Gunpowder Plot, although I doubt that the Independents were, as he says, "declining gentry." (Christopher Hill, from whose work as well as from that of Tawney, Stone, and Trevor-Roper I have learned a great deal, writes me that he has a forthcoming article which will take up this point.) However, Trevor-Roper minimizes the importance of the "improving gentry." There is too much contemporary comment, from Bacon to Harrington, on the rise of this class in wealth and, through its political machine, the House of Commons, in political power for it to be summarily dismissed, as Trevor-Roper does ("The Gentry, 1540–1640," 44–45), as "a repetition of dogma" and "general statements that some Members of the House of Commons were of greater consequence than many peers. . . ." (Actually, the letter to which he refers as an example of such a general statement states: "I heard a lord estimate they [the members of the House of Commons] were able to buy the upper house (His Majesty only excepted) thrice over. . . .") The rise of the "improving gentry" accounts for the fact that, even using a method of computation that does not permit Trevor-Roper's criticism of his previous one (and the new method does not seem better than the old one), Tawney is able to demonstrate ("Postscript," pp. 209–12) that of 2,547 manors in seven counties the percentage owned by gentry went up from 67.1 in 1561 to 73.3 in 1640 while the percentage owned by peers remained almost exactly the same (13.1 in 1561 and 13.4 in 1640). However, it is true, as Trevor-Roper showed in his criticism of Stone, that the extent of the decline of the nobility was exaggerated by Tawney and especially by Stone.

22. Tawney, *The Agrarian Problem in the Sixteenth Century,* pp. 193–94.

23. Greville, pp. 67–69.

24. Lawrence Stone, "State Control in Sixteenth-century England," *Economic History Review,* XVII (1947), 116–17. The

new aristocracy had another great source of revenue in the offices which it occupied. It was taken for granted that clients and suitors should pay officials for their influence and services. After the revolts of 1569–1572 the old nobility was largely excluded from office. When Leicester brought it about that Sussex was deprived of office, Sussex flew into such a fury of desperation that he forgot himself before the queen. Cf. Trevor-Roper, "The Gentry, 1540–1640," 32 and 39.

25. Greville, p. 117.

26. The bourgeoisie regarded Leicester's faction as a friend at court. In Heywood's bourgeois drama, *If You Know Not Me, You Know Nobody*, Part II, which was designed to glorify the building of Gresham's Royal Exchange and to celebrate the defeat of the Spanish Armada, Elizabeth appears with Leicester and Sussex. Sussex is given a few lines, while Leicester is given several speeches and treated most sympathetically. Sidney and Essex were both very popular with the London burghers. The London guilds were conspicuous at Sidney's great funeral.

27. *State Papers—Spanish—Eliz.*, October 16, 1579.

28. Sir Philip Sidney, "A Letter to Queen Elizabeth," *The Defence of Poesie, Etc.*, ed. George E. Woodberry (Boston, 1908), pp. 91–92.

29. Greville, pp. 52–54.

30. Greville, however, may be exaggerating Sidney's prescience. Although he was a counselor of James, presumably advising moderation in dealing with Parliament, his biography, which on his orders was not published till after his death, is an implicit criticism of James's policies and a nostalgic comparison of the golden days of Elizabeth with the degeneracy of the times. Greville wished to write a history of Elizabeth's reign, but James's official would not give him access to the state documents unless he would guarantee that his history would not reflect on Elizabeth's successor. Greville refused.

31. Emma Gurney-Salter, *Tudor England Through Venetian Eyes* (London, 1930), p. 78.

32. Greville, p. 203.

33. R. H. Tawney's introduction to Thomas Wilson, *A Discourse upon Usury* (London, 1925), pp. 33-34.

34. John U. Nef, *Industry and Government in France and England, 1540–1640* (Philadelphia, 1940), p. 1.

35. Tawney's introduction to Wilson, p. 58.

36. *Ibid.*, p. 157.

37. The usurer is often described as a Puritan in Elizabethan literature. See Wilson, p. 178; John Marston, *Works*, ed. A. H. Bullen (London, 1887), III, 38 and 271; Robert Greene, *The Life and Complete Works*, ed. Alexander B. Grosart (London, 1881–1883), XII, 104.

38. Tawney's introduction to Wilson, p. 165.

39. G. N. Clark, *The Wealth of England from 1496 to 1760* (Oxford University Press, 1946), p. 86.

40. For an account of the frequent laxness of the enterprising gentry and rich merchants in enforcing industrial regulation, see Nef, pp. 35-51.

41. Not only was there no thoroughgoing reform of the church, but its conservative hierarchy was left largely undisturbed. "What must we say," bitterly writes Beza to Bullinger in 1566, "when not only the papists are left in possession of the revenues of their benefices but even of their ecclesiastical offices upon merely taking an oath to maintain the reformation; so that the godly brethren are for the most part placed under the authority and compelled to submit to the jurisdiction of those who are in general both unlearned and in their hearts the most bitter enemies of true religion?"—*The Zurich Letters (Second Series)*, ed. Hastings Robinson, Parker Society Publications (Cambridge University Press, 1845), II, 130.

42. Malcolm William Wallace, *The Life of Sir Philip Sidney* (Cambridge University Press, 1915), p. 315.

43. J. E. Neale, "The Commons' Privilege of Free Speech in Parliament," *Tudor Studies*, ed. R. W. Seton-Watson (New York, 1924), p. 258.

44. *Ibid.*, p. 283.

45. *Ibid.*, pp. 284-85.

46. James Harrington, *Oceana* (London, 1887), p. 60.

47. Rowse, pp. 71–72, 82, 86.

48. Sir Thomas Wilson, *The State of England Anno Domini 1600*, Royal Historical Society Publications, Camden Third Series, LII, 39.

CHAPTER II

1. James Anthony Froude, *English Seamen in the Sixteenth Century* (London, 1895), pp. 115–20.

2. John Richard Green, *A Short History of the English People* (London, 1899), pp. 413–15. The bourgeoisie also fought Spain on the international money market. "Sir T. Gresham is said to have succeeded in delaying the sailing of the Armada for a year by a successful corner in bills."—W. Cunningham, *The Growth of English Industry and Commerce in Modern Times* (Cambridge University Press, 1912), II, 146.

3. Greville, p. 202.

4. T. C. Noble, *The Spanish Armada, 1588* (London, 1886), p. xii.

5. *Ibid.,* pp. xv–xvi.

6. Cf. William Haller, *The Rise of Puritanism* (Columbia University Press, 1938), pp. 330–31: "Under the conditions of Elizabethan court politics they ['the great nationalist and Protestant courtiers'] had found leaders of a kind in the Earl of Leicester and the unfortunate Earl of Essex, but they are best remembered in such shining figures as Sidney and Raleigh. . . . The descendants of the Elizabethan idealistic, patriotic, Protestant peers and gentlemen came forward, *mutatis mutandis,* to take the leadership of the Puritan party at the revolution."

7. A. F. Pollard, *The History of England (1547–1603)* (New York, 1910), p. 458.

8. Richard Hooker, *Of the Laws of Ecclesiastical Polity* (London, 1925), I, 128.

9. Pollard, p. 463.

10. R. H. Tawney and Eileen Power, *Tudor Economic Documents* (New York, 1924), II, 274.

11. *Ibid.,* II, 286–87.

12. *Ibid.*, II, 292.

13. *Ibid.*, II, 275.

14. *Ibid.*, II, 272.

15. Thomas Nashe, *Works*, ed. R. B. McKerrow (London, 1910), I, 212–13.

16. Pollard, p. 459.

17. The tone of the court seems to have deteriorated in the last years of Elizabeth, as the aged and frequently lonely and melancholy queen demanded more extravagant flattery and febrile amusement. Donne wrote in 1600: "I am no courtier, for without having lived there desirously I cannot have sinned enough to have deserved that reprobate name. . . . The court is not great but full of jollity and revels and plays as if it were not sick."—Evelyn M. Simpson, *A Study of the Prose Works of John Donne* (Oxford University Press, 1948), p. 310. Even after making allowance for the tradition of anti-court satire and for Donne's aggrievement at the disgrace of Essex, the picture we get from this letter is that of a court in which the presence of a Sidney, even a Sidney frustrated, as he often felt, would have been an anomaly.

18. Essex's son was to be a moderate leader of the English Revolution in its early stages. He was as popular with the London masses, who went to battle under the slogan of "to live and die with the Earl of Essex," as his father had been.

19. Edward P. Cheyney, *A History of England from the Defeat of the Armada to the Death of Elizabeth* (New York, 1926), II, 558.

20. "He seeks taxes in the tin," continues the ballad, "He polls the poor to the skin: / Yet he swears 'tis no sin."

21. *Correspondence of James VI of Scotland,* ed. John Bruce (Camden Society, 1861), p. 59.

22. Stone, "The Anatomy of the Elizabethan Aristocracy," *Economic History Review*, XVIII (1948), 19.

23. "Sir Anthony Weldon's Court and Character of King James," *Secret History of the Court of James the First,* ed. Sir Walter Scott (?) (London, 1811), I, 328–29.

24. A number of commercial magnates were permitted to buy peerages. Also, by selling knighthoods liberally James gained some much-needed money, at the expense of antagonizing most of the gentry, and encouraged the older families to bid for peerages in emulation. "Ancient gentlemen, finding themselves preceded by baser families . . . fell into that trap, gilded with the title of baronet, for which they were to pay a thousand pounds. . . ."—"Francis Osborne's Traditional Memoirs of the Reign of James I," *Secret History of the Court of James I*, I, 257. Cf. the ballad of the young courtiers of the king, "With new titles of honor bought with his father's old gold, / For which sundry of his ancestors' old manors are sold, / And this is the course most of our new gallants hold."

25. Lucy Aiken, *Memoirs of the Court of King James the First* (London, 1822), I, 227.

CHAPTER III

1. "The Tree of Commonwealth," p. 19. Quoted by Lewis Einstein, *Tudor Ideals* (New York, 1921), p. 53.

2. Lewis Einstein, *The Italian Renaissance in England* (New York, 1902), p. 214.

3. Tawney and Power, I, 326. See also Roger Ascham, *The Schoolmaster*, ed. Edward Arber (Boston, 1898), p. 109.

4. Einstein, *Tudor Ideals*, p. 53. The Duke of Norfolk stated in the spirit of this unnamed peer that "England was merry England before all this New Learning came in."—E. M. G. Routh, *Sir Thomas More and His Friends, 1477–1535* (Oxford University Press, 1934), p. 126.

5. Sir Thomas Elyot, *The Book Named The Governor*, ed. Henry Herbert Stephen Croft (London, 1880), I, 99.

6. James Cleland, *Institution of a Young Nobleman* (London, 1607), p. 134.

7. Sir Edmund Chambers has pointed out that the new aristocracy at the court of Henry VIII welcomed the learning which was rejected by the old aristocracy. Cf. his *Sir Thomas Wyatt and Some Collected Studies* (London, 1933), p. 100. The merchant princes also had ties with the early humanists. Sir Thomas

More was a member of the Mercers' Company of London, the textile exporters who composed the most powerful group of merchants of his time, and served it as a translator in its negotiations with Antwerp, and Colet left the trusteeship of St. Paul's School to the Mercers' Company.

8. Phoebe Sheavyn, *The Literary Profession in the Elizabethan Age* (Manchester University Press, 1909), p. 13. The importance of Sidney for the flowering of Renaissance literature has recently been stressed in John Buxton, *Sir Philip Sidney and the English Renaissance* (New York, 1954).

9. Lines 69–96.

10. Lines 571–88.

11. J. H. Hexter writes ("The Education of the Aristocracy in the Renaissance," *Journal of Modern History*, XXII [1950], 5–9): "Among the great crown servants who surround Elizabeth—the Cecils, the Bacons, Walsingham, Smith, Coke, Hatton, Sidney—there is scarcely one without a university education. Never before had the lay councilors and titled nobility of an English ruler been so learned. But these are the men at the top, the very apex of the pyramid of gentility. What happens if we descend a little? . . . [We find that] whatever the validity of the indictment at the beginning of the sixteenth century, it was certainly not true at its end that English gentlemen as a group were indifferent to formal schooling." It seems to me that this judgment is vitiated by the failure to draw a distinction between the old aristocracy and the new aristocracy. To be sure, Hexter in the course of his article mentions the names of some members of the old aristocracy who, accommodating themselves to new conditions, acquired the university education required for the holding of office. Yet the fact remains that for a century after he says that the indictment against the nobility of hostility to learning was no longer valid writers continued to make it. It would seem that this indicates the persistence of such hostility among many of the old families with feudal traditions. Aside from the question of opposition to formal schooling, see pp. 41–42 and notes for a discussion of the opposition of the old aristocracy to the ideas of Christian humanism. As for Hexter's statement con-

cerning the gentry, a similar qualification must be made. Shaftesbury's account of the life of Henry Hastings (quoted by Wallace Notestein, *The English People on the Eve of Colonization, 1603–1630* [New York, 1954], p. 57n.), the presentation of Sir Raderick in *The Return from Parnassus*, Samuel Butler's character of "The Bumpkin or Country Squire" (*Characters and Passages from Notebooks*, ed. A. R. Waller [1908], pp. 40–41) all give the picture of a rude, uncultured person who devotes himself entirely to hunting, the ancestor, in fact, of Fielding's Squire Western. Joseph Hall wrote in 1627 (*Epistles, the Sixth Decade,* quoted by Godfrey Davies, *The Early Stuarts 1603–1660* [Oxford University Press, 1938], pp. 267–68): "Our land hath no blemish comparable to the miseducation of our gentry." These were the provincial gentry immired in the swamp of rural idiocy. Gentry producing for port towns and urban centers, in which they often maintained town houses and had social connections with the burgess oligarchy, whom they frequently represented in Parliament, were subject to vitalizing influences.

12. The Puritan spirit was strongest in that section of the bourgeoisie engaged in banking, industry, and retail trade rather than in foreign trade. Cf. Miriam Beard, *A History of the Business Man* (New York, 1938), pp. 386–87.

13. Nashe, I, 213.

14. Douglas Bush, *The Renaissance and English Humanism* (University of Toronto Press, 1939), p. 85.

15. The humanists regarded the universe as a marvelous structure whose workings were to be studied in detail so that the craftsmanship of its divine creator might be better appreciated. The meaning of the universe in this view was like the "meaning" to be derived from the reading of a great poem—it lay in the perception of the total effect: the understanding of the beauty and the order of the universe enables one to perceive the divine wisdom of God; the meaning of the universe in the medieval view was more like the meaning to be derived from the deciphering of a cryptogram. Although the humanists sought scientific knowledge in the writings of the ancients rather than through experimentation, the humanist view of the universe

encouraged the growth of modern science, which, unlike medieval scholasticism, asks not why things are what they are but what is the natural law that governs their operation. In the seventeenth century and later, however, the authority of the ancients came more and more to be an obstacle to the advance of science, as an aristocratic elite combated the utilitarian, democratic, and anti-authoritarian implications of the Baconianism espoused by the Puritan middle class, although humanistic ideals continued to be maintained by such Puritan members of the enterprising gentry as Colonel Hutchinson and Lord Brooke and by such Puritan intellectuals as John Milton. See Francis R. Johnson, *Astronomical Thought in Renaissance England* (Johns Hopkins Press, 1937) and Richard Foster Jones, "Ancients and Moderns," *Washington University Studies, New Series,* VI (1936), no. 6, for useful discussions of the relations between humanism and science.

16. In their polemics against the feudalistic noble leaders of the Pilgrimage of Grace and their peasant followers, who vowed to expel "all villain blood from the King's grace and his Privy Council for the commonwealth and restoring of Christ's church," the humanists emphasized, to an unusually strong degree, the idea that, while the social hierarchy must be maintained, men were free to find what place they could within this hierarchy in accordance with their ability. "For them ['the obscure but talented authors of Henry's new order'], social rank would continue to exist, limited only by a man's abilities. As beneficiaries of the new order, they wanted to legalize their own rise, and they were anxious to maintain the privilege."—W. Gordon Zeeveld, *Foundations of Tudor Policy* (Harvard University Press, 1948), pp. 210–11. After the peasant rebellion of 1549 the emphasis was placed on the maintenance of the social hierarchy rather than on the freedom of opportunity within it. "The royal apologists couldn't have it both ways, and subsequent history was to prove that the break in the elaborate medieval social structure would not be repaired by a mere reiteration of the principle of degree."—Zeeveld, p. 224.

17. Elyot, I, 3–4.

18. Cf. "A Homily against Disobedience and Willful Rebellion" (1571), *Certain Sermons or Homilies, Appointed to Be Read in Churches in the Time of the Late Queen Elizabeth of Famous Memory* (London, 1864), p. 498, and Thomas Starkey, *A Dialogue between Cardinal Pole and Thomas Lupset*, ed. J. M. Cowper, Early English Text Society ed., 1878, p. 52.

19. Democracy, Elyot believes, must lead either to tyranny or to communism and chaos. Aristocracy, the other form of government besides monarchy recognized by Aristotle, must, on the other hand, lead to factionalism and civil war. He sees England (I, 23) as having been rent by internal war when it was divided into many kingdoms during the time of the primitive Britons. Welded into a monarchy by Edgar so that "reason was revived," the realm began "to show some visage of a public weal." It has continued as such since that period, although its condition has occasionally deteriorated. Such a period of deterioration was the War of the Roses, but since the realm now has a prince equal to the ancient princes in virtue and courage, it should become a public weal excelling all others. This same view of history lies behind Edward Hall's chronicle of the War of the Roses, to which Shakespeare was greatly indebted.

20. *Certain Sermons or Homilies*, p. 104.

21. Sir John Cheke, *The Hurt of Sedition*. In Raphael Holinshed, *Chronicles of England, Scotland and Ireland, 1587* (London, 1807), III, 990.

22. Elyot, I, 12.

23. Cf. Franklin Le Van Baumer, *The Early Tudor Theory of Kingship* (Yale University Press, 1940), p. 92.

24. The law of nature was regarded as the elementary principles of justice which God had written in the hearts of all men to be perceived by their unaided reason and upon which all good laws must be grounded. Cf. Starkey, p. 19. Sir John Hayward states (*An Answer to the First Part of a Certain Conference Concerning Succession*, London, 1603, Sig A, 4r) that the canons account natural law to consist of such precepts as these: "To worship God; to obey parents and governors, and thereby conserve common society; lawful conjunction of men and women;

succession of children; education of children; acquisition of things which pertain to no man; equal liberty of all; to communicate commodities; to repel force; to hurt no man and generally to do another as he would be done to." It will be noticed that obedience to the state, acquisition of private property, and the exchange of commodities are included among the rules which God has imprinted in men's souls.

25. This is shown most clearly in the "Homily Against Disobedience and Willful Rebellion," which was published shortly after the Northern Rebellion, the Pope's Bull of Deposition, and the Ridolfi plot. The homily refers directly to the Northern Rebellion, emphasizing that it was a crime against God, and contests the Pope's right to depose sovereigns.

26. Cf. Erasmus, *The Education of a Christian Prince* (Columbia University Press, 1936), p. 175, Elyot, I, 4–6, Baldassare Castiglione, *The Book of the Courtier*, tr. Sir Thomas Hoby, 1561 (London, 1928), pp. 275–77. Erasmus's treatise, like Castiglione's courtesy book, was highly popular among the humanists in England. More awaited its publication eagerly, Colet got a copy immediately after publication, and Henry VIII received a copy from Erasmus himself a year later. Elyot commended it as a book with which gentlemen of all times would be familiar.

27. Erasmus, p. 157, Castiglione, pp. 276–77.
28. *Ibid.*, p. 158, Castiglione, p. 276.
29. *Ibid.*, p. 162, Castiglione, pp. 276, 277.
30. *Ibid.*, p. 221, Starkey, p. 19, Castiglione, p. 277.
31. Elyot, I, 6, Erasmus, p. 212.
32. Erasmus, p. 212, Elyot, I, 6–7, Castiglione, p. 285.
33. *Ibid.*, pp. 226–27.
34. Starkey, pp. 3–4.
35. Erasmus, p. 15, Greville, p. 116.
36. Starkey, pp. 53–54.
37. Erasmus, pp. 163–64, Castiglione, p. 278.
38. *Ibid.*, pp. 156–57.
39. *Ibid.*, p. 173. Erasmus is evidently thinking of a governmental system similar to England's monarchy and the two Houses of Parliament. Cf. Starkey, pp. 169–70, 180–84, Sir Thomas

Smith, *De Republica Anglorum* (Cambridge University Press, 1906), pp. 16–17 and Sir Fulke Greville's comparison between England's "moderate form of monarchy" and France's "precipitate absoluteness," quoted above, p. 16.

40. Cf. Ruth Kelso, "The Doctrine of the English Gentleman in the Sixteenth Century," *University of Illinois Studies in Language and Literature,* XIV (1929), 29–30: "There seems . . . to be a tendency in the renaissance to lay more emphasis than had been laid before upon the part that personal worth plays in acquiring and maintaining nobility and less upon birth, which becomes desirable for its initial advantage rather than for its assured heritage of personal superiority. But though emphasis may have changed it would be a mistake to suppose that either in theory or practice gentle birth played a negligible part in determining a man's status. True nobility is almost always defined as that of race and virtue, and much of the insistence on virtue is intended not to comfort the lowly-born but to admonish the well-born who seem generally to have prided themselves on birth to the neglect of virtue." Thus the members of the new Tudor aristocracy, while insisting on their claims to ancient lineage (Sidney was bitter in his reply to anonymous detractors of his uncle Leicester who implied that the latter was of base ancestry), were able to excoriate the degeneracy of the old nobility. Cf. Spenser, *The Faerie Queene,* I, v, 51; II, iii, 40; II, xii, 79–80.

41. *Ibid.,* 68–69. The occupations which were permitted to the younger sons of the gentry and other needy gentlemen were those in which manual labor was not involved—law; agriculture, when the gentleman merely supervised the work; trade, if it was of the wholesale variety, particularly foreign trade, and the gentleman did not stand behind a counter; and, grudgingly, medicine. Cf. Sir Thomas Smith, pp. 39–40: "Whosoever studieth the laws of the realm, who studieth in the universities, who professeth liberal sciences, and, to be short, who can live idly and without manual labor and will bear the port, charge and countenance of a gentleman, he shall be called esquire, for that is the

title which men give to esquires and other gentlemen, and shall be taken for a gentleman."

42. The Italianates at court, led by Oxford, formed a faction opposed in politics, fashion, and literature to that of Sidney. Cf. W. J. Courthope, *History of English Poetry* (New York, 1897), II, 203, 210–11. They were young nobles who resented bitterly the rise to power of members of the new aristocracy and who flaunted their gaudy, outlandish clothing and their Italian affectations as a sign of their dissatisfaction with English society. Cf. Nashe, I, 185–86: "So long as pride, riot and whoredom are the companions of young courtiers they will always be hungry and ready to bite at every dog that hath a bone given him beside themselves. Jesu, what secret grudge and rancor reigns amongst them, one being ready to despair of himself if he see the prince but give his fellow a fair look or to die for grief if he be put down in bravery never so little. *Yet this custom have our false hearts fetched from other countries,* that they will swear and protest love, where they hate deadly and smile on him most kindly who subversion in soul they have vowed. . . . *Which of them all* sat in the sunshine of his sovereign's grace or *waxed great of low beginnings but he was spiteblasted, heaved at, and ill spoken of,* and that of those that bare them most countenance?" (My italics.) Cf. also B. M. Ward, *The Seventeenth Earl of Oxford* (London, 1928), p. 244n.

43. Spenser is referring to the Petrarchan sonnet cycles, written by those associated with the old aristocracy, in the chivalric tradition of adulterous love. The new Tudor aristocracy was inspired by the idealism of Castiglione's doctrine of neo-Platonic love, in which the courtier, the most rationally controlled of men, is able, through love guided by reason, to rise above the material world of the senses and finally to transcend reason itself. The Calvinism of the new aristocracy caused it, however, to emphasize one part of this doctrine—to regard love, that is, not as a series of stages through which one must pass to attain a vision of the divine beauty but as an ideal of life in which one devotes himself to what "seems on earth most heavenly." Spenser deals in *The Faerie Queene* with that form of neo-Platonic love

described by Castiglione which remains fixed to its earthly object. To this view of love he joins the Calvinist ideal of married love. See Paul N. Siegel, "The Petrarchan Sonneteers and Neo-Platonic Love," *Studies in Philology*, XLII (1945), 164–82 and "Spenser and the Calvinist View of Life," *Studies in Philology*, XLI (1944), 214–18.

44. The Italianate courtier guided himself by a code of honor that set him apart from ordinary mortals. This code demanded an extreme touchiness of spirit that sought redress for any slight in accordance with an elaborate system governing duels imported from Italy and Spain. Although Elizabeth interdicted the duel, the feudal tradition of redress by private action was still alive, and the cult became widely practiced in her last years and even more so during the reign of James. Cf. Fredson Thayer Bowers, *Elizabethan Revenge Tragedy, 1587–1642* (Princeton University Press, 1940), pp. 30–34. Although Sidney sought to fight a duel with Oxford after their quarrel during the French negotiations, he was opposed to the concept of honor as an extreme sensitivity to anything which might be construed as a slight, displayed by the rigid adherence to the "terms of honor" of a formalized system. Cf. his condemnation of "proud Anaxius" (*The Countess of Pembroke's Arcadia*, ed. Albert Feuillerat [Cambridge University Press, 1922], p. 439): "For, by a strange composition of mind, there was no man more tenderly sensible in anything offered to himself which in the farthest-fetched construction might be wrested to the name of wrong, no man that in his own actions could worse distinguish between valor and violence, . . . falsely accounting an inflexible anger a courageous constancy. . . ." The Italianates were also charged with maintaining enduring enmity while professing reconciliation and with revenging themselves in the vendetta manner by secret murder through the hiring of bravi or the use of poison. Oxford, it was stated by his former associates, planned to have Sidney killed by ruffians. Such methods were denounced even by those who retained a sympathy for the use of personal action to avenge deep injuries, especially if legal recourse was impossible. To counteract the continuing feudal tradition of personal action,

which weakened the authority of the state, Tudor homilists and moralists constantly inveighed against revenge. The basic text cited was Romans, xii, 17 and 19: "Recompense to no man evil for evil. . . . Dearly beloved, avenge not yourselves, but rather give place unto wrath; for it is written, Vengeance is mine, I will repay, saith the Lord."

CHAPTER IV

1. Samuel Rowlands, urging his fellow poets to belabor the "gross follies" of contemporary society, writes: "Leave Cupid's cut, women's flatt'ring praise, / Love's subject grows too threadbare nowadays."—"The Letting of Humors in the Head-vein," *Works* (Hunterian Club ed., 1874), I, 5. See also Joseph Hall, *Satires*, Book I, Satire 1; Edward Guilpin, "Satire Praeludium," *Skialetheia* (London, 1598); *Marston*, III, 269.

2. J. W. Saunders, "The Façade of Morality," *That Soueraine Light: Essays in Honor of Edmund Spenser, 1552-1594*, ed. William R. Mueller and Don Cameron Allen (Johns Hopkins Press, 1952), p. 7.

3. *The Return from Parnassus*, Part II, III, ii, 1216.

4. Part II, III, ii, 1273.

5. Part I, I, i, 157-58.

6. This refers to the fashion for erotic poems such as Shakespeare's *Venus and Adonis*, Marlowe's *Hero and Leander*, Marston's *Pygmalion*, and Nashe's *The Choice of Valentines*. Gullio is represented as an admirer of Shakespeare's love poetry, and Hall and Guilpin attack Nashe for having written *The Choice of Valentines* for a noble patron (Shakespeare's patron, the Earl of Southampton).

7. Part I, V, ii, 1488-93.

8. Part I, V, iv, 2152-56.

9. Cf. Hall, Prologue, Book I, addressing his satires: "Truth be thy speed, and Truth thy patron be," and Book I, Satire 1: "Nor can I crouch and writhe my fawning tail / To some great patron for my best avail / . . . Rather had I, albe in careless rhymes, / Check the misorder'd world and lawless times."

10. Ingenioso refuses the offer which the printer has made for

one of his libelous pamphlets with the words: "Forty shillings? A fit reward for one of your rheumatic poets!" When he details its libelous contents, the printer replies: "Oh, this will sell gallantly. I'll have it whatsoever it cost."—*The Return,* Part II, I, iii.

11. Louis B. Wright, *Middle-class Culture in Elizabethan England* (The University of North Carolina Press, 1935), p. 384.

12. Raymond M. Alden, *The Rise of Formal Satire in England* (University of Pennsylvania Press, 1899), pp. 230–32.

13. See Robert Anton's description (*The Philosopher's Satires,* London, 1616, p. 9) of the malcontents

> Who long retain their great Italian-hate,
> Witty in nothing, but things desperate
> To glut revenge, with studious memory
> Of shallow wrongs or slight injury.

14. See Z. S. Fink, "Jaques and the Malcontent Traveller," *Philological Quarterly,* XIV (1935), 237–52, and the chapter entitled "The Italianate Malcontent" in Paul N. Siegel, *Studies in Elizabethan Melancholy,* 1941, typewritten doctoral thesis in Harvard College Library.

15. Roger Ascham, *English Works,* ed. William Aldis Wright (Cambridge University Press, 1904), p. 221.

16. Cf. Anton, p. 10, and Thomas Lodge, "Wit's Misery," *Works,* Hunterian Club ed. (Glasgow, 1879), IV, 17–18.

17. Cf. Lodge, "Wit's Misery," IV, 85; Donne, *Fourth Satire,* 11, 30–48; Guilpin, "Satyra Quinta," *Skialetheia.* Christopher Marlowe, the greatest of these bohemian rebels, was a government spy.

18. The satirists portrayed several varieties of gulls, such as the malcontent traveler, the military swaggerer, the spruce coxcomb, and the seedy gallant, but they assigned many of the same attributes to each. For all of these social types were the products of the same milieu, and no doubt there was no sharp distinction between them in real life. The continental wars attracted penurious younger sons of both the nobility and the gentry, as well as unemployed university men, and the traveler,

real or pretended, easily passed over into the soldier, real or pretended. The same man might parade in Italianate finery when he was in funds and skulk in gloomy black as a malcontent when he was in the dumps.

19. See Marston, III, 271–75, 366–67; Nashe, I, 22, 220; Lodge, IV, 67-68.

20. Greene, XII, 104.

21. Nashe, I, 73.

22. The bourgeoisie and the lower classes, of course, did not practice this kind of idolization of one's mistress, which was one of the conventions of aristocratic love-making. What Marston is doing is to identify a class with humanity. In the traditional view virtue was supposed to be characteristic of the upper classes, who ruled over their natural inferiors as the soul directs the body. But now the "soul" of society was itself corrupted.

23. Marston, III, 379.

24. *Ibid.*, III, 264.

25. The reference, of course, is to Baldassare Castiglione, author of *The Courtier*. Cf. "Castilio Balthazar, a spruce courtier," in Marston's *Antonio and Mellida* and "Balthazar" in Guilpin's *Skialetheia*.

26. Marston, III, 350–51.

27. Cf. the first, fourth, eleventh, and twentieth elegies.

28. Cf. "Love's Progress" and "To His Mistress Going to Bed."

29. Cf. Louis I. Bredvold, "The Naturalism of Donne in Relation to Some Renaissance Traditions," *Journal of English and Germanic Philology*, XXII (1923), 471–502, which suggests that Donne's source for the doctrine is Montaigne. Cf. also the words of Basilius in Sidney's *Arcadia,* who, like Donne, makes the doctrine an excuse for libertinage in his plea that Zelmane should offer pity to him by "yielding grace" (p. 43): "Alas, let not certain imaginative rules whose truth stands but upon opinion keep so wise a mind from gratefulness and mercy, whose never failing laws nature hath planted in us."

30. Cf. Edward Guilpin, "Satyra Sexta," *Skialetheia:*

How art thou [reason] baffled? How comes this disgrace,
That by opinion thou art bearded so,
Thy slave, thy shadow—nay, outbearded too?
She, earthworm, doth derive her pedigree
From body's dirt and sensuality. . . .

31. Cf. *The Faerie Queene,* II, vii, 16.

32. Cf. Spenser's description ("Epithalamion," lines 185–203) of the "inward beauty" of his bride's "liuely spright," where "vertue raynes as Queene in royal throne, / And giueth lawes alone, / The which the base affections doe obay" and Sidney's encomium of his mistress, in whom he finds ("Astrophel and Stella," Sonnet IV) "all vices' overthrow, / Not by rude force, but sweetest sovereignty / Of reason."

CHAPTER V

1. Alfred Harbage, *Shakespeare's Audience* (Columbia University Press, 1941), p. 90.

2. John Stow, *A Survey of London,* 1603, Everyman ed., p. 492.

3. I, ii, 231–32.

4. I, ii, 161–62.

5. II, i, 87–89.

6. II, i, 99–103.

7. IV, ii, 94–104.

8. Alfred Harbage, *Shakespeare and the Rival Traditions* (New York, 1952), p. 141.

9. III, iv, 205–6.

10. A weakness of Harbage's admirable *Shakespeare and the Rival Traditions* is that it packs the plays of the popular repertory into one sealed compartment and the plays of the select repertory into another sealed compartment, not taking into account or explaining away plays like *Every Man in His Humour* and *The White Devil,* which were produced at the public theaters but influenced by the trends exhibited by the plays of the private theaters. Thus we are surprised when we come in the concluding chapter to his correct statement concerning Shakespeare (p. 295): "There is no mood or idea in the select

drama that is unexpressed in his. This is not to say that he combines and balances. Rather he reduces to proportion, places in perspective. He assimilates and transforms the thought of his antagonists at the same time that he excels their art." This is true not only of the tragedies but of the satiric comedies. In the satiric comedies we have the corruption of court and city excoriated by the verse satirists and the satiric dramatists. There is an interesting contrast between the world of Shakespeare's satiric comedy and that of his romantic comedy, a contrast which may be said to reflect symbolically the rise of a new reinvigorated aristocracy and its subsequent loss of vitality: in the world of his romantic comedy a simple gentleman gains by his great merit a duke's daughter or a great lady, a Sylvia, a Portia, a Rosalind, an Olivia; in the world of his satiric comedy a proud lord rejects a worthy gentlewoman, a Helena, a Mariana. *All's Well That Ends Well* and *Measure for Measure* differ, however, from the satiric comedies written for the private playhouses— *Troilus and Cressida*, I agree with Oscar James Campbell, is a special kind of play almost certainly written for an Inns of Court audience—in that elements of romantic comedy (foreign locales, devoted, long-suffering gentle-born maidens, unrealistic plots derived from folk material, happy marriage endings) are retained, even though the dramatic universe of which these elements are a part has changed. More than this, they differ from them in that they have religious overtones of redemption that derive from such popular prose exposés and warnings as Nashe's *Christ's Tears over Jerusalem* and Dekker's *The Seven Deadly Sins of London* and such similar popular plays as Greene's *A Looking-glass for London and England*. And at the end of them, vice is unmasked, social abuses are corrected, the audience is left edified and ethically satisfied.

11. Prologue of Marlowe's *Doctor Faustus,* line 5.

12. Marston, I, 99-100.

13. C. F. Tucker Brooke, *The Tudor Drama* (New York, 1911), p. 445.

CHAPTER VI

1. Joseph Wood Krutch, *The Modern Temper* (New York, 1929), p. 127.

2. There is evidence that Shakespeare had various connections with a group of aristocrats, members and stockholders of the Virginia Company, who were in opposition to James's policies. It seems certain that he knew, in addition to the Earl of Southampton, the Earl of Pembroke, and his younger brother, the Earl of Montgomery, and Christopher Brooke, and it is in varying degrees likely that he knew Sir Edwin Sandys, Sir Henry Neville, Sir Fulke Greville, and a number of others. See Charles Mills Gayley, *Shakespeare and the Founders of Liberty in America* (New York, 1917), pp. 8–39 and, for further discussion of the Calvinistic temper and the opposition to James of the leaders of the Virginia Company, Richard Beale Davis, *George Sandys: Poet-Adventurer* (Columbia University Press, 1955), pp. 280–81. Be that as it may, it is clear that Shakespeare's social environment made him look up to the new aristocracy as the leaders of society and caused him to accept the ideas formulated by the humanist theoreticians of this aristocracy. The son of a provincial burgher who, as presiding officer of the town council, must have been active during young William's childhood in mustering men to be sent to suppress the Northern Rebellion, Shakespeare as a playwright and actor in London must have learned to feel more strongly than ever about the need for maintaining the "king's peace" against all who would violate it. Each riot—and there were four such between 1588 and 1595—meant that for some weeks the theaters would be closed and his means of livelihood gone. Indeed his occupation would have been taken away from him altogether by the Puritans on the City Council, who wished to make the showing of plays illegal, were it not for royal favor and aristocratic protection.

3. *Shakespearean Tragedy* (London, 1949), pp. 38–39.

4. For disregarded premonitory dreams in Elizabethan drama, see Bain Tate Stewart, "The Misunderstood Dreams in the Plays of Shakespeare and His Contemporaries," *Essays in Honor*

of *Walter Clyde Curry* (Vanderbilt University Press, 1954), pp. 197–206.

5. *English Domestic or Homiletic Tragedy* (New York, 1943), p. 18. For such indications of divine providence in the tragedies, see pp. 113–15, 138–40, 156–59, 166–86, 223–24, 227.

6. Cf. Sylvan Barnet, "Some Limitations of a Christian Approach to Shakespeare," *ELH*, XXII (1955), 85. For other objections to the reading of Shakespearean tragedy as having Christian implications, see H. B. Charlton, *Shakespearian Tragedy* (Cambridge University Press, 1948), pp. 10–11; Clifford Leech, *Shakespeare's Tragedies and Other Studies in Seventeenth Century Drama* (London, 1950), p. 18; J. A. K. Thomson, *Shakespeare and the Classics* (London, 1952), pp. 253–54. These critics have based themselves on some well-known theories of tragedy. Compare Leech, p. 18, and Barnet, 82 and 84, with W. MacNeile Dixon, *Tragedy* (London, 1924), pp. 37–38; Charlton, pp. 10–11, Leech, pp. 10–11, and Barnet, 92 with I. A. Richards, *Principles of Literary Criticism* (New York, 1948), p. 246; Thomson, pp. 253–54 and Barnet, 87, with F. L. Lucas, *Tragedy* (London, 1949), p. 108. I trust that in the course of this chapter I have answered their objections in passing.

7. For the Elizabethans the Roman Empire was part of the divinely preordained scheme of things. Cf. Hugh Latimer, *An Apology for the Power and Providence of God* (London, 1635), p. 506: "Surely, if by Fortune we should understand God's providence, we may safely say that for the effecting of His own purposes (though happily unknown to them) rather than for an extraordinary worth or merit in them he conferred upon them the Empire of the world; as Augustus Caesar was by God's special providence directed in taxing the world that so, every man repairing to his own city, Christ by that means might be born in Bethlehem."

8. See, however, for poetically fitting retribution in *King Lear* Robert B. Heilman, *This Great Stage* (Louisiana State University Press, 1948), pp. 41–51, 53–57 and 150–51.

9. Cf. Miles Coverdale, "The Spiritual and Most Precious Pearl," *Works*, Parker Society ed., p. 138: "God tempereth and

frameth the punishment even like unto the sin, so that they do agree together as well in form and likeness as in proportion and quality." For other quotations illustrating the doctrine that Divine Providence inevitably visits the consequences of their actions upon sinners, see Lily B. Campbell, *Shakespeare's Tragic Heroes: Slaves of Passion* (Cambridge University Press, 1930), pp. 16–20.

10. "Preface to Shakespeare," *Shakespeare Criticism*, ed. D. Nichol Smith (Oxford University Press, 1946), p. 89.

11. For such retribution in *Hamlet*, see pp. 114–15 and n; in *Othello*, pp. 138–40; in *Macbeth*, pp. 156–58; in *King Lear*, pp. 166–170.

12. Malvolio's Puritanism is only the mask for his self-seeking which Puritanism was so often charged with being, and he is ready to assume another mask whenever he has need. "Marry, sir," says Maria (*Twelfth Night*, II, iii, 151–60), drawing his character, "sometimes he is a kind of puritan. . . . The devil a puritan that he is, or any thing constantly, but a time-server." So, too, the villainously hypocritical and grasping Shylock would have reminded the Elizabethans of the Puritan usurers of their own day. See Paul N. Siegel, "Shylock and the Puritan Usurers," *Studies in Shakespeare*, ed. Arthur D. Matthews and Clark Emory (University of Miami Press, 1952), pp. 129–38. In *Measure for Measure* the "outward-sainted" Angelo (III, i, 89), who has waiting to be unloosed beneath the gravity of his bearing a predatory passion which causes him to act tyrannically upon assuming power, would also have been recognized as one whose approach to life is that of the Puritan. See Donald J. McGinn, "The Precise Angelo," *Joseph Quincy Adams Memorial Studies*, ed. James G. McManaway, *et al.* (Washington, D. C., 1948), pp. 129–39.

13. See pp. 120–21.

14. Perhaps I should add Bradley's own footnote (p. 19n.) as an explication of my statement: "I do not dream of suggesting that in any of his dramas Shakespeare imagined two abstract principles or passions conflicting, and incorporated them in persons. . . ."

15. See pp. 99–101, 112–16, 125–31, 147–54, 161–69, 178.

16. See pp. 116–17, 140–41, 158–60, 187–88.

17. Charlton, pp. 109–10, 117–18, 143–44, 218–20.

18. Cf. S. L. Bethell, *Shakespeare and the Popular Tradition* (New York, 1948), pp. 42–61.

19. The Elizabethans followed Boethius and the Middle Ages in emphasizing the mutability of the things of this world, over which fortune prevails, while maintaining that the uncertainties of life, beyond human foresight, are in reality part of the divine scheme of things. Spenser's "Cantoes of Mutabilitie" is the *locus classicus*. The humanist treatises of moral philosophy and religious consolation account for the misfortunes of the good by the doctrine that adversity teaches them to rise above worldly things and to grow in love for their fellow men and God. Cf. "A Dialogue of Comfort against Tribulation," *The Works of Sir Thomas More* (London, 1557), p. 1149; Peter de la Primaudaye, *The French Academy* (London, 1594), p. 326; Sir Francis Bacon, "Of Adversity." Thus Hamlet and Lear learn from their ordeals. This contributes to a sense of reconciliation on our part, although it does not wipe away our memory of their pain. Desdemona and Cordelia, unlike the heroes of Shakespearean tragedy, suffer through no fault of their own, but they are Christ-like figures who exemplify the Christian virtue of accepting entirely unmerited calamities with unshrinking fortitude and undiminished love.

20. *Certain Sermons or Homilies,* pp. 63, 66, 83, 122, 139, 157, 498.

21. Cf. Lily B. Campbell, *Shakespeare's "Histories": Mirrors of Elizabethan Policy* (The Huntington Library: San Marino, California, 1947). Miss Campbell, however, tends to regard the plays too much as detailed allegories. Shakespeare himself poked fun at straining for extended historical analogies when he had Fluellen say (*Henry V,* IV, vii, 32–35), "If you mark Alexander's life well, Harry of Monmouth's life is come after it indifferent well; for there is figures in all things," proving his point with the argument that Henry V was born in Monmouth and Alexander was born in Macedon, that the Wye is at Monmouth

and there is also some river or other at Macedon, that Alexander killed his friend Cleitus in his cups and Henry turned away Falstaff in his right wits. Aside from Shakespeare's view of historical analogy, a dramatist writing for a popular audience under the conditions of Elizabethan stage censorship could not very well have written subtle and intricately constructed allegories of the politics of the day. He would have seen the advantage, however, of giving an added fillip to his audience's interest in the past by implying a historical parallel to important contemporary happenings of which the past events in their broad outlines were reminiscent, which everyone would recognize, and to which the government censor would not object allusions being made—and this, I believe, was what Shakespeare did.

22. Furness Variorum ed. of *Othello*, p. 308n.

23. See p. 227, n. 11.

24. IV, i, 169–71, 239–42. The Bishop of Carlisle immediately before Richard's entrance in this scene had linked him with Christ, saying (IV, i, 125, 126, 144) that if Richard, "the figure of God's majesty" and His "deputy-elect," is deposed, England will be called "the field of Golgotha and dead men's skulls." But, although England must suffer for the deposition, York indicates that Richard, in bearing with gentle fortitude the indignities inflicted upon him by the masses as, stripped of his crown, he rides through the streets, is a Christlike figure whose passion serves God's ultimately beneficent purpose:

> But dust was thrown upon his sacred head;
> Which with such gentle sorrow he shook off,
> His face still combating with tears and smiles,
> The badges of his grief and patience,
> That had not God, for some strong purpose, steel'd
> The hearts of men, they must perforce have melted,
> And barbarism itself have pitied him.
> But heaven hath a hand in these events,
> To whose high will we bound our calm contents.
> (V, ii, 30–38)

The description of Richard's "tears and smiles" in his "grief and patience" resembles that of the "smiles and tears" of

216

Cordelia, another Christlike figure (see above, pp. 132–34), in her "patience and sorrow." (*King Lear*, IV, iii, 18–21.)

25. G. Wilson Knight, *The Wheel of Fire* (London, 1949), p. 235 and n.

26. See pp. 125–27, 131, 132, 134, 136, 143–45, 186, 225, 226, 227–28, 229. In *Hamlet*, the first of the great tragedies, the only biblical analogue I have found is Claudius' reference (III, iii, 37–38) to his resemblance to Cain.

27. Richards, p. 246.

28. He noted Shakespeare's use of "current religious ideas" in *Macbeth* and *Hamlet* (pp. 172–73): "The horror in Macbeth's soul is more than once represented as desperation at the thought that he is eternally 'lost'; the same idea appears in the attempt of Claudius at repentance; and as *Hamlet* nears its close the 'religious' tone of the tragedy is deepened. . . ." Bradley's use of quotation marks with "lost" and "religious" is an attempt to save his concept of Shakespearean tragedy as essentially secular. If we listen, however, with our ears open to the implications of words that for the Elizabethans would have had a profoundly religious significance, the plays take on new overtones. When Richard III, for instance, concludes his speech of bravado to his troops with (V, iv, 312–13), "March on, join bravely, let us to 't pell-mell; / If not to heaven, then hand in hand to hell," the ringing couplet becomes more than a rhetorical flourish; it is seen to be dramatically ironic: Richard really is going to his eternal damnation, as Margaret had prophesied.

29. Oscar James Campbell, "The Salvation of Lear," *ELH*, XV (1948), 107.

30. G. Wilson Knight has shown (*The Shakespearian Tempest* [Oxford University Press, 1932], *passim*) that Shakespeare uses throughout his drama certain imagery (raging tempests, oceans swallowing up land, rivers in angry flood overflowing their banks, unrestrained weeping) to suggest disturbances in the natural order of the universe, of the state, and of man, and other imagery (harmonious music, gentle breezes, still or softly flowing water) to suggest the smooth operation of natural law on the universal scale, social concord, the well-integrated per-

sonality, love. This symbolic imagery springs naturally from the way of thinking Shakespeare inherited. Cf. Hooker, I, 156–58: "Since the time that God did first proclaim the edicts of His law upon it, heaven and earth have hearkened unto his voice, and their labour hath been to do His will: He 'made a law for the rain' [Job xxviii. 26]; He gave His 'decree unto the sea that the waters should not pass His commandment.' [Jer. v. 22]. . . . [Because of] divine malediction, laid for the sin of man . . . swervings are now and then incident into the course of nature. . . ." See also E. M. W. Tillyard, *The Elizabethan World Picture* (London, 1943), pp. 94–99 for a discussion of the medieval and Renaissance concept of the universe and of the state as a musical harmony.

31. See pp. 126–31.

32. A. C. Bradley, *Oxford Lectures on Poetry* (London, 1909), pp. 87–88.

33. "Most subject is the fattest soil to weeds," says Henry IV of Hal (2 *Henry IV*, IV, iv, 54–56), "And he, the noble image of my youth, / Is overspread with them." Just as monarchy, the best form of government, can be transformed into tyranny, the worst form of government, so the kingly nature, in its very richness, can, under unfavorable circumstances, go to seed more thoroughly than ordinary human nature.

34. Douglas Hewitt, "The Very Pompes of the Divell—Popular and Folk Elements in Elizabethan and Jacobean Drama," *Review of English Studies*, XXV (1949), 21.

35. Herbert Weisinger, *Tragedy and the Paradox of the Fortunate Fall* (Michigan State College Press, 1953), p. 225n.

36. William Empson, *Some Versions of Pastoral* (Norfolk, Conn., n. d.), pp. 84–85.

37. Cf. Reginald Scot's statement ("A Discourse of Devils and Spirits," 1584, *Discovery of Witchcraft* [London, 1651], p. 384) that the story in Genesis of Adam's temptation and fall is "set down in the manner of a tragedy." Chaucer's monk, following the highly influential *De Casibus Virorum Illustrium* of Boccaccio in including Adam's fall among his stories of those "yfallen out of heigh degree / Into myserie," had said that of "worldly

man" no one had had such "heigh degree" as Adam (*The Complete Works of Geoffrey Chaucer*, ed. F. N. Robinson [Cambridge, Mass., 1933], p. 226). According to his definition, then, Adam's tragedy was not only the first in the history of mankind but also the greatest.

38. Sir James George Frazer, *The Scapegoat* (New York, 1935), pp. 226–28. Gilbert Murray finds (*The Classical Tradition in Poetry* [Harvard University Press, 1930], pp. 64–65) that the Greek tragic hero is "derived both from the Life Spirit—call him Dionysus or what you will—who comes to save the community with the fruits of the New Year, and from the polluted Old Year, the *Pharmakos* or Scapegoat, who is cast out to die or to wander in the wilderness, bearing with him the sins of the community." The situation of Hamlet, Lear, and Richard II is not unlike that of the scapegoat in the Elizabethan folk ceremonies who was accorded regal honors and then derisively expelled, a custom related to that of having a fool preside over revels and giving him the honors of a king. Hamlet, isolated amidst the sycophantic court of Claudius, who has deprived him of the throne, is in a sense a prince in name only and is, as he says (III, ii, 401), fooled to the top of his bent—that is, treated as a fool, a deranged person, to the limits of his endurance. Lear, with only a nominal kingship, flouted by his daughters, driven out into the storm, and wandering about crowned with nettles and weeds, also endures the utmost of humiliation. The Fool suggests more than once that they could exchange places. So, too, Richard II speaks of himself (IV, i, 260) as "a mockery king." The derisive treatment of Hamlet, Lear, and Richard II as mock kings parallels not only the Elizabethan folk ceremonies but the passion of Christ, who was crowned with thorns, given a reed for a scepter, and mockingly hailed as the king of the Jews.

CHAPTER VII

1. Hamlet, like the other malcontent revengers, exhibits the symptoms of pathological melancholy. Cf. Lawrence Babb, *The Elizabethan Malady* (Michigan State College Press, 1951), pp.

107n. and 108: "All of the melancholic traits appearing in Hamlet, it should be noted, were traditional and commonplace. It is not necessary to assume that Shakespeare had read a book on melancholy. . . . His morose brooding, his weary despondency, his suicidal impulses, his cynical satire, his sudden changes of mood and unpredictable fits and starts of rash activity are all in keeping with the Elizabethan idea of the melancholiac. The melancholy man, moreover, is traditionally a person who reflects rather than acts, who is painfully circumspect and very much inclined to 'thinking too precisely on the event.' "

2. For description of the black clothes and affected negligence of dress of real-life Elizabethan malcontents, see Donne, Satire IV; Marston, III, 274–75; Nashe, I, 169–70; Lodge, IV, 17–18.

3. Bowers, pp. 39–40. In his "Hamlet as Minister and Scourge" (*PMLA*, LXX [1955], 740–49) Bowers sought to consider the light his study of Elizabethan revenge tragedy and its background of contemporary ethical thought and social history threw on the greatest of Elizabethan revenge tragedies. Hamlet waits agonizedly for the opportunity to kill Claudius as an act of public justice rather than of private revenge, he concludes in this article. Such an opportunity will be provided for him by divine providence if he is to be a minister of God, who acts as an avenger without staining his soul, but Hamlet fears that his role is to be that of the scourge of God who, while acting as the agent of divine retribution, does so by committing the sin of murder. "We may see . . . the anomalous position Hamlet conceives for himself: is he to be the private-revenger scourge *or* the public-revenger minister? . . . If he anticipates [God's will] and revenges, he risks damnation. If he does not revenge, he must torture himself with his seeming incompetence. In moments of the deepest depression, it could be natural for doubts to arise as to his role, and whether because of his 'too too sullied flesh' he may not in fact have been appointed as a scourge, in which case his delay is indeed cowardly."—745. The weakness of this theory is the weakness of so many other theories about Hamlet: it attributes to him thoughts which Hamlet himself does not express or imply. In

not a single line does he wonder if his position is that of a criminal avenger or of a shining, unstained instrument of God's justice; at no time is it indicated that the reason for his delay is that "as minister," he is "waiting on the expected opportunity which should be provided him, and not finding it."—745. Other works seeking to illuminate *Hamlet* by studying Elizabethan attitudes toward revenge are John E. Hankins, *The Character of Hamlet* (University of North Carolina Press, 1941); G. R. Elliott, *Scourge and Minister* (Duke University Press, 1951); J. J. Lawlor, "The Tragic Conflict in *Hamlet*," *Review of English Studies, New Series*, I (1950), 97–113. I do not agree with the central thesis of any of these works, but I am indebted to each of them for information and insights.

4. Bowers, *Elizabethan Revenge Tragedy*, pp. 40 and 184.

5. *Ibid.*, p. 40.

6. "An Homily against Disobedience and Wilful Rebellion," *Certain Sermons*, p. 502.

7. "An Exhortation to Obedience," *Certain Sermons*, p. 108.

8. Hamlet resembles the other malcontent avengers in being temporarily overwhelmed by his awful responsibility and beset by doubt and hesitation. Cf. Ashley H. Thorndike, *"Hamlet* and Contemporary Revenge Plays," *PMLA*, XVII (1902), 204.

9. Cf. Primaudaye: "All private revenge . . . is vicious and forbidden by God. . . . There is no sin that can avoid punishment and that findeth not a judge even in him that committed it . . ." and "The conscience of a wicked man is unto him in stead of an accuser, a witness, a judge, and a hangman. . . . The violence of man's conscience cometh from God. . . ." Quoted by Lily B. Campbell, "Theories of Revenge in Renaissance England," *Modern Philology*, XXVIII (1931), 287, 286.

10. Robert H. West has shown in "King Hamlet's Ambiguous Ghost," *PMLA*, LXX (1955), 1107-17, that the ghost is not theologically consistent: there can be no doubt that he comes from purgatory, yet a purgatorial spirit would not call for revenge. *Hamlet* was not written to be studied by students of theology but to be seen by a popular audience which was accustomed to have stage ghosts come from an afterworld to demand revenge and which, moreover, had its own folk ghost lore

Cf. Robert H. West, *The Invisible World* (University of Georgia Press, 1939), pp. 51–52: "Apparitions thus popularly credited were not so much conceived to be from the Christian havens for souls as from the more immediate and gruesome charnel house and grave. . . . This idea that the souls of the dead were swayed by earthly passions and frequented the resting places of their bodily organs . . . was one that persisted despite the theologians. . . . It was essential to theory of necromantic ghosts and treasure-guarding ghosts and revenge ghosts. . . ." The humanized, if majestic, *Hamlet* ghost, which, while confined to purgatorial fires during the day, is "doom'd for a certain term to walk the night" (I, v, 10), and which Hamlet says was cast up from the sepulcher underneath which his father was buried (I, iv, 48–51), has many of the features of this earth-bound folk spook. The fact, however, that it is established—after disturbing questions concerning its authenticity, making dramatic use of contemporary speculation to increase the tension of doubt and fear, have been settled—that it came from purgatory would have added to the vibrancy of the dramatic credence the audience gave it, for the Elizabethan man in the street, however loyal to the Church of England, remembered enough of the "old faith" to permit the representation of a ghost from purgatory to work upon his imagination. Yet his religious sensibilities would not have been shocked by a ghost from purgatory calling for revenge, for officially he did not believe in purgatory.

11. Cf. also the midnight soliloquy of the villainous atheist in Tourneur's *The Atheist's Tragedy, or The Honest Man's Revenge* (IV, III): "I could now commit / A murder were it but to drink the fresh / Warm blood of him I murdered."

12. Gentillet, *A Discourse . . . Against Nicholas Machiavel,* tr. Patericke (London, 1608), Part III, max. 6. Quoted by Bowers, p. 52.

13. The reckoning with an afterlife distinguishes Hamlet from the Kydian avenger. Hieronimo, debating within himself whether to leave vengeance to God or to return wrong for wrong (*The Spanish Tragedy,* III, xiii, 1–11), decides that death,

the worst result that can come from resolute action, can come as easily to the man who exercises patience as to the one who seeks revenge. Unlike Hamlet, he thus overlooks justice in another world and becomes a criminal revenger. One crime opens the way to another, as stated in the line from Seneca he quotes to justify his revenge, but the person committing the second is as subject to divine retribution as the person committing the first.

14. Cf. George Lyman Kittredge's gloss in his *Sixteen Plays of Shakespeare* (New York, 1946), p. 1083.

15. *All's Well That Ends Well*, III, ii, 30. Bertram accepts the guidance of Parolles, through whose Italianate pretensions and furbelows Lafeu, the elderly counselor of the king, sees without much difficulty. See II, iii, 211–17.

16. Thorndike, 215.

17. In the words "we defy augury" Hamlet expresses, as S. F. Johnson has pointed out ("The Regeneration of Hamlet," *Shakespeare Quarterly*, III [1952], 204), a rejection of prognostications, such as those made by the augurs of pagan Rome, of the workings of a fate indifferent to man to which he is subject; in the remainder of the speech he expresses an acceptance of a divine providence, whose mysterious ways he cannot fathom but on whose merciful justice he can rely. The echoes in the passage of Montaigne and, more remotely, of Marcus Aurelius and Seneca (which would have been detected only by the learned in the audience, if by them), need cause us only to make the qualification of Johnson: "This is not deadening fatalism but good Christian doctrine, if somewhat colored later by neo-stoicism."

18. Such poetic justice is also visited on those who serve him. Polonius, worldly wise, officious, foolishly proud of his cunning and his deviousness, delighting in his spying on his own son and on Hamlet, is fittingly killed as he is eavesdropping. With all of his trickery and superficial wisdom this busybody has not understood the nature of the deadly struggle into which he has intruded himself. "Take thy fortune," says Hamlet (III, iv, 32–33), as he finds him dead behind the arras, "Thou find'st to be

too busy is some danger." So, too, Rosencrantz and Guildenstern, twin yes-men without regard for old friendship in their desire for advancement, in seeking to lure Hamlet to his death drive on to their own destruction. Claudius instructs them (IV, iii, 56), "Tempt him with speed abroad." But in hurrying Hamlet aboard ship they are themselves unknowingly hurrying to their own death, which, as Hamlet says (V, ii, 57), they invite upon themselves in their eagerness to be used by Claudius. Laertes also is, as he says (V, ii, 317–18), "justly kill'd with mine own treachery," the victim of his own plot, "as a woodcock to mine own springe."

19. Polonius' death added to the uncertainty with which the audience regarded Hamlet. In the passage which Bowers made the jumping-off point for his theorizing in "Hamlet as Minister and Scourge," Hamlet, looking down upon the slain Polonius, says (III, iv, 173–75): "For this same lord, / I do repent: but heaven hath pleased it so, / To punish me with this and this with me, / That I must be their scourge and minister." He accepts here without questioning, as he does until his return from his ocean voyage, his role as the divine agent who, in punishing the wicked, must himself sin and be punished. It is in this sense that he spoke of himself earlier (II, ii, 613) as being "prompted to my revenge by heaven and hell." But the slaying of Polonius is scarcely the "premeditated murder in the first degree, not manslaughter" that Bowers says it is (741). When Polonius suddenly calls for help from behind the arras, it must seem to Hamlet that he has fallen into a trap and that the call is a signal for the king's men. His reaction is swift and defensive, not at all premeditated. His lightning thrust through the arras must certainly have been regarded by the Elizabethans in a different light than, say, Antonio's deliberate stabbing of the boy Julio in Marston's *Antonio's Revenge*. Yet the person behind the arras, although Hamlet does not know it, is an unarmed old man, and the audience may well have wondered if this is the first of a series of killings by a criminal avenger. Hamlet's expression of repentance is, however, an indication that this is not so.

20. I. J. Semper, *Hamlet without Tears* (Dubuque, 1946), p. 99.

21. G. R. Waggoner, "An Elizabethan Attitude toward Peace and War," *Philological Quarterly*, XXXIII (1954), 33.

22. Caroline Spurgeon, *Shakespeare's Imagery* (New York, 1935), 316–19.

23. Paul A. Jorgensen, "Shakespeare's Use of War and Peace," *Huntington Library Quarterly*, XVI (1953), 336.

CHAPTER VIII

1. Speaking to the degenerate gentleman Roderigo, who would be contemptuous of those who have to do with business calculations, he says (I, i, 19, 31) that the courtly Cassio is "a great arithmetician," a "debiter and creditor" and a "counter-caster"—that is, one who is trained to handle military accounts and not a real soldier. Like so much of what Iago says, this is the ironic reverse of the truth: his is the coldly calculating spirit of the mercantilist.

2. This section of the chapter is a version of my article "The Damnation of Othello," *PMLA*, LXVIII (1953), 1068–78, that is somewhat expanded, in part to meet the stimulating criticisms of E. C. Pettet and F. G. Schoff, who were kind enough to write to me setting forth in detail their objections to it.

3. "If any wretch have put this in your head," says Emilia to Othello (IV, ii, 15–16), speaking of her husband without knowing it, "Let heaven requite it with the serpent's curse!" The words remind us of the Genesis account.

4. One Christian tradition, later made use of by Milton, was that Satan's envy of Adam in his bliss impelled him to tempt him. Cf. Kathleen Ellen Hartwell, *Lactantius and Milton* (Harvard University Press, 1929), p. 59.

5. *Microcosmus* (London, 1603), p. 62.

6. Kittredge glosses "This sorrow's heavenly; / It strikes where it doth love" (p. 1307): "My sorrow is like that which God feels when he punishes the guilty: he loves the sinner, yet punishes the guilty: Cf. Hebrews, xii, 6; 'Whom the Lord loveth he chasteneth.'" There is profound irony in Othello's comparing

himself to God as he makes ready to do that which is forbidden by God.

7. Harley Granville-Barker, *Prefaces to Shakespeare* (Princeton University Press, 1947), II, 80. Granville-Barker anticipated my thesis that Othello is to be regarded as damned (p. 114): "Othello wakes as from a nightmare only to kill himself, his prospect hell." Cf. also S. L. Bethell, "Shakespeare's Imagery: The Diabolic Images in *Othello*," *Shakespeare Survey*, ed. Allardyce Nicoll, V (1952), 78–79. Before Bradley cast his potent spell it was not considered to be obvious to all that Othello remains spiritually innocent in spite of his murder. The question was, in fact, so long debated in earlier Shakespearean criticism that the *Edinburgh Review* of July 1840 could say: "The character of the Moor, in which the explication must be sought [i.e., an explication of the play that would provide a 'moral justification of its horror'], has been interpreted more contradictorily than any other in the range of the poet's works, *Hamlet* itself not excepted." Cf. the Furness Variorum edition of *Othello*, p. 419. For examples of the view that Othello, despite his goodness, is overcome and destroyed by the evil within him, see Furness, pp. 419–20, 420, 421–22, 422–23, 425–28, 431–32, 444–45, 452–53.

8. *Certain Sermons*, p. 490: "We read in the gospel that Judas was so sorrowful and heavy, yea, that he was filled with such anguish and vexation of mind for that which he had done that he could not abide to live any longer. Did not he also, afore he hanged himself, make an open confession of his fault, when he said, *I have sinned, betraying the innocent blood?* . . . It is evident and plain, then, that although we be never so earnestly sorry for our sins, acknowledge and confess them, yet all these things shall be but means to bring us to utter desperation except we do steadfastly believe that God our heavenly father will, for his son Jesus Christ's sake, pardon and forgive us our offences and trespasses and utterly put them out of remembrance in his sight. Therefore . . . they that teach repentance without Christ and a lively faith in the mercy of God do only teach Cain's or Judas' repentance."

9. Cf. Calvin, *Institutes of the Christian Religion*, tr. Henry Beveridge (Edinburgh, 1845), III, iii, 4: "Their [Cain's, Saul's, and Judas'] repentance, therefore, was nothing better than a kind of threshold to hell, into which, having entered even in the present life, they began to endure the punishment inflicted by the presence of an offended God."

10. Modern editors generally follow the Quarto reading of the lines (V, ii, 346–48) in which Othello speaks of himself as "one whose hand, / Like the base Indian, threw a pearl away / Richer than all his tribe." Richmond Noble (*Shakespeare's Biblical Knowledge* [New York, 1935], pp. 91–93) argues convincingly, however, for the Folio reading "base Iudean." "Iudean" would refer to Judas Iscariot, who, like Othello, killed himself in despair at his guilt and whose kiss of betrayal, bringing death to Christ, is recalled by Othello's words (V, ii, 358) "I kiss'd thee ere I kill'd thee." "Just as Judas threw away his Saviour, the most precious possession of his Tribe, so he (Othello) destroyed what had been his most precious blessing." "Pearl" not only refers to Christ but alludes to the "pearl of great price" (Matthew, xiii, 46), the kingdom of heaven and the soul whose abode it is. Cf. *Macbeth*, III, i, 68–69: "And mine eternal jewel / Given to the common enemy of man," i.e., his immortal soul given to the devil, who (Rev., xii, 9) "deceiveth all the world."

11. *Boethius' Consolation of Philosophy*, tr. George Colville (1556), ed. Ernest Belfort Bax (London, 1897), pp. 51–52. Desdemona's words of resignation (IV, ii, 128), "It is my wretched fortune," express Christian endurance of adversity as God's will. She is, as "A Sermon of Christian Love and Charity" recommended (*Certain Sermons*, p. 65), following the example of Christ in taking his "cup of death" with the words "Thy will be done." In the next line, in answer to Iago's question "How comes this trick upon him [Othello]?" she replies, "Nay, heaven doth know." Men are in the dark, but heaven knows all things, permits the suffering of the good for its own purposes, and will perform justice—this is the feeling communicated to the audience, as it observes Iago's malevolently ironic pretense of ignorance met by Desdemona's faith in an all-seeing providence. Al-

though Desdemona does not speak in the theological terms of the good angel of the moralities, she is a Christian figure. To Othello's question "Are not you a strumpet?" she replies (IV, ii, 82–85):

No, as I am a Christian:
If to preserve this vessel for my lord
From any other foul unlawful touch
Be not to be a strumpet, I am none.

She is here, as she continues to be in her cry (IV, ii, 88), "O, heaven forgive us" in response to Othello's unjust accusation and in her hope (IV, ii, 135) "heaven pardon him" for the unknown villain who has calumniated her, "made one with Christ," in the words of "A Sermon against Whoredom and Uncleanness" (*Certain Sermons*, p. 122): "And a little before he [St. Paul] saith, *Do ye not know, that your bodies are the members of Christ? Shall I then take the members of Christ and make them the members of a whore?* . . . How unseemly a thing is it then to cease to be incorporate or embodied and made one with Christ. . . ."

12. Thomas Adams, *The Devil's Banquet* (London, 1614), pp. 58–59. Quoted by Bowers, p. 31.

13. So, too, adherence to the Italian aristocratic code of honor makes Othello lose his virtue, the only true source of honor. When, broken by his sense of guilt, he is disarmed, he says (V, ii, 245–46), "But why should honour outlive honesty? / Let it go all." "Honour" here means "reputation for valor," and "honesty" means "honorable character." Why keep one's escutcheon unblemished when one's soul is black with guilt? Elsewhere (V, ii, 294) he speaks of himself with bitter irony as an "honourable murderer." He had thought that he was acting in honor and had proved to be a base murderer.

14. Kenneth Muir has shown ("Freedom and Slavery in *Othello*," *Notes and Queries*, CXCIX [1954], 223–28) the importance of the words "free" and "slave" and their synonyms in *Othello*.

15. *Richard II*, II, i, 40–42.

CHAPTER IX

1. Cf. the Elizabethan utterances that the Christian prince is an image of God, cited on p. 203, n. 29. Chivalric love poetry had punned on the grace rendered by Cupid conceived of as both a feudal lord and as a god.

2. Cf. the Elizabethan utterances that the tyrant is an image of Lucifer, cited on p. 203, n. 35. One of the traditional reasons advanced to explain the rebellion of Lucifer was that, out of jealousy, he "challenged the place of the Messias." Cf. Scot, p. 362.

3. The Discourses of Niccolò Machiavelli, ed. Leslie J. Walker (Yale University Press, 1950), I, 363.

4. Primaudaye, The French Academy, "Epistle to the Reader."

5. Innocent Gentillet, A Discourse upon the Means of Well Governing, tr. Simon Patericke (London, 1608), pp. 109–10.

6. John Donne, Complete Poetry and Selected Prose, ed. John Hayward (New York, 1949), p. 371.

7. Cf. Richard's "Tears then for babes; blows and revenge for me." (Henry VI, Part III, II, i, 86)

8. See Lilian Winstanley, Macbeth, King Lear & Contemporary History (Cambridge University Press, 1922). Miss Winstanley, straining to see Macbeth as a vast, closely detailed symbolic rendition of contemporary history, indulges in many far-fetched analogies and in much dubious logic. However, she has vividly shown the terrific impact the Gunpowder Plot made on the public consciousness; the comparison that James made between it and the murder of his father, Darnley, by Bothwell; the parallels drawn by contemporary historians between Darnley's murder and the murder of Duff, details of which Shakespeare drew upon from Holinshed and used in the depiction of the murder of Duncan; the conviction of the younger Bothwell, James's cousin and hated enemy and the center of Catholic plots against him, of dealing with witches to achieve his death; the proclamation of the Scottish Privy Council that the Gunpowder Plot was diabolically inspired. These and other points indicate that the audience would have recognized the charged

atmosphere of the times as having entered into *Macbeth*'s making.

CHAPTER X

1. Greene, XII, 142.
2. Cf. *Richard II*, II, i, 31–32.
3. Lear, it would seem, could not be acted as holding Cordelia in his arms all this time: the attitude would be too strained and unnatural. He must have laid her down when he asked for a looking glass, and in order to put the feather to her lips, he must kneel beside her. The position reminds us of the blessings he and Gloucester received when they knelt before and contributes to the dramatic effect.
4. There are some interesting parallels between the scene in which Pericles awakes from a state of inanition out of grief for the death of his daughter, this scene, and the one in which Lear awakes to the sight of Cordelia that illustrate how *King Lear* in some ways prefigures the tragicomedies while differing essentially from them. Pericles awakes to Marina's singing, as Lear had awaked to the sound of music and found Cordelia. He blesses her, as she kneels before him, and asks for fresh garments, the sign of the resumption of his kingship, as the fresh garments on Lear when he awoke are the sign of his restoration. In his ecstasy it seems to him that he hears a "heavenly music" (*Pericles*, V, ii, 234), which is unheard by his faithful old counselor Helicanus and by Lysimachus, who will take his place as the ruler of Tyre, just as the dying Lear's ecstatic vision of Cordelia as living is not perceived by Kent and Albany. It is as if in his beatitude he is attuned to the music of the spheres which mortals cannot ordinarily hear. The ravishing music sends him into a slumber. From a living death he had been roused by Marina into a waking dream, and now he sinks once more into insensibility—his dream rounded with a sleep, to use Prospero's famous words about human life (*The Tempest*, IV, i, 156–58)—but this time he experiences while his senses are inert a vision of divinity that enables him to regain his wife Thaisa. The family reunion after Marina and Thaisa have

seemingly been dead, besides which the miseries of life are unimportant, as Gloucester's and Lear's having been reunited to
their children in a new love justifies their agonies, signifies the
reconciliation gained from the perception of the continuity of
life in the rebirth of one's self in another form in one's children
and from the promise that rebirth in this world is the analogue
of a new life in another world after death. In *King Lear* and the
other tragedies it is the vicarious suffering and death represented
in the agricultural folk plays which are the center; in *Pericles*
and the other tragicomedies it is the awakening from death
which is the center—or, in terms of the Christ story, it is the
analogy with the crucifixion which is the center of the tragedies
and with the resurrection which is the center of the tragicomedies. The recurring theme in Shakespeare's last plays of
royalty lost and then recovered, as if from death, is the final
expression of his faith in the restoration of the conditions of
the Elizabethan compromise.

5. Oscar James Campbell has shown ("The Salvation of Lear,"
ELH, XV [1948], 93–109) that *King Lear* derives from the
homily, frequently dramatized in the moralities, of man de-
serted in the face of death by the fair-weather friends riches
and worldly relationships and accompanied and sustained by
one for whom he has done little, variously represented as faith,
hope, charity, or good works.

6. W. H. Clemen (*The Development of Shakespeare's Imagery*
[Harvard University Press, 1951], p. 135n.) refers to a study by
L. Schmetz which "notes the frequent occurrence of quantitative
and mercantile terms as well as the use of calculating compara-
tives in the language of the two sisters (cf. 'disquantity,' 'remainder,' 'want,' 'need,' 'scanted,' 'prize,' 'use,' 'business,' 'safe
and politic,' 'expense and waste of his revenues' (I.i.72, 281–282;
I.iv.272–273, 348, 353; II.i.102; II.ii.121–130; II.iv.241, 264,
266)."

INDEX

INDEX

INDEX

INDEX

Feudalism: in "North Parts," 5; and new aristocracy, 12, 54; and Christian humanism, 54; and tradition of revenge, 206–7. *See also* Shakespeare
Fielding, Henry, 200*n*11
Fink, Z. S., 208*n*14
Forgiveness. *See* Shakespeare
Fortune. *See* Mutability
Frazer, Sir James George, 97, 219
Frobisher, Sir Martin, 14, 18
Froude, James Anthony, 196*n*1

Garnet, Henry, 160
Gayley, Charles Mills, 212
Gentillet, Innocent, 105, 149, 229*n*5
Gentleman, ideal: qualities of, 51–52; ancestry, 204; occupations permitted, 204–5. *See also* Shakespeare
Gentry: Parsons on, 25–26; Tawney, Stone, and Trevor-Roper on, 191–93; James's policy towards, 198*n*24; education of, 199–200
Gentry, enterprising: and Tudor monarchy, 3; rise of, 5, 8–10; in House of Commons, 21; "seadogs" of coast, 27; Parliamentary struggle of, 30–31; and new aristocracy, 39–40
Gentry, feudalistic: economic position weakened, 10, 23–24
Gorboduc, 74, 75
Granville-Barker, Harley, 129, 130, 226
Green, John Richard, 196*n*2
Greene, Robert, 58, 61, 162–63, 195*n*37, 211
Grenville family, 11
Gresham, Sir Thomas, 17, 74, 194*n*26
Greville, Sir Fulke, Baron Brooke, 13, 15, 16, 17, 28, 118, 189*n*6, 194*n*30, 212
Grey, Arthur, Lord Grey de Wilton, 39
Groat's Worth of Wit, 61
Guilpin, Edward, 55, 207*n*1

Gull's Hornbook, 74
Gurney-Salter, Emma, 194*n*31

Hall, Arthur, 22, 56
Hall, Edward, 202*n*19
Hall, Joseph, 55, 200*n*11, 207*n*1
Haller, William, 196*n*6
Hamlet, 87, 90, 92, 99–118, 217*n*28
Hankins, John E., 221*n*3
Harbage, Alfred, 71, 72, 74
Harrington, James, 22, 24, 54, 193*n*21, 195*n*46
Harrison, William, 72, 190*n*16
Hartwell, Kathleen Ellen, 225*n*4
Harvey, Gabriel, 149
Hatton, Sir Christopher, 4, 35, 199*n*11
Hawkins, Sir John, 28
Hayward, Sir John, 202*n*24
Heaven. *See* Shakespeare
Heilman, Robert B., 213*n*8
Hell. *See* Shakespeare
Henry III, 16
Henry V, 44, 215–16
Henry VI, Part III, 149, 150
Henry VII, 41
Henry VIII, 6, 8, 12, 13, 22, 35, 38, 41, 54, 201
Herbert family, 11
Hero, the. *See* Shakespeare
Heywood, Thomas, 75, 117, 194*n*26
Hewitt, Douglas, 218*n*34
Hexter, J. H., 199–200
Hierarchy: universal, 45; social, 45–48; Henrician humanists on mobility within, 201. *See also* Shakespeare
Hill, Christopher, 193*n*21
Hoby, Sir Thomas, 53
Holinshed, Raphael, 184, 202*n*21, 229*n*8
"Homily Against Disobedience and Willful Rebellion," 47
"Homily of Repentance," 131
Honor: sought by courtier, 53; Italianate code of, 206–7. *See also* Shakespeare
Hooker, Richard, 31, 76, 196*n*8, 218*n*30

INDEX

Howard family, 38
Humanism, Christian: world view of new aristocracy, 44; view of society, 44–48; and transition between feudalism and capitalism, 54; Marston on, 65; and drama, 78; and science, 200–1; and 17th-century enterprising gentry, 201. *See also* Shakespeare
Huntingdon, Henry Hastings, Earl of, 26
Hutchinson, Colonel John, 201
"Hymn of Heavenly Love, An," 144

Ignatius His Conclave, 150
Individualism. *See* Shakespeare
Infanta of Spain, 35, 36
Italianism: characteristics, 59–60; and old aristocracy, 59–60, 205; satirized, 59–62; and London gallants, 60; and Puritanism, 61–62; and "Machiavellianism," 61–62; and malcontentism, 61–62; and Jacobean drama, 78; code of honor, 206–7. *See also* Shakespeare

James I, 30, 34, 37, 38, 39, 194*n*30, 198*n*24, 206*n*44, 212, 229*n*8
Jew of Malta, 148
Johnson, Francis R., 201
Johnson, S. F., 223*n*17
Johnson, Samuel, 86
Jones, Richard Foster, 201
Jonson, Ben, 58, 77, 78
Jorgensen, Paul A., 225*n*23

Kelso, Ruth, 204*n*40
King. *See* Prince
King Lear, 87, 90, 93, 148, 161–88, 230–31
Kinlosse, Edward Bruce, Lord, 39
Kittredge, George Lyman, 117, 223*n*14
Knight, G. Wilson, 217*n*25, 217–18
Krutch, Joseph Wood, 81, 212

Latimer, Hugh, 213*n*7
Laud, William, 36
Law of nature: governs creation, 46; to guide prince, 49, 50, 102; rejected by Donne, 68–69; defined, 202–3. *See also* Shakespeare
Lawlor, J. J., 221*n*3
Leech, Clifford, 213*n*6
Leicester, Robert Dudley, Earl of, 4, 5, 6, 12, 13, 14, 15, 16, 26, 36, 41, 43, 194, 196*n*6, 204*n*40
Life of Sir Philip Sidney, 189*n*6
Lodge, Thomas, 208*n*16
A Looking-Glass for London and England, 211
Love: universe drawn by God's, 45; and courtier, 64; Donne's mockery of ideals of, 66–70; chivalric tradition of and old aristocracy, 205; neo-Platonic and new aristocracy, 205–6; taught by adversity, 215*n*19. *See also* Shakespeare
Liljegren, S. B., 190*n*12
Lok, Henry, 56
Louis XV, 16
Loyola, Ignatius, 150
Lucas, F. L., 213*n*6
Lucifer, set pattern for man, 88–89. *See also* Analogy, biblical, *under* Shakespeare
Lust, Marston on, 63–65. *See also* Shakespeare
Lyly, John, 56, 74

Macbeth, 87, 90, 107, 142–60, 217*n*28
McGinn, Donald J., 214*n*12
Machiavelli, Niccolo, 61, 105, 149, 150, 229*n*3
"Machiavellianism": and Italianates, 59, 61–62; and Puritans, 61–62; in revenge tragedy, 102; Greene on, 162–63. *See also* Shakespeare
Malcontents: Italianates attacked as, 59, 61–62; Puritans attacked as, 61–62; did not accept hier

INDEX

archy, 62; danger in peacetime,
117. *See also* Shakespeare
Marlowe, Christopher, 77, 149, 162,
208*n*17
Marston, John, 55, 63–65, 70, 77,
78, 117, 195*n*37, 209*n*22
Mary, Queen of Scots, 26, 30, 38
Mazzini, Guiseppe, 62
Measure for Measure, 211, 214*n*12
Middle class. *See* Bourgeoisie
Miller, Arthur, 90
Milton, John, 201
Mirror for Magistrates, A, 184
Misfortunes of Arthur, The, 75
Montgomery, Earl of, 212
Morality plays. *See* Shakespeare
More, Sir Thomas, 41, 42, 76, 198–
99, 215*n*19
Mulcaster, Richard, 43
Muir, Kenneth, 228*n*14
Murray, Gilbert, 219*n*38
Mutability, part of divine scheme
of things, 215. *See also* Shake-
speare

Nashe, Thomas, 34, 44, 117, 197*n*15,
211
Nature, Donne's presentation of,
68–70. *See also* Shakespeare
Naunton, Sir Robert, 5, 189*n*3
Neale, J. E., 195*n*42
Nef, John U., 195*n*34
Neville, Sir Henry, 212
Newcastle, William Cavendish,
Duke of, 5
Nicolas, Sir Harris, 189*n*4
Nobility: Elizabeth's policy to-
wards, 5, 194; Parsons on, 25–
26; in Civil War, 29; chal-
lenged by Puritans, 31; rehabil-
itated by James, 37–38; prince
to discourage idleness of, 50
Noble, Richmond, 227
Noble, T. C., 196*n*4
Norden, John, 118
Norfolk, Thomas Howard, Duke of,
4, 5, 12, 38, 198*n*4
Northampton, Henry Howard, Earl
of, 38, 39, 197*n*23

Northumberland, Henry Percy,
Earl of, 10, 37, 38, 190*n*9
Notestein, Wallace, 200*n*11
Nottingham, Charles Howard of
Effingham, Earl of, 39

Ocland, Christopher, 56
Othello, 87, 88, 90, 93, 119–41
Oxford, Edward de Vere, Earl of,
4, 5, 12, 26, 38, 59, 74, 205*n*42,
206

Pace, Richard, 42
Palmerin of England, 76
Paradoxes and Problems, 161
"Pardoner's Tale," 84
Parma, Alexander Farnese, Duke
of, 28
Parsons, Robert, 25, 26, 29, 197*n*23
Passion: imperils universal order,
46–48; to be ruled by reason,
49. *See also* Shakespeare
Peele, George, 56
Pembroke, Henry Herbert, Earl
of, 15
Pembroke, William Herbert, Earl
of, 11, 43, 212
Percy family, 11
Pericles, 230–31
Philip II of Spain, 15, 25, 26, 27,
28
Pius V, Pope, 25, 27
Plato, 69
Poetaster, 77
Poetic justice. *See* Retribution,
divine
Pollard, A. F., 30, 196*n*7
Power, Eileen, 196*n*10
Primaudaye, Peter de la, 149,
215*n*19
Prince: in Christian humanist view,
48–51; and old aristocracy, 49;
God's vicegerent, 49; fashions
society in own image, 49–50;
displays qualities of God, 50.
See also Shakespeare
Protestants: Sidney on, 16; among
gentry, 26; attitude towards
Elizabeth, 30

INDEX

INDEX

INDEX

INDEX

Warwick, Robert Rich, Earl of, 29
Webster, John, 125
Weisinger, Herbert, 96, 218n35
Wentworth, Peter, 34
West, Robert H., 221-22
Westmoreland, Charles Neville, Earl of, 10
Whitgift, John, Archbishop, 31, 35
William of Orange, 16, 27
Wilson, Thomas, 195n33
Wilson, Sir Thomas, 24, 196n48
Winchester, William Paulet, Marquis of, 26

Winchester, John Paulet, Marquis of, 29
Winstanley, Lilian, 229n8
Winter's Tale, The, 181
Wolsey, Thomas, 14
Worcester, Edward Somerset, 4th earl of, 39
Worcester, Edward Somerset, 6th earl of, 5
Wright, Louis B., 208n11

Zeeveld, W. Gordon, 201
Zurich Letters, The, 195n41